THE NEW ORLEANS SISTERS
OF THE HOLY FAMILY

THE NEW ORLEANS SISTERS OF THE HOLY FAMILY

African American Missionaries to the Garifuna of Belize

EDWARD T. BRETT

University of Notre Dame Press
Notre Dame, Indiana

University of Notre Dame Press
Notre Dame, Indiana 46556
www.undpress.nd.edu

Published in the United States of America
Copyright © 2012 by the University of Notre Dame Press
All Rights Reserved

The author and publisher express their gratitude to the Sisters of the Holy Family and to Sister Mary Carolyn Leslie, Archivist, for permission to reproduce the photographs in the gallery.

Matt Whetsell, La Roche College, provided the maps in chapter 1.

Library of Congress Cataloging-in-Publication Data

Brett, Edward Tracy, 1944–
 The New Orleans Sisters of the Holy Family : African American missionaries to the Garifuna of Belize / Edward T. Brett.
     p. cm.
 Includes bibliographical references (p.   ) and index.
 ISBN 13: 978-0-268-02230-3 (pbk. : alk. paper)
 ISBN 10: 0-268-02230-5 (pbk. : alk. paper)
 ISBN-13: 978-0-268-15834-7
 1. Sisters of the Holy Family (New Orleans, La.) — Missions — Belize.
 2. Sisters of the Holy Family (New Orleans, La.) — History.
 3. Catholic Church — Missions — Belize. 4. Missionaries — Belize. I. Title.
     BV2843.B8B74   2012
     266'.27282 — dc23
                    2012006671

∞ *The paper in this book meets the guidelines for permanence and durability of the Committee on Production Guidelines for Book Longevity of the Council on Library Resources.*

To the Sisters of the Holy Family and all other religious sisters who

have served in Central America

and who have made a difference in the lives of many;

and to Father Edward L. Cleary, O.P. (1929–2011)

colleague, mentor, and dear friend

Contents

Acknowledgments ix

Introduction 1

PART I
THE PRE-VATICAN II PERIOD

Chapter 1
Foundation and Growth in New Orleans 13

Chapter 2
Mother Austin Jones and the Early Mission 26

Chapter 3
Trouble with the Bishop 40

Chapter 4
The 1920s to the Second Vatican Council 51

PART II
THE POST-VATICAN II YEARS

Chapter 5
Changes in the 1950s through the Early 1970s 65

Chapter 6
Problems over Language and Inculturation   85

Chapter 7
Mission Experiences of Three Holy Family Sisters   108

Chapter 8
Withdrawal from Belize   125

Conclusion   143

Appendix A
Holy Family Sisters Who Have Worked in Belize   156

Appendix B
Holy Family Sisters from Belize   160

Appendix C
Reflections of Three Lay People Who Were Taught by the Holy Family Sisters in Belize   163

Notes   172

Bibliography   206

Index   215

Acknowledgments

Many people have generously given their time and expertise so that the story of the Sisters of the Holy Family and their 110-year mission in Belize could come to light in this book. I thank all of those listed in the bibliography whom I corresponded with or interviewed. A special thanks, however, goes to Sister Carolyn Leslie, S.S.F., the archivist for the Holy Family Sisters, who through my eight years of research on this book provided me with hundreds of documents—many of which I would never have found on my own—and set up countless interviews for me with members of her congregation who, she realized, had valuable information to share. Of this latter group I am especially grateful to Sisters Sylvia Thibodeaux, Clare of Assisi Pierre, Judith Therese Barial, and Jean Martínez, and to the former mayor of Dangriga, the Honorable Sylvia Flores, who is an associate member of the Holy Family Congregation. Indeed, when I first interviewed Sisters Judith and Clare in 2003 and saw their eyes sparkle as they reminisced about their years in Belize, I knew that this was a research project worth undertaking.

Special thanks goes to Sister Angelyn Dries, O.S.F., Diane Batts Morrow, Father Cyprian Davis, O.S.B., Sister Patricia Byrne, C.S.J., Sister Sally Witt, C.S.J., and Father Robert Carbonneau, C.P., for reading all or parts of my manuscript. These fine historians pointed out mistakes and misconceptions in my work and also, along with David Miros of the Jesuit Midwest Province Archives, brought to my attention important books and articles of which I had been unaware. I am also grateful to Charles Nolan, who played a crucial role in helping me gain admittance to the Holy Family Archives, and to my brother-in-law Kurt Whitson, who, without being asked to do so, saved every article for me that appeared in the New Orleans newspapers over the last decade that treated the Holy Family Sisters.

My appreciation also goes out to my colleagues at La Roche College, especially Paul Le Blanc, Joshua Forrest, Sister Michele Bisbey,

C.D.P., Sister Mary Christine Morkovsky, C.D.P., Sister Rita Yeasted, S.F.C.C., Edward Bobinchock, and Anna Marie Neutrelle, and to Father Edward L. Cleary, O.P., of Providence College, for the many discussions I had with them concerning my research and writing. These discussions and my colleagues' input certainly made this a better book. I am likewise grateful to the staff of the La Roche College Library— LaVerne Collins, Darlene Veghts, Jacqueline Bolte, Marilyn McHugh, and Caroline Horgan—who obtained for me countless books and articles and always did so with good cheer. I am also grateful to Elizabeth Williams, my former student, for helping me track down several hard-to-find books and articles. My thanks also go out to Sister Barbara Flores, S.C.N., and Sister Ellen Doyle, S.C.N., for their help concerning the apostolate of the Sisters of Charity of Nazareth in Belize.

I would be remiss if I did not acknowledge my daughters, Erin Brett and Tracy Brett Dunlap, and my son-in-law, David Dunlap, for their ongoing support when it comes to my research projects and for almost always listening politely when I would get carried away on the topic of the Holy Family Sisters. Thanks also should go to my two young grandsons, Scott and Samuel Dunlap, for at least trying to be quiet when their grandfather was working on the computer or reading something about the Holy Family Sisters.

The person who is most deserving of my appreciation, however, is my wife, Donna. She has read every word of every draft of this book (and everything else I have written), checking my grammar and style and making insightful suggestions to clarify or expand on the text. Before I began my work on the Holy Family Sisters, she had coauthored a book and several articles with me on the Catholic Church in Central America. My collaboration with her on these projects has certainly made me a better historian.

Introduction

In the mid-1980s, my wife and I decided to write a book on U.S. missionaries who had been murdered in the 1970s and 1980s in Central America. Aside from a few short magazine and newspaper articles, we had never before written about modern-day missionaries, so, like any reputable historian would do, we began a search to uncover and read everything we could find that dealt with the history of U.S. Catholic missions and missionaries in Latin America. The one work that proved to be of immense value to us was Gerald Costello's *Mission to Latin America: The Successes and Failures of a Twentieth-Century Crusade*.[1] It greatly influenced our approach in composing our book and has influenced my scholarship ever since. Aside from Costello's study, however, there were not many other books that we found on U.S. Catholic missions that could be termed serious, professional history. Granted, there were some histories of specific religious congregations' mission enterprises, but they were usually in-house productions printed by small publishers who charge a fee for their services. They were often hagiographical in tone and usually devoid of meaningful analysis. To put it bluntly, they were amateurish, usually replete with historical misconceptions and of little worth to a serious historian.

When my wife and I consulted the standard books on U.S. Catholic history, we were again disappointed. Although they included some information on European missionaries who came to work in what would become the United States, they contained almost nothing on U.S. Catholic foreign mission enterprises.[2] To make matters worse, the archives of religious congregations were often poorly organized. They contained valuable information on Catholic mission history, but the researcher had to have patience and plenty of time to track down what he or she needed.[3] Nevertheless, despite these problems we were eventually able to complete our book.[4] From our research efforts, however, I had come to believe that American missionaries had played a significant role, especially in the twentieth century, in shaping U.S. Catholic perceptions of other cultures. Furthermore, I came to realize that American missionaries had influenced how their fellow U.S. Catholics — both clergy and laity — viewed the foreign policy of their own government.[5] Even more important, I was convinced that the American Catholic missionary movement had had an important role in the overall history of the U.S. Catholic Church, yet historians had given little attention to this field of study.

The National Conference of Catholic Bishops' Committee on the Church in Latin America took a step in remedying this situation when it commissioned Sister Mary McGlone to draw up a study of the relationship between the North American and Latin American Catholic churches, with special emphasis on how that relationship has impacted the United States. The book that resulted from her efforts, *Sharing Faith across the Hemisphere*,[6] which appeared in 1997, also includes valuable appendices on the involvement in Latin America of U.S. dioceses, parishes, religious orders, and congregations as well as Catholic colleges and universities.

The year 1997 also saw the publication of *American Women in Mission: A Social History of Their Thought and Practice,* by historian Dana Robert. This innovative work not only highlighted the contributions made by female missionaries, both Catholic and Protestant, to U.S. mission history, but it also showed convincingly that women missionaries were far more than mere auxiliaries to their male counterparts. They provided services to indigenous people that could not be offered by men due to cultural mores and other reasons, and, in so doing, they often developed a closer relationship with the common people, especially with women, than did the male missionaries.[7]

The publication in 1998 of Sister Angelyn Dries's *The Missionary Movement in American Catholic History* represented a major advance in U.S. Catholic mission studies.[8] In this important work, Dries lists virtually every American mission enterprise—those conducted by male and female religious congregations, those directed by dioceses, and those that were lay-oriented—and provides basic information on their history. Moreover, she convincingly shows that Catholic missionaries had a profound influence on the development of a distinct U.S. Catholic identity and, as a consequence, that U.S. mission history is an intricate subset of American Catholic history in general and therefore needs to be thoroughly investigated by scholars of American religion and culture. She states emphatically that U.S. Catholic mission history is a new, under-researched field that needs further exploration, and she expresses the hope that her book might encourage other historians to make use of hitherto largely ignored U.S. Catholic missionary archives.[9]

I was searching for a research project when I read Dries's seminal study. My interest was aroused when I came across two brief paragraphs on the missionary work in Belize of the Sisters of the Holy Family.[10] These sisters, based in my former hometown of New Orleans, are an African American congregation who in 1898 agreed to staff a school for "black Carib" children in the Stann Creek District of what was then British Honduras. In 1998, after a hundred years, their mission still flourished. I had read of Protestant African American missionaries and their work in Africa and the Caribbean, but this was the first time I had ever come across any reference to African American Catholic missionaries. I knew of several white U.S. congregations of sisters who had taught black children in underdeveloped countries and who thought that their work had been somewhat impeded as a result of racial differences. Here was an opportunity to study black sisters teaching black children. Would their encounter with their black students differ from that of the white missionary sisters? I was intrigued and thought that perhaps this was a research topic worth pursuing. A study of African American Catholic missionary nuns ministering to "black Caribs" in Central America could make a unique contribution to the history of the U.S. Catholic missionary movement. I next wrote to Charles Nolan, the archivist of the Archdiocese of New Orleans and a fellow historian whom I had known years earlier when I still lived in southern Louisiana. He informed me that the sisters had considerable archival sources on their Belize mission at their motherhouse in New Orleans. Through my contact with Nolan, who had coauthored a book and several pamphlets on the Holy Family Congregation, the sisters agreed to grant me access to their archives. As time went on they also allowed me to interview former missionary sisters and Garifuna (black Carib) sisters who were stationed in New Orleans.

Not long after I entered into my new research project, I realized that I knew little about the history of black Catholics in the United States. For my study to be of any value, it had to be written in a way that placed it in the overall context of the U.S. black Catholic experience. But just as with U.S. Catholic missionary history, I soon found that this African American subset of U.S. Catholic history had until very recently been almost totally ignored by American historians and historians of U.S. Catholicism.

In the first half of the twentieth century, the Josephite John Gillard had authored two studies on black Catholicism.[11] Although these works were the first of their kind and contained much important information, they were replete with prejudiced and paternalistic notions that were unfortunately almost universal among white American priests at that time, even among the Josephites whose mission was to minister to African Americans. In 1955 the Jesuit Albert S. Foley contributed a collection of short, descriptive biographies of over half of the seventy African American priests ordained between 1854 and 1954.[12] The book, *God's Men of Color,* has its weaknesses, which result at least in part from the fact that Foley was forced to compromise his work and submit to church officials who insisted that he sanitize his writing in order to avoid any embarrassment to the institutional church. In an article that appeared over three decades after *God's Men of Color* had been published, Foley was finally able to reveal the details of the censorship and restrictions that he had endured in his attempt to write black Catholic history in a pre–Vatican II environment. This article vividly illustrates a major reason why the subfield of African American Catholic history was all but nonexistent throughout most of the twentieth century.[13]

The late 1980s saw the beginning of a renaissance in black Catholic history. In 1988, Marilyn W. Nickels's *Black Catholic Protest and the Federated Colored Catholics, 1917–1933: Three Perspectives on Racial Justice* was published.[14] The fact that the work was completed in 1975, but not published until thirteen years later, shows that in the United States, even as late as the 1970s, African American Catholic history was still considered to be of little relevance. Nickels's book is important in that it shows that black Catholics in the early part of the twentieth century were unwilling to accept a place of inferiority in the U.S. Catholic Church. Led by the layman Thomas Turner, they fought to end discrimination in their church and to obtain black priests for their parishes. Their efforts were not in vain. After countless petitions to Rome, the Vatican interjected itself into U.S. church politics and played a major role in creating a seminary for African Americans in Mississippi.

In 1990 two valuable studies appeared. The first, *Desegregating the Altar: The Josephites and the Struggle for Black Priests, 1871–1960*,[15] by Stephen J. Ochs, is more than simply a dry history of the Josephites. After presenting a solid overview of African American Catholic history, Ochs carefully documents the long struggle by black priests. In contrast to Foley's *God's Men of Color*, he makes no attempt to whitewash this embarrassing chapter of U.S. Catholic history. On the contrary, he paints a vivid picture of the racism and timidity that permeated the institutional U.S. Catholic Church when it came to issues of justice for black Catholics.[16]

Shortly after the appearance of *Desegregating the Altar*, Cyprian Davis's groundbreaking study, *The History of Black Catholics in the United States*, was published.[17] Just as Angelyn Dries's book was a major advance in the field of mission history, so is Davis's pioneer study destined to be the fountainhead for many future specialized studies. Largely based on information that he gleaned from an enormous number of archives throughout the United States and Europe, Davis's book is a comprehensive, meticulously researched history of the African American Catholic community. It is not an exaggeration to say that it is the work that was needed in order to give black Catholicism its rightful place within the context of U.S. Catholic history and the history of American religion.

Up to this time, however, save for a few articles and pamphlets, little of professional quality was written on African American female religious congregations.[18] This gap was especially unfortunate because, with the absence of a black clergy well into the twentieth century due to the church's refusal to ordain African Americans, it was these religious women who represented the African American face of institutional Catholicism for both black and white Americans. The gap was partly filled in 2002 with the publication of *Persons of Color and Religious at the Same Time: The Oblate Sisters of Providence, 1828–1860* by Diane Batts Morrow.[19] Largely based on documents found in the sisters' archives in Baltimore, the book presents a detailed history of the first thirty-two years of the oldest surviving African American religious congregation. Morrow does more than merely present a narrative history, however. She skillfully intertwines the latest scholarship on issues of race and gender into her monograph, and in so doing she demonstrates how the sisters were able to survive by negotiating with a church and a secular society that more often than not had little sympathy for them. But Morrow goes further by adroitly addressing conflicts within the Oblate Sisters' community that resulted from ethnic, class, and skin color differences. A masterful study, Morrow's book influenced my own approach in my work on the Holy Family Sisters, whose history I would find had much in common with the Oblates of Providence.

As with U.S. Catholic missionary history and that of African American Catholicism, the history of U.S. female religious and their congregations has been largely neglected until the last few decades. As historian Carol Coburn writes, "With the exception of early congregational in-house histories often written for novices, American women religious have been virtually 'invisible' in American Catholic history until recently."[20] This began to change, however, in the early 1980s. Evangeline Thomas's *Women Religious History Sources: A Guide to Repositories in the United States* and Elizabeth Kolmer's *Religious Women in the United States: A Survey of the Influential Literature from 1950 to 1983* laid a foundation upon which other scholars could build.[21]

The study of Catholic religious sisters was given a major boost, however, when the Conference on the History of Women Religious was formed in 1989. Scholars interested in the history of female religious could now formally gather together once every three years to present research papers and discuss the latest ideas and techniques concerning their subfield of history. A by-product of these meetings was that the study of women's religious history became more analytical, nuanced, and sophisticated. No longer was it studied in isolation; it was now examined in a way that intertwined it within the larger context of U.S. and world history.

With the additional aid of the newly formed field of feminist studies, which provides models of how to view history through the lens of gender, a plethora of rich scholarship on women religious and their contributions to the U.S. Catholic Church have appeared within the last two decades. Consequently, religious sisters are no longer "invisible," and the struggles they underwent to control their own destiny in a male-dominated, patriarchal church are finally seeing the light of day.[22] In the last three decades, historians have proven beyond a doubt that female religious, beginning with the coming of the Ursulines to New Orleans in 1727, have played a major role, albeit usually out of the limelight, in the development of the American Catholic Church. Moreover, these historians have made it clear that, contrary to what had previously been assumed, U.S. Catholic sisters had always been far more than mere ancillary assistants to the male clergy. Many excellent histories of female religious congregations, including that of Morrow, have now been written,[23] but little has appeared on these congregations' contribution to the U.S. foreign missionary movement.[24] Thus, it is hoped that the pages that follow will fill this void at least in a modest way, while also adding a small contribution to the fields of black Catholic history and of women religious.

The letters, reports, and other documentation dealing with the founding and growth of the Holy Family Sisters' mission in Belize, which are located in New Orleans in the congregation's archives, form the principal source for my study.[25] These resources, covering a 110-year span from 1898 to 2008, have been almost entirely ignored by previous scholars, thus making them especially valuable for my project.[26] Interviews that I conducted with Holy Family Sisters and letters that they wrote to me in answer to my questions constitute the second most important primary source. Most of the nuns who communicated with me in this fashion are North Americans, but several are Garifuna or Belizean Creoles. Some began serving in what was then British Honduras in the 1940s; others worked in Belize in the period following the Second Vatican Council, when long-accepted notions of what constituted good missionary techniques were giving way to new ideas. Still others served the people of Belize in the 1980s and 1990s and into the twenty-first century when the sisters were confronting mission challenges with creative innovations. This personal correspondence provided me with factual information crucial to my study; however, it was also vital in that it shed light on the transformation that took place over time in the congregation's mission outlook. Letters and testimonies from Belizeans who were not Holy Family Sisters constitute the final type of primary sources. Some of these came from lay people and others from Sisters of Charity, whose congregation has worked in Belize in recent years. This correspondence was important in that it provided me with the perspectives of people who had been influenced by the Holy Family Sisters but were not members of their congregation.

Part I of this book treats the sisters' missionary work in the period before the Second Vatican Council. The first chapter discusses the foundation and growth of the congregation in New Orleans prior to the sisters' decision to accept a teaching commitment in what was then British Honduras. This chapter is essential to my study in that it provides the reader with basic facts on the charism of the Holy Family Congregation and also with an understanding of how the sisters coped with the racism and gender problems that they were forced to endure because they were African American women. Chapter 2 treats the early history of the British Honduras mission, concentrating especially on Mother Mary Austin Jones, the superior of the Holy Family Sisters, who was responsible for expanding the congregation's work into the mission field. Highlighted in this chapter is the significance of the contract between Mother Austin and the first bishop of Belize, which detailed the sisters' rights vis-à-vis those of the bishop. The third chapter treats the conflict between the second bishop of Belize and the Holy Family Congregation over finances and missionary personnel. Here I contend that the sisters prevailed in this struggle because Mother Austin had had the foresight to demand a written contract from this bishop's predecessor. At the end of this chapter I also examine the relationship of the first two bishops of Belize with the white, New Orleans–based Mercy Sisters—the first Catholic female religious missionaries in British Honduras—and compare it with that of the bishops and the Holy Family Sisters. Chapter 4, the last chapter of Part I, takes the story of the mission from the 1920s to the Second Vatican Council. Here the sisters' accomplishments are evaluated from the perspective of what leaders of the institutional church in the pre–Vatican II era believed constituted success in the mission arena.

Part II deals with the Belizean mission from the eve of the Second Vatican Council through the post–Vatican II years. Chapter 5 addresses the effects that the Council had on women religious in general and on the Sisters of the Holy Family in particular. It also documents and analyzes the sisters' amalgamation of their Catholic high school with those of two Protestant denominations in the Stann Creek region of Belize. This chapter makes it clear that following Vatican II the Holy Family Sisters were united in their eagerness to amend their missionary efforts so that they conformed to the spirit of the Council.

Chapter 6 treats the congregation's failure to understand and adjust to the sense of ethnic pride that had recently come to permeate its Garifuna (Carib) members as a result of the Belizean struggle for independence from Britain and to a modern spirit within the Catholic Church emanating from the Council. It is here that I attempt to explain the reasons behind the sisters' failure to "read the signs of the times," thereby causing a preventable rift to develop within the congregation.

Chapter 7 presents case studies of three of the congregation's missionary sisters in an attempt to illustrate how the Holy Family Congregation, beginning in the 1980s, learned to adapt to and assimilate into their own lives the culture of the people whom they served. It especially emphasizes the creative innovations that the Holy Family community, true to the spirit of Vatican II, introduced into the Belizean educational system. It likewise shows why these innovations were so important to the people of Belize.

The final chapter chronicles the congregation's efforts to keep its missionary work alive and meaningful when faced with an ever-growing shortage of new religious vocations. Finally, following the conclusion, there are three appendices: the first lists all Holy Family Sisters who have served as missionaries in Belize; the second lists all members of the congregation who were natives of Belize; and the third gives the testimonies of three lay people who had been taught by the sisters in Dangriga (Stann Creek).

The Sisters of the Holy Family are unique in that they were the first African American Catholics to serve as missionaries. It is my hope that the hitherto unknown story of their missionary efforts in Belize will enhance the already distinguished reputation that they have earned for themselves through their work with poor blacks in the United States.

Part I

The Pre-Vatican II Period

CHAPTER 1

FOUNDATION AND GROWTH IN NEW ORLEANS

On March 31, 1898, Mother Superior Mary Austin Jones of the Holy Family Sisters, her traveling companion Sister Mary Ann Fazende, the postulant Addie Saffold, and four soon-to-be-missionary sisters boarded a steamer, the *Stillwater,* at New Orleans.[1] The intended destination of the seven African Americans was Stann Creek (today called Dangriga), a settlement on the Atlantic Coast of British Honduras (since 1973 called Belize), south of Belize City. There, the four missionaries—Sisters Mary Rita Mather, Mary Dominica Bee, Mary Emmanuel Thompson, and Mary Stephen Fortier—with the help of Saffold, who would work for a year in the sisters' preschool program,[2] were to run Sacred Heart primary school for mostly black Carib (Garifuna) students,[3] whose ancestors had first settled the area in the 1790s.[4] An English Jesuit, Brother Daniel Reynolds, had started the school,[5] and it was the Jesuit Order that since the 1860s had labored virtually alone in evangelizing the Caribs,[6] a close-knit people descended from shipwrecked African slaves and indigenous Caribbean islanders.

After an uneventful voyage, the steamer docked at Belize City on April 3, where the seven religious women stayed overnight with the

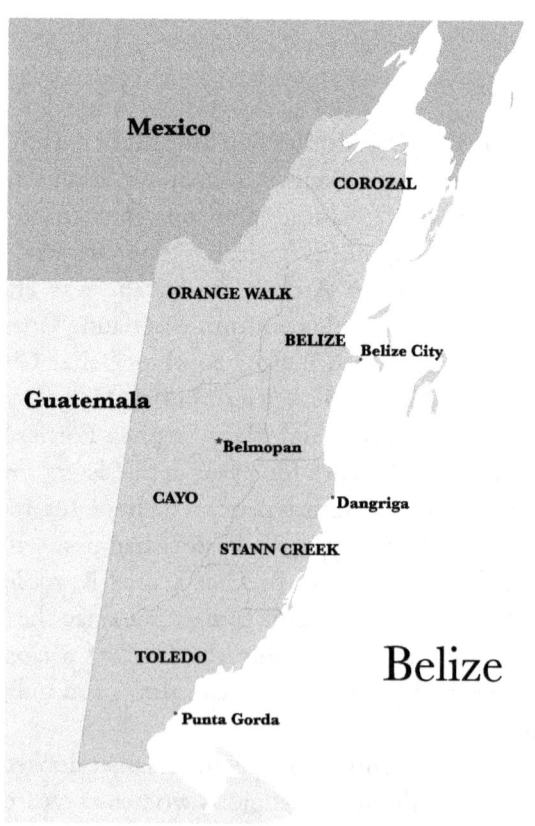

Maps by Matt Whetsell

Sisters of Mercy, a white congregation, who, like the Holy Family Sisters, were also from New Orleans. The Mercy nuns were the second Catholic religious order to enter British Honduras and had been teaching at St. Catherine's and Holy Redeemer primary schools since 1883. In 1886 they had opened St. Catherine's Academy, the oldest Catholic secondary school in Belize.[7] The next morning, after a "hearty breakfast" provided by the Mercy community, the Holy Family nuns were given a tour of St. Catherine's convent and "select school."[8] At about 3:00 p.m., the seven companions reboarded the *Stillwater*, which had finally finished unloading the bulk of its cargo. After sailing south for an additional thirty-six miles, the nuns reached their destination.

Because Stann Creek had no wharf, but only a pier for small craft, all seven religious had to be lowered from the ship into a rowboat (called a "dorey" by the natives) about a mile offshore. Since they were dressed in their bulky habits, this transfer was not only a frightening experience but also an adventure that became part of the congregation's folklore. When they reached the pier, Jesuit Fathers C. J. Leibe and Matharus Antillach greeted them, as did a large contingent of townspeople. After a most impressive welcome, they were shown to their convent, a small frame building with a zinc roof, prepared for them by the Jesuits and the families of the merchants of the town, "who left nothing undone to make everything as comfortable as possible."[9] On April 12 the sisters took charge of Sacred Heart, which by British Honduran law served as a public school. They also opened a select school for students who could afford to pay tuition.[10]

On April 15, after making sure that all was in order, Mother Austin returned to New Orleans with her traveling companion. Sister Mary Francis Borgia Hart, in her in-house history of the Holy Family community, sums up the mother superior's impressions of her first trip to British Honduras: "The primitive condition of the people, the unique reception given to the Sisters and the nature of the work which was to be done for God's glory, so impressed the Mother, that Stann Creek and the Caribs won a place in her zealous heart, and until her death, its needs and the frequent replacements of its personnel claimed her attention, and were always the first to be served."[11] Perhaps Mother Austin realized that the mission begun by the four sisters whom she had left behind was a historic first, in that it was the earliest missionary endeavor by Catholic African Americans, male or female.[12] From extant sources, however, it is clear that she and her sisters were well aware of the hurdles they would face. Consequently, using pragmatic mechanisms they had developed in their struggle to survive in nineteenth-century New Orleans, they would overcome racial and gender discrimination and in some ways would even turn these negatives to their advantage. As a result, the congregation would enjoy over a century of remarkable missionary success.

Before addressing the Holy Family Sisters' ministry in Belize, however, it should prove useful to look at the unique origin and early history of this congregation. This, in turn, necessitates a review of Henriette Delille, the foundress of the religious community, and the peculiar environment from which she came.

Henriette was born in New Orleans in 1812. Although we are not completely sure who her father was, it is virtually certain that he was a member of the Creole class, that is, he was a white gentleman probably of French or Spanish descent. Her mother, Marie Josephe Dias, was a Creole *femme de couleur libre* (free woman of color) whose parentage was of mixed race, on the paternal side Caucasian and on the maternal a mixture of African and white. Just like Henriette, her mother was the offspring of a white Creole and a *femme de couleur libre.* Her maternal grandmother, Henriette Leveau, and great-grandmother, Cecile Dubreuil, although born into slavery and later freed, were likewise of mixed race, but her great-great-grandmother, Nanette, was an African slave.[13] Thus, for three generations her ancestors had an arrangement known as *plaçage* (placing). They did not marry—interracial marriages were illegal—but instead voluntarily entered into a liaison whereby the *femme de couleur libre* was kept by her Creole lover as his mistress. Herbert Asbury, in his racy *The French Quarter: An Informal History of the New Orleans Underworld,* claims that it was indeed rare for a young Creole gentleman not to have a *femme de couleur libre* as his paramour.[14] Sometimes these relationships remained for life but this was uncommon. Almost always the male partners in these arrangements "came and went . . . leaving the women to raise their children with little or no support."[15]

Young free women of color usually received a practical education while also being schooled by their mothers in the ways of seduction.

When they were old enough, they would be elaborately dressed and escorted by their mothers to so-called quadroon balls to be paraded before young white male suitors. A gentleman who fancied one of the girls would then reach an understanding with her mother. When the *plaçage* was finalized, she was usually set up in a small apartment. After 1832, the most famous and ornate quadroon balls were held every Tuesday and Friday night at the Orleans Ballroom. Quadroon balls began to decline in popularity about 1850 and by the end of the Civil War had virtually ceased to exist. It is no coincidence that in 1881 the Holy Family Sisters purchased the Orleans Ballroom and transformed it into a convent and school for black girls.[16]

This, then, was the peculiar society into which Henriette Delille was born. She was the youngest of four children, one of whom died while still an infant. While the different fathers of her surviving sister and brother have been identified, the name of hers is not certain, although it seems most probable that he was Jean-Baptiste Delille. What does seem clear, however, is that he took little if any interest in his daughter.[17] Moreover, since Henriette's older sister, Cecile Bonille, contracted into a *plaçage* in 1824, it is virtually certain that the same fate was planned for her.[18]

That this was not to be was in part due to Sister Marthe Fontière, a French Dame Hospitalière who opened a school for free girls of color in New Orleans in 1823. According to oral tradition passed down by the Holy Family Sisters, it seems that Fontière allowed some students, including Henriette and her close friend, Juliette Gaudin, to assist her in her ministry, which included teaching catechism to children and to adult female slaves. Fontière and her work so impressed her two teenage helpers that they resolved to dedicate themselves to a life of religious service.[19]

For the next few years, Henriette and Juliette continued their ministry to the poor while holding firm to their desire for the religious life. In 1836 they were two of a small group of free women of color to join Marie Jeanne Aliquot in forming a religious confraternity dedicated to serving poor blacks. But soon Aliquot, who was white, left the group, possibly due to Louisiana racial laws. Most of the other members, discouraged by the hardships and prejudice they encountered, eventually followed her lead. The remnant—Delille,

Gaudin, and a few other *femmes de couleur libre*—struggled on. On November 21, 1836, they organized themselves under the name of the Congregation of the Sisters of the Presentation of the Blessed Virgin Mary and drew up "Rules and Regulations" for their confraternity, committing the "sisters" to a common purpose: "to care for the sick, help the poor and instruct the ignorant."[20] It is evident from the details of the "Rules and Regulations" that the "Sisters of the Presentation" were no more than a pious association of laywomen. Nevertheless, the fact that they chose to call themselves "sisters" indicates that their goal was to eventually transform themselves into a traditional community of vowed religious.

In 1842 the small band of *femmes de couleur libre* moved closer toward this goal when Père Etienne Rousselon, the diocesan vicar general and the women's spiritual director-chaplain, leased a group home for them near St. Augustine Church, where he was pastor. Delille, Gaudin, and a third member, Josephine Charles, who up to this time had been residing at home with their families, could now live together in community. The women had not been permitted by the archbishop to take formal vows of poverty, chastity, and obedience, however, nor had they gone through a novitiate program. Thus, they were not recognized as a vowed religious congregation, but rather, according to the official diocesan directory, as a "pious association for the relief of the indigent and sick."[21] Rousselon named Delille head of the new community and, following his suggestion, the women changed their name from the Sisters of the Presentation to the Sisters of the Holy Family.

In 1847, Henriette and her companions, along with several of their financial supporters, incorporated themselves with the state of Louisiana as the Society of the Holy Family. This move was important because it gave "the sisters" a legal basis for their ministry. In 1850, using her inheritance and money borrowed from Marie Jeanne Aliquot, Delille purchased a residence for her community on Bayou Road.[22] The building was spacious enough to allow the "sisters" to open a school for *femmes de couleur libre*.

By this time the Society of the Holy Family was providing an invaluable service to the Archdiocese of New Orleans through its ministry to black slaves and free people of color. Archbishop Antoine

Blanc was fully aware of these efforts and as a result seems to have been willing to help the pious women fulfill their dream of becoming a vowed religious community. This had to be done with great discretion, however, due to the laws and social mores of the time. Thus, there is little extant evidence to help us understand exactly how and when Delille and her companions became a diocesan-approved congregation of sisters. According to the oral tradition of the Holy Family Sisters, Père Rousselon convinced the Religious of the Sacred Heart at St. Michael's Convent in Convent, Louisiana, between New Orleans and Baton Rouge, to allow Delille to make her novitiate year with them in 1850. Upon her return to Bayou Road, she then served as novice mistress for her Holy Family companions.

Although there is conclusive evidence that Delille spent time living with the Religious of the Sacred Heart, there is no documentation that she did so to fulfill the novitiate requirement so that her community could become vowed religious.[23] Nevertheless, as Cyprian Davis notes, although we do not know all the particulars of Delille's stay at St. Michael's Convent, "there is little doubt that somehow Henriette and her companions received enough formation to satisfy the archdiocese that they might make religious vows," and very likely they did so in 1851 or 1852.[24] However, as Davis points out, those vows must have been taken privately, since Delille is not listed during her lifetime as a "sister" in any official church document.[25] Indeed, this fact has led historian Tracy Fessenden to question whether Delille was ever actually considered a vowed religious sister by the institutional church of her time.[26] At any rate, under civil law the three women were definitely not recognized as "sisters" since they were non-Caucasian.[27] We do know that at this time they began to wear a simple black cotton dress and black bonnet as their uniform. It was not until 1876, however, that they were finally allowed by the archbishop to wear an official religious habit publicly;[28] and it was not until March 19, 1887, that the archbishop of New Orleans finally approved the formal rule of the congregation.[29]

Sister Borgia Hart tells us that in the early years the sisters' "presence on the streets [of New Orleans] was hailed with ridicule; for, in the minds of the early inhabitants . . . Colored Sisters were simply an anomaly."[30] Nevertheless, they persevered; and during the yellow fever epidemic of 1853, they so courageously nursed the sick that they earned some credibility and respect.[31]

Throughout the antebellum period, the small group of sisters struggled for survival. Occasionally a woman would join the three cofounders, but the congregation's tenuous situation and the long hours of arduous work expected of its members in service to the poor took their toll, and the woman usually left the community. By the end of the Civil War there were only five Sisters of the Holy Family. And indeed, during the war, spent by years of backbreaking toil and anxieties, Mother Henriette died on November 16, 1862. Her obituary, which appeared on the first page of the archdiocesan newspaper, *Le Propagateur*, is revealing:

> Last Monday there died one of those women whose obscure and retired life has nothing remarkable in the eyes of the world but is full of merit before God. Miss Henriette Delille had for long years devoted herself without reserve to the instruction of the ignorant . . . and principally of the slaves. To perpetuate this sort of apostolate so difficult yet so necessary she had founded with the help of certain pious persons, the House of the Holy Family, a house poor and little known except by the poor and the young and, which for the past ten or twelve years, has produced, without fanfare, a considerable good which will continue. . . . Worn out by work, she died at the age of fifty years after a long and painful illness borne with most edifying resignation. The crowd gathered for her funeral testified by its sorrow how keenly felt was the loss of her who for the love of Jesus Christ had made herself the humble and devoted servant of the slaves.[32]

The fact that Mother Henriette's obituary appeared on page 1 testifies to her importance within the Catholic community of New Orleans. The large crowd reported to have attended her funeral mass likewise is a testament to the success of her congregation's much-needed apostolate to the poorest of the poor, the black slave.

At the same time, one cannot help but notice that in the obituary Henriette is referred to as "Miss" and never as "Mother" or "Sister," and her congregation is called the "House of the Holy Family" rather than the "Sisters of the Holy Family." The avoidance of titles that would designate Henriette and her associates as "real religious" is testimony to the racial prejudice that the Holy Family Sisters had to face not only at that time but also for at least a century thereafter. Sister Audrey Marie Detiege in her pamphlet on Henriette Delille emphasizes this point:

> [N]othing would be written in newspapers, journals, letters, or minute books of the deliberations of ecclesiastical or civil authorities about these Sisters. Whenever the Sisters of the Holy Family were referred to in a Catholic newspaper or directories, they were always called a "group of pious, colored females or women" who gave religious instruction or took care of the poor and indigent of their race. In the Catholic Directories, where all the nuns working in the Diocese of New Orleans were listed, the names of the Sisters of the Holy Family never appeared until the 1870s. And when they finally were listed with the other nuns of the Diocese, they were last in rank with the word colored behind their name or (col.).[33]

The obituary's declaration that Henriette's life was obscure and the work of her followers little known and done without fanfare, but resulting in considerable good, is also telling. Because of the unfortunate reality of racial prejudice, Mother Henriette and her sisters thought it wise to work in a low-keyed manner so as not to attract notice from those who might want to find an excuse to impede their efforts.[34] Indeed, it seems to the author that her congregation throughout its history has adhered to this approach. While not a conservative religious community, its members have avoided being in the vanguard with those religious congregations who call for a more progressive church. They have tried to steer clear of controversial issues, choosing instead to adhere as much as possible to the original focus of their founders, that is, restricting their apostolate to teaching and ministering to mostly poor black children and the elderly. This low-keyed approach has worked well for them over the years and has resulted in an unusual degree of success.

The death of Mother Henriette was followed five months later by that of Marie Jeanne Aliquot and in 1866 by that of Père Rousselon. Since these were the congregation's two greatest friends and benefactors, the sisters' future looked bleak. This grim outlook was further complicated by the fact that after the Civil War white Creoles, who had previously intermixed culturally with Creoles of color, allied with white Americans to become staunch proponents of racial segregation. Indeed, Sister Mary Bernard Deggs, the first historian of the Holy Family Sisters, writing in the 1890s, notes that even other women religious discriminated against them, especially the Sisters of St. Joseph, who "tried all that they could to make us take off our habits."[35] Nevertheless, the community struggled on. To meet their daily expenses the small group was forced to contract with New Orleans businesses to take in sewing. This meant that following their daily prayer obligations, along with a long day of teaching or ministering to the elderly, the sisters were often compelled to sew late into the night in order to finish their orders by deadline.[36]

But all was not grim. Due to cultural and legal restrictions in the antebellum period as well as to self-imposed color and class restrictions, only women from the small Creole *gens de couleur libre* class had been allowed to enter the Holy Family community. Consequently, there was a caste-like separation between the sisters and the poor African American people whom they served. In 1870, however, this division ended when Chloe Preval, the housekeeper of Archbishop Jean-Marie Odin, became the first former slave and the first dark-skinned woman to be admitted to the congregation.[37] But this did not happen without controversy. When the majority of the sisters voted not to accept Preval, Father Gilbert Raymond, the congregation's chaplain and spiritual director, used his superior status as priest-advisor to the nuns to override Mother Juliette Gaudin's authority as superior general. He rented a second, separate residence on Chartres Street and moved Sisters Josephine Charles, Elizabeth Wales, and Marie Magdalene Alpaugh there. These were the three sisters who had voted to admit Preval. He then declared the Chartres residence the new motherhouse of the congregation and appointed Charles the new superior general, thereby placing her above Gaudin, whose authority was now reduced to local superior of the older, Bayou Road house.

Needless to say, Gaudin was furious and Charles was uneasy with the situation in which Father Raymond had placed her. Nevertheless, Preval was now admitted as the fourth member of the Chartres convent.

The four sisters at the new house were financially on their own. They received no monetary help from Mother Juliette and her community and had to rely solely "upon the charity of kind persons for provisions as well as for furniture."[38] Sister Mary Bernard Deggs notes how dire their situation was when she states that Mother Josephine "did not have a nickel when she was sent to [the] house." The sisters there could not even buy firewood to cook their meals. They only survived because their first two postulants, who "were as dark as the head of a jet pine," brought dowries that together came to $806.[39] Thus, for all practical purposes, the Holy Family Congregation was split in two and remained so from 1870 to 1883.[40]

According to Sister Borgia Hart, the majority of the sisters had rejected Preval because she had dark skin and had been a former slave.[41] Historians Virginia Meacham Gould and Charles E. Nolan however, believe that the situation was more complicated. They speculate that she was not admitted because she was the archbishop's housekeeper and would continue to be so as a sister. Simply stated, the majority of the sisters did not want to be identified as a community of domestic servants, since this would compromise their hard-won status as religious sisters.[42] At any rate, regardless of the reason for Preval's initial rejection by the congregation's majority, there is no denying the fact that her acceptance was a significant development for the Holy Family Sisters. Had the barrier between the more privileged sisters from the *gens de couleur libre* class and that of the larger black population not been removed, the Holy Family Sisters would have found it increasingly difficult, if not impossible, in the post–Civil War period to carry out their ministry. Most probably, they would not have survived.

In 1873 the Holy Family Sisters expanded beyond New Orleans when they accepted a request to open a school for African American girls in Opelousas. Similar schools in other southern Louisiana locations soon followed. In 1876 they again responded to the needs of the black community when they consented to take on the responsibility for an orphanage for black girls in New Orleans. Less than two decades later they took on a second orphanage, this one for boys.

These expansions exerted a tremendous financial strain on the congregation, but the sisters accepted this burden because they realized how crucial their education ministry was to the children of newly freed slaves. To survive, the congregation sought and received permission from the archbishop to send sisters to northern churches to solicit donations. But this did not provide enough, and eventually the community was forced to resort to other forms of alms collecting. Sister Borgia Hart explains:

> Begging or soliciting alms in food, clothing, money or useful articles was a necessity. Wherever a large number of persons were being paid, two Sisters, or at least a Sister and an orphan, were present with outstretched hand to receive the nickel or dime given by the recipient of a pay envelope. Sometimes, as for example, on the pay days of the police and the school teachers, the Sister collectors took their stand at the paying center or at the City Hall at eight o'clock, and as each person came to be paid at the hour convenient to himself, continuing until five in the evening, those asking for donations were forced to remain at their post all day until closing time without even a drink of water. In addition to begging in the markets and groceries there was the round to be made at stated times in office buildings, in railroad offices, in banks, and in some homes whose charitable inmates were ready at the appearance of the Sisters to give their share.[43]

The sisters earned additional revenue by tailoring clothing for some clergy, doing their laundry, and making the communion hosts for virtually every Catholic church in New Orleans. They also continued to sew baby clothes, tablecloths, and other items for various shops. Yet since the people to whom they ministered—poor black children and adults—had little money to pay them for their services, they were perpetually burdened with their own bills. Sister Mary Bernard Deggs expresses just how desperate their situation was:

Many were the times the foundresses had nothing to eat but cold hominy that had been left from some rich family's table.... [T]heir clothing . . . was more like Joseph's coat that was of many pieces and colors darned, until darn was not the word.... Many a night did our dear sisters, after working all day, pray that some dear friend would send them a few spoonfuls of sugar.... Many ladies, knowing how poor we were, often sent us old shoes or boots to wear in the yard when it rained.[44]

This, then, was the precarious condition in which the Sisters of the Holy Family found themselves when Sister Austin Jones was elected mother superior and they were called upon by Bishop Salvatore Di Pietro of British Honduras to send sisters to open a school for black Carib (Garifuna) children in Stann Creek. Their ministry had always been restricted to southern Louisiana and they could barely make ends meet. Could they take on the additional burden of missionary work in a primitive foreign land?

CHAPTER 2
―――

MOTHER AUSTIN JONES AND THE EARLY MISSION

Mother Austin was the first mother superior of the Holy Family Sisters who spoke English rather than French as her first language. She was also the first who did not descend from the Creole class of *gens de couleur libre*. Thus, in many respects her election marks the finalization of the congregation's gradual transition from a Creole African French orientation to one that was more African American. Indeed, Sister Bernard Deggs, in her history of the Holy Family Sisters, sums up Mother Austin's importance to her community when she labels her the "most capable" and "most successful" of the congregation's mother superiors.[1]

Born on May 7, 1861, in Donaldsonville, Louisiana, as Mary Ellen Jones, she entered the Holy Family community in 1877 and was formally professed in 1879. Following three years of religious training, she was assigned to St. Mary's Academy in New Orleans as principal. Her intelligence, administrative ability, and disposition for the religious life did not go unnoticed; in 1891 she was elected mother superior even though she was only thirty years of age. Thus, she became the youngest mother superior in the congregation's history. So successful was she in that office that she was elected six consecutive times. Her tenure only ended with her death in 1909.

Jones had entered the congregation at the end of Reconstruction. By that time the Fifteenth Amendment had given blacks the right to vote, and a significant number had been elected to political office. Congress had passed the Civil Rights Act of 1875, outlawing racial segregation in "public accommodations." And equally important to the Holy Family Sisters, several new postulants had joined their community. In short, it was a time of great hope for the sisters.[2]

By the 1890s, however, when Mother Austin took up the reins of leadership in her religious community, optimism had vanished along with Reconstruction. In 1883 the U.S. Supreme Court had outlawed the Civil Rights Act of 1875, and by 1885 most southern states had passed laws requiring separate schools for blacks and whites. By the mid-1880s only a few decaying public schools for black children still remained open in New Orleans, and white officials had ended public education for black students after completion of the sixth grade. In 1896 the Supreme Court would legalize racial segregation in its infamous Plessy v. Ferguson decision, a forerunner of "separate but equal." Two years later the "grandfather clause" would be written into the Louisiana Constitution, thereby disenfranchising African Americans. Indeed, by the time Jones was elected mother superior, Jim Crow laws had been put into effect throughout the South, thereby ensuring that the black population would be relegated to a status that was little better than slavery. Those who were not willing to accept their inferior status with docility would more likely than not have to face the wrath of the Ku Klux Klan.[3] To make matters worse for the Holy Family Sisters, the Klan despised Catholics almost as much as it did blacks. Yet, faced with such a bleak environment, Mother Austin would not only hold her congregation together, but under her skillful tutelage it would also grow in numbers as never before and significantly expand its apostolate to poor blacks. New schools and orphanages would be opened in New Orleans. The sisters would expand their labors to include the teaching of boys and to construct better facilities for the indigent elderly. For the first time the sisters would go beyond southern Louisiana, opening schools in Texas and Arkansas.[4] Yet Mother Austin's bold decision to accept Bishop Salvatore Di

Pietro's invitation to send sisters to Stann Creek in British Honduras was perhaps her most significant achievement.

Di Pietro, a Sicilian Jesuit, had come to British Honduras in 1869 and was shortly thereafter appointed Jesuit Superior for the colony, a position he held off and on until he was named the vicar apostolic (first bishop) of Belize on April 16, 1893. This was the same year that the order's superior general in Rome transferred Jesuit jurisdiction in British Honduras from the English to the U.S. Missouri Province.

In 1897, Di Pietro traveled to New Orleans with a request that the Holy Family congregation consider taking charge of a school that his order had reluctantly begun in Stann Creek for Garifuna children. Methodist missionaries had recently moved into the area and opened a church and school. The Jesuits, in keeping with the policy of Ignatius Loyola, their founder, had only planned to open schools for the Spanish-speaking sons of the Central American elite. It was hoped that their graduates would become the future leaders of the various isthmian countries. Educating Garifuna (Garinagu) had not been part of their strategy,[5] because, in accordance with the prejudice of the times, they believed that "black people generally are not fitted for any higher education than that afforded by the public schools."[6]

Methodist competition in Stann Creek, however, forced them to alter their plans. A Jesuit brother, Daniel Reynolds, was charged with launching an elementary school, which was staffed by four laymen and one laywoman. It was soon apparent, however, that these teachers did not have the time or adequate training to instruct the large number of students who enrolled. Moreover, religious sisters would obviously be better able to instill in their youthful charges an understanding of the Catholic faith. Thus, Di Pietro asked the Mercy Sisters of New Orleans, who already were staffing a Spanish-speaking and an English-speaking school in the capital, for help. But they were unwilling to expand their mission commitment to Stann Creek. Their reluctance may have resulted from racial prejudice, for their high school in the capital, St. Catherine's Academy, only accepted light-skinned students. On the other hand, members of their congregation were already teaching in a free school for black children in Jamaica, and their superior in New Orleans, Mother Austin Carroll, prided herself on the fact that her sisters took on the instruction of black children in a few southern Louisiana Catholic elementary schools. St. Catherine's had earlier become entangled in a battle between Irish and German factions in the U.S. Catholic Church, which eventually involved the Vatican. With the problems this caused Carroll and her congregation, it seems safe to conclude that, racial prejudices aside, the last thing that the Mercy Sisters needed was another teaching mission in British Honduras.[7]

The bishop next approached the Holy Family congregation. His invitation "struck deep into the hearts of the Sisters" because, when their Rule had been drawn up decades earlier, a line had been inserted stating that, "God Blessing His work, the Congregation of the Holy Family might [someday] extend to other countries."[8] The sisters also remembered that their co-founder and second mother superior, Juliette Gaudin, had been intensely interested in the Propagation of the Faith and its associated Catholic missionary work.[9] Also, two sisters from Belize City, Sister Aimee de Jesus Thompson and Sister Mary Gerard Sorel, had by 1897 already entered the Holy Family congregation in New Orleans. Thus, Mother Austin presumably had some knowledge of British Honduras by the time Di Pietro had asked for their help.[10] Consequently, the mother superior and her congregation agreed to consider the bishop's appeal.

Numerous pages of correspondence would pass between the sisters and Di Pietro over the following year before the sisters felt secure enough to extend their operations and an arrangement could finally be worked out. Two items from this correspondence are especially interesting. The first is a letter from the sisters to Di Pietro, and the second is a contract between Mother Austin and the bishop. The letter begins by stating that the sisters would be happy to accept the bishop's invitation to work in British Honduras. But Mother Austin then adds, "for our own security as well as to prevent difficulties and troubles for you, we humbly propose" that you agree to the following conditions: All sisters working in British Honduras would always be under the jurisdiction of the motherhouse in New Orleans and not under the bishop. The mother superior in New Orleans would have absolute power concerning which sisters are sent or recalled and who is appointed or removed as the superior. "Furthermore as we are not known in your diocese and being there without resources," each sister would be paid no less than twenty dollars per month. And finally, "Considering that in your Lordship's diocese no convent for our Sisters is built yet and that with the salary of 20 Dollars no house rent can be paid," the diocese will provide the sisters with a residence rent-free.[11]

When Di Pietro accepted most of the sisters' conditions, a contract was drawn up. The bishop agreed to receive four sisters "to take full charge of the parochial schools of Stann Creek." He would "pay their passage in coming and give them for their services in teaching sixty dollars a month." Since this was twenty dollars less than the sisters had asked for, the nuns would be permitted to "open a select school and teach music, and whatever money comes from the private school will be theirs." Each music pupil would be required to pay two dollars per month for lessons. The sisters would also be provided with a furnished house for use as a convent for as long as they remained in Stann Creek. The Stann Creek community would be a branch house of the convent in New Orleans and, as such, would be under the jurisdiction of the mother superior there for all matters concerning religious life. In other matters the sisters would be dependent on the vicar apostolic in Belize. If a sister is to be recalled to the United States, it should only be done after the mother superior in New Orleans has consulted with the vicar apostolic, and no sister can be withdrawn without another being sent to take her place. Finally, "according to the Education Code of the Colony," the sisters would be required to allow pupil teachers to work at their school. The government would pay these pupil teachers, but the head instructor must provide them with at least four hours of special lessons per week. For this service the head instructor would receive "a small remuneration from the government."[12]

These two documents are highly significant because they demonstrate the astuteness of Mother Austin and her sisters concerning practical matters of financial security and jurisdiction. It is a well-known fact that in the nineteenth and early twentieth centuries, many female religious congregations throughout the United States had accepted invitations from bishops to teach in schools only to find that they were expected to pay the mortgage or rent for their convent, or that the salaries provided by the diocese were not enough to cover basic needs.¹³ Likewise, bishops sometimes interfered in a paternalistic way in appointments and transfers of sisters and at times even took control of convents, separating nuns from their congregations and turning them into diocesan religious communities under direct episcopal jurisidiction.

Mother Austin and her sisters were determined to make sure that no bishop or priest would be in a position to control their fate. Likewise, as black nuns,¹⁴ they especially had to be careful not to allow themselves to be subjected to the authoritarian whims of a parish pastor or diocesan bishop. The Holy Family Sisters were a community without financial stability; Jones well knew that unanticipated expenses in British Honduras could destroy them. If they were going to venture into the foreign mission field, then they would have to have an agreement in writing as to their rights and the bishop's responsibilities to them. Indeed, as will be shown in the following pages, Mother Austin's insistence on a detailed contract spelling out the rights and responsibilities of the sisters vis-à-vis those of the bishop would prove to be crucial to the survival of the British Honduras mission.

On the Monday after Easter 1898, as the sisters were settling into their new Sacred Heart Convent in Stann Creek, Bishop Di Pietro journeyed to the town to make sure that all was going well. In a letter to "Your Grace" (presumably the archbishop of New Orleans), he notes that he found everything in order:

> Yesterday they opened the schools, both parochial and select ones. They had 177 [students] in the first and 7 in the second. Many more are expected. The select school will increase up to 15, and six or eight pupils are ready for music lessons. Calculating on this they can make over 100 dollars a month, [an] amount quite sufficient for supporting in this town, in consideration of what the people are bringing to them nearly every day in provisions.¹⁵

Di Pietro ends his letter with a prediction that great things will come from the sisters' labors in Stann Creek: "According to what I heard and what I said it seems to me that the foundation of the Sisters of the

Holy Family in Stann Creek will be a success. The work will civilize not only the children but the adults and I feel confident that in a short time we will see a remarkable change in the town."[16]

His poorly chosen word "civilize" aside, Di Pietro's prediction that the sisters would make a profound difference in Stann Creek was right on the mark. The major reasons for their future success would be their hard work and competence. But another factor undoubtedly was that they were in the unique position of being black Catholic missionaries serving a black clientele. Mission historian Angelyn Dries indirectly indicates how important this is when she quotes a Sister of Charity working among poor Bahamian islanders in the early 1920s. The sister notes with frustration: "It is difficult for white people . . . to penetrate into the racial life of the negro." Elaborating on this remark, Dries adds that as close as the white Charity Sisters came to the islanders, the black people to whom they ministered always "kept them distant" when it came to that part of their lives involving their African roots.[17] The African American Holy Family sisters would not have this problem at least to the degree that white sisters would. Thus, their black racial identity, which caused them to suffer discrimination in the United States, turned into an advantage in British Honduras.

But success for the sisters would not be easy. Once the initial euphoria that accompanied their arrival was over, the missionary nuns settled into their daily routine of teaching. The sisters were unable to obtain some of the staples that they had become accustomed to in the United States, such as milk and meat. Realizing this, Mother Austin, until she died in 1909, had a supply of meat sent to them weekly on a United Fruit Company steamer. This worked fine in the winter months, but in the summer, even though the meat was kept on ice while in transit, it often arrived spoiled and inedible.[18]

The hot and humid tropical climate took a heavy toll on these missionary nuns, especially since their rule required them to wear a heavy, black habit with starched head, neck, and shoulder linen. The women also proved susceptible to the disease-carrying insects of the British colony. Shortly after the first sisters' arrival, some of them contracted malaria. This and other tropical health problems would plague the Holy Family community in British Honduras throughout the early decades of their mission. Indeed, in the early years, before health conditions improved in the colony, sisters were frequently forced to return to New Orleans either temporarily or permanently due to sickness.[19] The expense of these trips to and from the United States, as will be seen, would eventually cause the mission to go into debt and the sisters to incur the wrath of the episcopal successor to Bishop Di Pietro.

Death would come to three of the sisters while serving in Stann Creek. Sister Mary Bernard Baker, a young nun who was sent to British Honduras less than a year after her profession, died in November 1908, only seventeen months after her arrival. Sister Mary Edmond Ogaldez, the first Garifuna to enter the community, died in August 1912, only sixteen months after returning to Stann Creek from New Orleans, where she had completed her novitiate. And in February 1935, Sister Mary of Lourdes Gray succumbed when a lingering malarial fever developed into "black water fever"; she had served in Stann Creek for eight years.[20] The three sisters are buried side by side in the town cemetery.

Upon their arrival, the four pioneer missionary sisters were faced with a crisis that was unforeseen. They discovered that their pupils spoke a patois mixture of Indian, English, French, and African dialects and did not understand English very well.[21] In order to be understood, the sisters attempted to learn the native language but found it too difficult. Thus, they felt that they had no choice but to teach their classes wholly in English and hope that the children would eventually come to comprehend this "foreign language." At first the students had trouble, but within a comparatively short time they adjusted. Although the children continued to speak in their own tongue outside the classroom, when at school they learned to use English little by little. This is apparent from the fact that, in accordance with British custom, each pupil had to be examined annually by an official appointed by the Crown. Despite the fact that the exams were conducted totally in English, the sisters' charges "gradually attained a fairly good average and were able to compete favorably with other pupils who had not this handicap."[22] In hindsight, this early language crisis probably was a blessing in disguise. Had the young Garifuna at Sacred Heart not learned to master English, most would have been faced with limited job opportunities as adults. Having a command of English meant that they could pursue higher-paying jobs or more advanced educational opportunities in other parts of British Honduras and even in the United States. On the other hand, since the sisters only spoke English, they would be limited in their relationship with the Garifuna people whom they had come to serve.

The fact that the Holy Family missionary sisters did not realize that the Garifuna did not speak English as their first language illustrates how little they knew upon their arrival about the people of Stann Creek and their culture. The Garifuna, who descend from escaped African slaves and Carib/Arawak Amerindians, originated in the seventeenth century on the Caribbean island of St. Vincent. Both France and Britain claimed the island, but in 1783 it was ceded to the British. There followed a series of so-called Carib wars, in which the Garifuna sided with the French settlers. When the Garifuna were finally subdued in 1796, the British deported most of them to the Bay Islands of Roatán and Bonacca, off the coast of Honduras. Of the five thousand or so who were deported, only about half survived the journey. Since these islands were infertile and too small to support the new arrivals, the Garifuna asked the Spanish for permission to cross over and settle on the mainland at what today is Trujillo, Honduras. Thus, over the next century the Garifuna people spread out along the Caribbean coast of Honduras, British Honduras, Guatemala, and, to a lesser degree, Nicaragua. Those who migrated to British Honduras settled mostly in Punta Gorda, Stann Creek, and Seine Bight, where they survived as subsistence farmers and fishermen. As foreign fruit-exporting companies expanded into their region, however, many Garifuna lost their land and were forced to seek employment in the low-paying lumber industry. With few local jobs available, larger and larger numbers were compelled to leave the country to find work.

When the Garifuna first entered Honduras, they adopted the Catholicism of the Spaniards, but blended it in a syncretic form with their earlier African religious beliefs. Drums, often accompanied by rattles made from dried gourds, were important in their religious rituals and overall culture. Dances, especially the *punta*, were performed on holidays and at most social events. The main staples of the Garifuna diet were cassava bread (*ereba*), which is usually eaten with fish and pounded plantains (*hudutu*), and a sticky, sweet rice (*bimecacule*). In general, throughout their history, life has been hard for the Garifuna, who were often discriminated against by other ethnic peoples in British Honduras who viewed them as "peculiar, foreign." Prior to the 1980s, U.S.-born Holy Family missionaries knew little of this rich culture when they arrived in Dangriga (Stann Creek). On-the-job training was the norm. But because the sisters in British Honduras, like other female religious congregations, lived a semi-cloistered life, it was difficult for them to adjust to their new environment and fit in fully with the people whom they served.

Like nearly all the schools in British Honduras, Sacred Heart was a government school. One had to qualify to be a teacher by passing examinations given by the Department of Education. Consequently, upon their arrival the four pioneer sisters each had to apply to the Board of Education for a "1st Class Provisional Certificate" permitting them to teach for six months. After that, they were given an "Honorary Teacher's Certificate, First Class," signifying that they held a high-school diploma and had passed their government exams. They were then qualified to teach at the primary school level.[23]

British Honduran primary schools consisted of six "standards." Their completion was the equivalent of finishing eighth grade in the United States. The sisters taught their students English grammar, reading, writing and composition, history, geography, elementary science, mathematics, nature study, drawing, needlework, handicrafts, physical education, and religion. In other words, they taught a curriculum that was basically the same as that in their schools in the United States. Such an American-based curriculum was standard fare for U.S. missionaries in the nineteenth and most of the twentieth century. The Mercy Sisters' set of courses at St. Catherine Elementary and Holy Redeemer School in Belize City did not vary from what their congregation taught in New Orleans and elsewhere in the United States;[24] and, as Sylvia M. Jacobs tells us in *Black Americans and the Missionary Movement in Africa*, Protestant African American missionary schools in Africa were also based on U.S. models.[25]

Once a student completed sixth standard, he or she had to go to Belize City for high school, since there were no high schools elsewhere in the country. But since very few students could afford this move, many simply kept repeating the sixth standard, often as many as three times since there was nowhere else for these students to go.[26] In addition to their work in the larger school, the sisters also taught a small number of special students whose parents were able to pay tuition in a "select school," but archival records do not record how much the sisters earned from this private school. And, as we know, the missionary nuns also gave music lessons to those who could pay the two-dollar fee. Select schools and music lessons had long been a common way for financially strapped female religious communities in the United States to supplement their income. Thus, the Sisters of the Holy Family were merely transporting a well-established, near-universal tradition to British Honduras, a tradition that enabled underpaid religious women to survive. But it appears that the Stann Creek select school was closed around 1911.[27] This meant that a significant source of income was lost to the already financially strapped sisters.

In keeping with their contract and British law, the sisters also provided instruction to pupil teachers. Much later, in 1943, with the help of Father John Knopp, S.J., pastor of Sacred Heart Parish, the Holy Family community would gain formal approval from the Department of Education to begin their own pupil-teacher training school, and in 1945 the government agency would classify Sacred Heart School as a Pupil-Teacher Training Center. Students who graduated from sixth standard were eligible for this five-year program. They would receive ten hours of instruction weekly, going to class from eight to nine o'clock in the morning and from four to five o'clock in the afternoon. In between they would assist the certified teachers in their classroom duties. For these services, they would be paid a small salary by the government. When the pupil-teachers passed a series of national tests given at the end of each school year, they were certified as teachers by the Department of Education. Sister Mary of the Rosary Heisser, writing in 1973, claims that the sisters' Pupil-Teacher Training Center "was second to none in preparing teachers for our schools in the Stann Creek area and throughout the country."[28]

It was certainly a godsend for both the young participants and the sisters who taught them. Because until the 1950s there were no high schools outside of the capital city, Stann Creek primary-school graduates, lacking the necessary funds, would have had little if any chance to become teachers had it not been for the nuns' pupil-teacher training program. Equally important, once enough new teachers were trained and certified, the Holy Family Sisters were able to open several additional schools without needing a large increase in religious personnel. Indeed, no more than ten Holy Family Sisters ever served in the Stann Creek district at one time, yet the sisters would train generations of capable teachers sufficient to educate students throughout the entire district and beyond.[29]

In addition to operating the select and free schools, the sisters also ran a "baby school" for parents who needed preschool care for their children. Prior to the coming of the sisters, preschoolers remained with their parents or grandparents as the adults worked on their subsistence farms. Needless to say, this was not a good situation for either worker or baby. Initially, Addie Saffold was assigned to run the "baby school." Both the success of her work and the need for a preschool in Stann Creek are attested to in a letter from Father Matharus Antillach to Mother Austin, dated March 17, 1899, following the return of Saffold to New Orleans where she was to make her novitiate:

> I am very [word missing, presumably "sad"] that we had to lose Miss Addie and the good Sister Emmanuel; especially perhaps, Miss Addie, because I do not see how I can supply [sic] for her absence from the Infant School. I am afraid that we are going to lose many children on account of her departure. The people are not yet aware that she is not to come back; however, some suspect it, and intend to draw up a petition for her return. This is sufficient proof of the people's esteem, and of her beneficial influence over young and old.[30]

Father Antillach now gets to the point. Saffold's work is crucial to the community in Stann Creek and he wants her to return immediately:

> I myself respect her great and [word missing, possibly "fervent"] desire of entering the Novitiate, and if it be necessary for her to remain away from us for some time, there is no one more ready to acquiesce than I am, still, if you should see that she might

make her novitiate or her Postulantship here among us, I should be ever so pleased. It is true such a course would be an exception to your Rules and Customs; still, there would be good reasons for making this exception, as she has been living as long a time among the Sisters, following their daily order, and experiencing the [word missing, presumably "same"] inconveniences as they, practicing, moreover, those principal virtues which are required by your Institute. She would have all the opportunities here as she would have there; teaching, of course; and visiting the sick.[31]

Antillach ends by stating that he will accept whatever decision Mother Austin makes.[32] She wisely did not acquiesce to the Jesuit's plea and allow Saffold to make an informal novitiate in Stann Creek, a fact that speaks well of her leadership capability and the determination of the Holy Family leadership not to capitulate to the clergy when it came to the internal affairs of their congregation. Saffold began her novitiate the day after Antillach's letter was mailed. She was given the religious habit and name, Sister Mary Matthew, on January 30, 1900. Unfortunately, she died on October 7 of that same year while still a novice.[33]

Rita Mather, the first local superior of the Holy Family Sisters in Stann Creek, in addition to her duties as community superior, took on the additional task of running the "baby school." The children would be left with Sister Rita in the early morning. She would bathe and feed them, and teach them the alphabet, their numbers, and their prayers. Sister Emmanuel, who had returned from New Orleans, would assist her. There is nothing in the sisters' archival records indicating whether or not they were paid for their preschool services, but most probably they were not. Sisters Emmanuel, Dominica, and Stephen were each charged with teaching one of the school's standards. In its first few years of existence, Sacred Heart was limited to Standard Three.[34]

In summary, the first pioneer sisters worked from sunup to sundown under very trying conditions, thereby paving the way for the ninety or so Sisters of the Holy Family who would follow them in service to the people of Dangriga (Stann Creek). They did nothing that was innovative; they adhered to the congregation's original charism and employed the same curricula and teaching methods as did their fellow sisters in southern Louisiana. There was one difference, however. In their schools in the United States, the sisters had no choice but to conform to the segregation required by law. They would not be so restricted in British Honduras. Although their pupils would primarily be Garifuna and black Creoles, Sister Borgia Hart notes with obvious pride: "There were no separate schools for natives. Europeans, Mexicans, and Central Americans were taught together."[35] In other words, Sacred Heart was open to anyone who needed instruction regardless of race or ethnic background.

CHAPTER 3

TROUBLE WITH THE BISHOP

On November 5, 1899, following the death of Bishop Di Pietro, Frederick C. Hopkins, an English Jesuit, was consecrated vicar apostolic for British Honduras, an office he would hold until April 9, 1923, when he, along with two Pallottine Sisters, drowned in a tragic boating accident.[1] During much of this time he would be embroiled in a conflict with the Holy Family Congregation over finances and personnel.

We first see documented evidence of problems in a 1910 letter from Hopkins to Mother Elizabeth Bowie, the successor to Mother Austin. Hopkins informs the mother superior that he is arranging "a scheme for founding a house for your Sisters in Punta Gorda," a coastal town south of Stann Creek in the Toledo District. This move, he claims, should keep the sisters from having to make expensive journeys from New Orleans to Stann Creek and back "when the Sisters need a change."[2] A later letter that will be discussed below indicates that what Bishop Hopkins actually had in mind was the establishment of a second branch of the Holy Family Sisters, one that would primarily be made up of Garifuna and Creoles and be under his jurisdiction rather than that of the motherhouse in New Orleans.

Hopkins next complains of Mother Elizabeth's plan to have Sister Mary Helena Plaisance return to New Orleans to take her vows: "The Stann Creek Convent cannot afford this expense as [the sisters] are already in debt. Last year I gave them $100 as a present to help them. This year I cannot do it as I have two schools and a presbytery building all of which I have to help. . . . I do not like to interfere in any way between you and your Community but if Sister Helena could take her vows in Stann Creek it would save expense."[3] Hopkins adds that Sister Bernadette Elback, the head of the Holy Family community in British Honduras, would "be glad to be relieved of the responsibility of being Superior," due in part to poor health but also to her inability to keep the sisters' expenses in line with their revenues.[4]

A letter from Sister Bernadette to Archbishop James H. Blenk of New Orleans, written six years later, shows that contrary to the wishes of Hopkins, she was still superior of the sisters in Stann Creek. It also shows that her community remained in desperate financial straits: "We are having hard times here since this Cruel War [World War I]. The people with whom we work are so very poor, it is sad to see, as for ourselves, we can hardly live. . . . Please beg Our dear Lord in His Divine Mercy to send us some money from somewhere."[5] The continuing debt of the Stann Creek sisters coupled with their frequent travel caused Hopkins to write another letter in January 1917 to Mother Elizabeth, one that was far less cordial than the one he had sent in 1910. He notes that it had come to his attention that the mother superior planned to have all four of the Stann Creek nuns visit her in New Orleans during the school break, "as you have not time to make the trip down here." As he continues, he cannot contain his anger: "I beg to represent to you, Rev. Mother, that such a journey would cost them at least $250 and they have not the money to pay for it. According to agreement with Mother Austin . . . we were to pay the Sisters $60 a month, $720 yearly. As a fact they were paid $1060 besides the $200 received [as a gift to the sisters] from Mother Katherine Drexel [foundress of the Sisters of the Blessed Sacrament]." But even with this extra money, he continues, the sisters are still unable to make ends meet. Consequently, since the church in British Honduras cannot afford to pay either the sisters' debts or their travel expenses, "I hope then that you will give us the pleasure of receiving a visit from yourself instead of wishing the Stann Creek Community to visit you."[6]

When Archbishop Blenk, who had always supported the sisters, died, Hopkins wrote to Father Jules B. Jeanmard, the chancellor and interim administrator of the New Orleans Archdiocese, hoping that his fellow cleric would see the matter from his perspective. His letter of October 1917, along with Jeanmard's response, goes far in shedding light on this conflict.

The vicar apostolic opens by stating that he is writing because it is useless to correspond with Mother Elizabeth; she "does not well understand the proper relations between the Ordinary [bishop] of this Vicariate and the Religious of the Holy Family residing here."[7] He next lists a whole series of instances when his wishes were ignored not only by Mother Elizabeth but by Mother Austin as well. When he complained to Mother Austin that Sister Rita Mather, the first local superior of the Stann Creek sisters, was "not sufficiently educated to take charge of a Government-aided school" and therefore needed to be replaced by a more qualified nun, she ignored him for several years. After another superior had finally been sent and eventually had to be replaced, he asked Mother Elizabeth not to send back Sister Rita, but his plea was ignored. Later, when the competent Sister Borgia Hart was placed in charge of the school and he asked that she not be replaced, she was transferred anyway, "without a word to me." Now, Sister Bernadette is in charge and under her direction the Stann Creek convent has gone more than $500 in debt. She "has begged over and over again to be relieved of the office but no change has been made, and when I have written to Rev. Mother Elizabeth she has not answered me on this matter."[8]

But, Hopkins continues, the large debt "is not entirely the fault of Sr. Bernadette"; rather, it is due to the excessive number of trips that the sisters make to and from New Orleans. It cost $81.25, for instance, for two sisters who recently made the journey. Fortunately this time, and this was a first, the father of one of the nuns paid part of the bill. Another sister was recalled for an assignment in New Orleans. Since she returned to work in the United States, the motherhouse should have incurred the $31.80 cost of her trip but it did not. Not only are these excessive trips expensive, but the sisters also at times return late for the beginning of the school year, thereby depriving the students at least for a short period of their teachers. Indeed, the Jesuits at Stann Creek, who have many more expenses than the sisters, live more frugally. Yet, says Hopkins, when he complained to Archbishop Blenk, the prelate took the side of the nuns.[9]

Shifting gears, Hopkins next accuses the sisters of sometimes going out alone on visitations to families in the area. When he warned Sister Bernadette that such visits should never be made unless the sister is accompanied by a female companion of no less than twelve years of age, he was ignored. The superior herself was so rash as to spend several days alone during a vacation at the home of a Protestant family. Finally, Hopkins suggests that if the sisters would only open a novitiate in British Honduras for Caribs, thereby creating a separate community of indigenous sisters, then the problem of costly travel to New Orleans would be eliminated.[10]

Jeanmard soon responded in a letter that is both significant and revealing: significant in that it sympathetically presents the nuns' side of the story, revealing in that it invokes the racist misconceptions of the time to "excuse" the sisters' supposed shortcomings. He begins by expressing sympathy for Hopkins and commiserating on how difficult it must be to oversee a poverty-stricken mission church fraught with so many difficulties. Next came the racism that the Holy Family Congregation had always had to contend with even within the church: "On the other hand I also must take into consideration the conditions as they exist among the Sisters of the Holy Family. These religious are recruited from a race that never can become inured to extreme hardships, such as Your Lordship describes in your letter and which the Mother General has explained to me *viva voce*."[11] Indeed, weakness resulting from racial inferiority is precisely why Hopkins should indulge them: because they cannot endure the heat of British Honduras, they must be allowed "a change of climate at stated intervals, [or] else they become unfit for further service." Mother Elizabeth understood this and so did Archbishop Blenk; "hence his recommendation that they should be allowed to come home for a visit, annually, if possible."[12]

Jeanmard now becomes more blunt:

> Your Lordship mentions the cost of such journeys. No doubt, they are quite expensive, but what about the health of the religious? You speak of Sr. Borgia. She could not return to Stann Creek, because her health was so seriously impaired that she needed, and still needs, a period of recuperation.[13]

> Mother Elizabeth deeply regrets that the convent in Stann Creek should be burdened with debt. . . . [B]ut she lays the blame on the conditions as they exist in that far-away and hardly accessible mission where the Sisters cannot find sufficient revenues that would permit them to recuperate from the fatigues of the climate and from the incessant labors in the school room.[14]

As far as the sisters' visitations without a female companion, Mother Elizabeth feels grieved that her charges were disobedient. "She puts the blame for this on the local superior's neglect in enforcing the rules of the community."[15]

The New Orleans chancellor next responds to a new contract (no longer extant) that Hopkins had enclosed with his letter, probably hoping that Jeanmard, as acting head of the archdiocese, would persuade Mother Elizabeth to sign it. It was obviously meant to replace the contract that Bishop Di Pietro and Mother Austin had mutually signed in 1889, which Bishop Hopkins saw as a constraint:

> Speaking of the contract of which you enclose a copy, Mother Elizabeth thinks it is evidently one-sided and that it would not hold good in any Court of Equity, no matter what Canon Law might consider it. This contract would make it practically impossible to recall a Sister although the state of her health or the good of the community would make such a recall imperative.[16]

Having dismissed the proposal of another contract, Jeanmard turns to the suggestion that the sisters open a novitiate for Garifuna girls. He concedes that a novitiate might be a good idea but adds that the bishop would have to find another congregation to run it. "It goes without saying that the Sisters of the Holy Family at Stann Creek could not open such a novitiate, because they are not sufficiently numerous, nor could the motherhouse spare any additional subjects."[17] As for Hopkins's proposal that the Holy Family Sisters in British Honduras become a separate community from that in New Orleans, the chancellor writes it off as impractical:

> To carry into effect your plan . . . for the erection of a separate community of Holy Family Sisters, will be fraught with

insurmountable difficulties. Of the four religious, who are at present in Stann Creek, three would demand to return to New Orleans, nor could they be forced to belong to another community against their own volition.... Small chance, then, that the few Sisters, with all the work to perform, would be able to have a novitiate at Stann Creek for Carib girls.[18]

Jeanmard closes with a frank suggestion:

> May I venture an advise [sic]? Let the Sisters have their own way. They will find means to provide for the occasional trips to New Orleans. In the meantime you might succeed in inducing another community to take charge of the Caribs at Stann Creek, a community that might make their habitat amongst these deserving children of Holy Mother Church without the necessity of traveling such a great distance to reach their motherhouse.[19]

There is no written record of whether Hopkins took the advice of Jeanmard. If the bishop attempted to persuade another female congregation to come to Stann Creek to replace the Holy Family Sisters, he was unsuccessful. Moreover, no Holy Family novitiate was ever established in Belize even though many native Belizeans entered the congregation over the next half-century.[20] We do know that despite the bishop's negative feelings toward Sister Bernadette, she continued as superior of the Stann Creek sisters until 1935, when she was replaced due to poor health.[21]

Mother Elizabeth and her successors continued to hold firm to the contract agreed to by Mother Austin and Bishop Di Pietro, although by the 1930s sisters under temporary vows who were assigned to Stann Creek no longer returned to New Orleans to take their final vows. Instead, they now took them at the Sacred Heart mission church.[22] Aside from this concession, there does not seem to have been much change in the policy of the sisters concerning occasional visits back to New Orleans. What we do have is a short letter from Hopkins to Mother Elizabeth written about a month after the vicar apostolic received his reply from Jeanmard, in which he congratulates Mother Elizabeth and the Sisters of the Holy Family on the seventy-fifth anniversary of the founding of their congregation.

Financial constraints are mentioned, but in a less belligerent way than before. Indeed, Hopkins seems almost apologetic when he writes: "On such an occasion I would have liked the Sisters of Stann Creek to have taken a part in your domestic celebration, but the difficulty of communications and the exorbitant price the Steamship Companies are charging were prohibitive. It would have cost them at least $350 to go [to New Orleans] and return."[23] Instead, he informs the mother superior that the Jesuits and the sisters at Sacred Heart School will commemorate the jubilee in Stann Creek by having a bazaar in which all proceeds will go to the sisters.[24]

Although this letter seems to represent the end of the contention between the Holy Family Congregation and the bishop of Belize, before moving on, two facets of the conflict must be given more attention. First, one must concede that Hopkins's charge, that some of the Holy Family Sisters sent to work in British Honduras were not sufficiently educated, may well have been true. Nevertheless, the bishop should have realized that under Louisiana's racially segregated Catholic and secular school system, there was no way for them to have had as good an education as, for example, the white New Orleans–based Mercy Sisters, who worked in Belize City. This should have been understood and accepted by Di Pietro and the Jesuits when they asked the Holy Family Congregation to take on the Stann Creek assignment. Evidently it was not understood by Hopkins, who seems to have expected more from the sisters than was reasonable considering the limitations placed on them by the racism of the day.[25]

It must also be pointed out, however, that the Holy Family Sisters brought a positive dimension to their mission work that the Mercy Sisters and other white congregations could not bring to theirs. It certainly offset whatever negative factor might have existed concerning education. The Holy Family missionaries gave the Catholic Church in British Honduras a unique opportunity that existed nowhere else. For the first time in modern history, indigenous black people from the developing world received Catholic missionaries who were of their own race. One need only remember the frustration of a white Sister of Charity, cited in chapter 2, who complained that racial barriers kept the sisters from penetrating into the world of the poor black Bahamians whom they served.[26]

The Sisters of the Holy Family did not have this problem. Due to the prejudice they were forced to deal with daily in the United States for no other reason than the color of their skin—Jim Crow laws, the absence of political power or equal treatment before the law, the lack of respect accorded them even by white church officials, a history of involuntary physical deprivation within their religious community—they were better able than white missionaries to understand the sufferings of the poverty-stricken people to whom they ministered. In other words, they had personally experienced some of the same poverty and indignities that indigenous black people were obliged to live with every day. They also had a long history of teaching the poorest of the poor back home in New Orleans. This was rarely the case with white missionaries.

The second point that needs to be emphasized is that, although Hopkins complains about the Stann Creek sisters' debt and their frequent trips to New Orleans, his bone of contention is primarily about the question of authority. Hopkins makes this clear when he writes to Jeanmard that Mother Elizabeth "does not well understand the proper relations between the Ordinary of this Vicariate and the Religious of the Holy Family residing here." Simply put, as in most dioceses in the pre–Vatican II church, the bishop wanted final power when it came to female religious communities operating within his jurisdiction. Mother Austin, who indeed well understood the problems that could arise if the sisters had no recourse against an autocratic bishop or pastor, had made sure that her sisters had a contract spelling out in detail the Stann Creek community's rights and responsibilities in relation to those of the bishop. Hopkins did not want to be limited by this contract. Consequently, his conflict with the sisters was principally the result of his attempt to force them to grant back to him the prime authority that Di Pietro had conceded to Mother Austin. Throughout the conflict, both Mother Austin and Mother Elizabeth, while remaining respectful, held firm. And with the contract of 1898 as their trump card, they emerged from the game as the clear winners.

It should be noted that while Bishop Hopkins was pressuring the Holy Family Congregation to allow him to create a second branch of the Holy Family Sisters separate from the New Orleans community and under his sole jurisdiction, there was also pressure on the New

Orleans–based Mercy Sisters to sever their ties with their community in Belize City. Evidence for this comes from several sources. In 1918, Bishop Hopkins published a short article in *The Catholic Historical Review* on the history of the Catholic Church in British Honduras. Although he says very little about the four female religious congregations that served in the tiny British colony,[27] he does comment in passing that in 1914 "it was decided" that the New Orleans–based Mercy Sisters, after thirty-one years in British Honduras, would withdraw from the colony and that their convent in Belize City would become an independent Mercy foundation. The bishop further states that this decision was based on the fact that the New Orleans motherhouse did not have a sufficient number of nuns available to properly staff their schools in his diocese.[28] In his *History of the Catholic Church in Belize,* Richard Buhler, S.J., adds: "In 1914 the Sisters of Mercy decided to open a novitiate in Belize [British Honduras] for young ladies wishing to enter religious life."[29] Prior to this time, women from British Honduras who wished to become Sisters of Mercy went to New Orleans for their novitiate.

Mercy Sister Yvonne Hunter, writing in the 1980s, sheds additional light on the separation of the two communities by providing details that were missing in Hopkins's and Buhler's works. In 1891 there were twelve Mercy Sisters in Belize City maintaining two schools, St. Catherine's Academy and Holy Redeemer. This was the same year that, against the wishes of Mother Austin Carroll, the congregation's superior, the New Orleans Mercy Congregation, was divided in two with Mobile, Alabama, becoming a separate foundation.[30] This division meant that there were considerably fewer sisters in the New Orleans branch and therefore fewer who could be spared for service in British Honduras.[31] In 1891, Bishop Di Pietro also asked Mother Austin to provide him with financial help and more sisters. When she responded that she was unable to do so, Di Pietro wrote to the Vatican Congregation for the Propagation of the Faith (Propaganda Fide) in Rome asking for the Mercy community in British Honduras to be made an independent foundation with its own novitiate.[32] His request was denied, however, since the Mercy motherhouse in New Orleans opposed it.[33] Di Pietro next pressed Mother Austin to turn over the title of her congregation's property in Belize

City to his diocese. The Mercy Sisters, who had spent about $10,000 over several years on this land and its buildings, did not want to give it up. Nevertheless, due to episcopal coercion, they were forced to do so.[34]

A few years after Hopkins became bishop, he traveled to New Orleans where, even though he knew that the Mercy Sisters were short on personnel, he pressured Mother Austin Carroll to expand her congregation's commitment in British Honduras by agreeing to staff a new school in Corozal in the northernmost part of the colony. She reluctantly acquiesced, but since the New Orleans motherhouse could spare no more than one sister from the United States, two were taken from the convent in Belize City, thereby adding one more hardship to the already overburdened sisters there. But Hopkins soon claimed that three Mercy Sisters were an insufficient number for Corozal and pushed for two more. Hopkins's ever-increasing requests angered Archbishop Blenk of New Orleans, who thought that the Mercy Congregation's primary responsibility should be to staff schools in his archdiocese. Not wanting to incur the wrath of the archbishop, and perhaps realizing that the New Orleans prelate had inadvertently presented her with a way out of her dilemma, Mother Austin informed Bishop Hopkins that she had no choice but to terminate her congregation's commitment in Corozal. This evidently did not placate Blenk, however, for in 1910 he wrote to the Propagation of the Faith, asking that the Mercy communities in New Orleans and Belize City be separated. But just as it did with Di Pietro earlier, Propaganda Fide denied his request because the Mercy Sisters opposed it.

Needless to say, this decision and the reason for it did not sit well with Blenk, who now made it virtually impossible for Hopkins to raise more money from New Orleans for the Mercy schools in Belize City. It was now Hopkins's turn to petition the Propagation of the Faith. Contending that the Belize City convent needed more sisters and financial help than the motherhouse in New Orleans could supply, he asked Propaganda Fide to reconsider its earlier decisions and to allow the Mercy convent in British Honduras to become an independent foundation. This time, Rome granted the request, and the Mercy community in British Honduras officially separated from the New Orleans motherhouse in 1914.[35]

What is recorded on the transition in the St. Catherine Convent Archives in Belize City is most revealing:

> August 16, 1913: The Bishop came for Mass. After breakfast he assembled all the Sisters in the Community Room and . . . declared this House a Foundation and independent of St. Alphonsus Convent of Mercy, New Orleans, and nominated Sister M. Stanislaus O'Donovan Reverend Mother Superior. Next week he expects several postulants [whom he personally recruited from Ireland and the United States]. He will appoint a Spiritual Father to train them in the religious life.[36]

Both the New Orleans–based Mercy Sisters and Holy Family Sisters had been put to the test by hierarchical attempts to gain power over their missions in British Honduras. But unlike the Holy Family Sisters, who had had the foresight to obtain a written contract from Bishop Di Pietro and therefore were able to control their own fate, the Mercy Sisters had not had such presence of mind. In the documentation unearthed from the Archives of St. Catherine Convent in Belize City, it is clear that the New Orleans–based Mercy Sisters wanted to maintain their connection with and control over their British Honduras mission. But caught between the conflicting wills of a bishop and archbishop—who for their own reasons wanted the two Mercy communities to be separated—the wishes of the sisters had little chance of prevailing. The Belize City convent became an independent foundation. Archbishop Blenk no longer had to spare Mercy Sisters for the mission in British Honduras. Bishop Hopkins, on the other hand, could now "nominate" the new local convent's mother superior and also appoint a new "Spiritual Father" to train his handpicked novices.[37] In other words, he now had dominant power over the Sisters of Mercy in his diocesan jurisdiction.

CHAPTER 4

THE 1920S TO THE SECOND VATICAN COUNCIL

There is little in the sisters' archives documenting their mission in British Honduras from the 1920s through the 1950s. We know that in 1924, when Mother Mary of Sacred Heart Jourdan visited Stann Creek to survey the mission, "she had the pleasure of witnessing the results of years of toil when five stalwart young Carib men called upon her introducing themselves as former pupils of the school."[1] All had had successful careers: three were government employees, one a clerk of the court, and another an owner of his own store. "But what pleased her most of all was the fact that each was a practicing Catholic faithful to Sunday Mass and a frequenter of the Sacraments. Four were fathers with families while the fifth had forgone marriage in order to take care of his widowed mother."[2] Mother Elizabeth Bowie, who after a respite of twelve years was again elected mother superior, likewise visited the mission, this time in 1935. Twenty-four years had passed since she had last been in the British colony. She was well pleased with how the mission had advanced; improvements had been made in the school plant and the number of students had increased. The town itself had progressed nicely. After a three-week stay, she returned to the United States, bringing with her two Belizean women for the novitiate.[3]

We know from the Sacred Heart School Records that in 1936 the school had 413 students. A letter from Belize Bishop Joseph Murphy to Mother Elizabeth, written in that year, notes that Sacred Heart was overcrowded and that plans by the Jesuits to build a much-needed addition had not come to fruition because money from U.S. donors had decreased significantly due to the Great Depression. We also know from this letter that tropical sickness still haunted some of the sisters and forced their return to New Orleans.[4]

Disasters seem to get more attention than do successes. Thus, much detailed information is found in the archives concerning the fire that destroyed the sisters' convent along with Sacred Heart Church on January 26, 1942. On that Monday morning, sometime between 1:00 and 2:00 a.m., Sister Bernardine Stanford was awakened by noise coming from the church. When she looked out the convent window, she found the church ablaze. She quickly alerted the other sisters, who grabbed what was most important and escaped before the flames reached the wooden-framed convent. Some townspeople braved the smoke and fire to save most of the furniture downstairs, but almost everything that was upstairs was lost. Since the convent was completely destroyed, the sisters had no idea where they would stay. But their anxieties were relieved somewhat when William Bowman, a Stann Creek merchant, generously offered the eight sisters the temporary use of his large home, where the sisters remained for a month. They then rented the upstairs floor of a building in the heart of town. It was far too small to house all of them comfortably, and privacy was limited by the fact that the downstairs was occupied by the shops of two merchants. Nevertheless, the sisters had no recourse but to reside in these crowded quarters for the next five years. But at least they were fortunate enough to have a friend such as Bowman, who paid their rent.

In their accounts of this tragic fire, the Stann Creek sisters point out with pride that only one day of classes was lost. On Tuesday morning, although exhausted and despondent from the horrors of the day before, all of the sisters reported on time to their classrooms to teach a student body that now numbered 589.

Then, on April 1, 1947, the sisters were finally able to leave their crowded "temporary" quarters and move into a new two-story, concrete convent that could house up to twenty sisters. It was larger and less susceptible to natural disasters than had been their old wooden residence. It had been built for the sisters by the Jesuits of the Missouri Province at a cost of $20,000, and it had taken so long to be completed because building materials had not been available due to scarcities during World War II.[5]

The Sacred Heart School Records also tell us that in 1947 twenty-one candidates in the improved pupil-teacher training program had passed their government examinations.[6] Similar successes would occur in the following years, so much so that the sisters' program would provide enough teachers to allow the state school system to expand greatly in the Stann Creek District in the 1950s.

When judged within the pre–Vatican II context of what constitutes a flourishing missionary endeavor, the Sisters of the Holy Family's Stann Creek apostolate was nothing short of amazing. Prior to the Second Vatican Council, the role of missionary women was seen, at least by the institutional church and its male leadership, as ancillary to that of the missionary priest.[7] The latter was to evangelize and administer the sacraments; the former was to supplement the priest's work by establishing and teaching in Catholic schools or serving as nurses in hospitals or clinics.[8] The Sisters of the Holy Family were, of course, called on to do only the first. So how effective were they in this role?

As noted earlier, by 1936 the enrollment at Sacred Heart had grown to 413 students. Indeed, because of the rapidly increasing number of students, in 1931 the motherhouse in New Orleans deemed it necessary to increase to six the number of sisters assigned to Stann Creek. Enrollments continued to climb, and in 1940 two more sisters were added. In 1945, Sacred Heart was enlarged with the addition of a new wing and in 1946 the enrollment broke 700 for the first time. By 1948 it had reached 725: 345 girls, 290 boys, 80 children under five in the infant school, and 10 students over sixteen presumably in the pupil-teacher training program.[9] In 1955 the enrollment had grown to about 1,100.

So crowded was Sacred Heart that in 1952 the sisters opened a second primary school, Holy Angels, at Pomona in Stann Creek Valley. In the following year, the sisters took a major step when they opened Austin High School, the first girls' high school in the country outside of the capital city. To help with their new responsibilities two more sisters were assigned to Stann Creek, bringing the total to ten. But enrollments continued to climb, necessitating the building of a third primary school, Holy Ghost, in 1964. By 1973, at the high point of their operations, the ten Holy Family Sisters were running three primary schools and one high school in Stann Creek with a combined enrollment of 2,200 students.[10] Thus, from 1936 to 1973 the number of students taught by the sisters had grown more than fivefold, yet the sisters were effectively handling this increased load with only four more nuns than they had had in 1936. This, of course, was possible because of their pupil-teacher training program. Its graduates were being hired as lay teachers, thereby enabling the Holy Family nuns to run their four schools with fully qualified teachers.

Since a major objective of pre–Vatican II mission work was to encourage native vocations to the priesthood and religious life,[11] we can also judge the success of the sisters by reviewing their achievements in this category. By the end of the 1950s, thirty-eight women from British Honduras had entered the Holy Family Congregation, eighteen of whom later worked in Stann Creek. By the end of the century, fifty had entered; twenty-two of these were at one time or another assigned to the Belizean mission.[12]

Sister Barbara Marie Francis, who was born in Stann Creek in 1919, was one of these women. Her father, a Jamaican, was a superintendent of railways based in Stann Creek. Since her parents were Protestant, they chose to send her to private school rather than to Sacred Heart. After graduating from elementary school, she moved with her mother and sister to Belize City so that she could attend St. Hildy's College, which was the Anglican high school. Her father stayed behind in Stann Creek, but during the two-month school vacations the rest of the family would join him. While alone in Stann Creek, recalls Sister Barbara Marie, he became friends with the Holy Family Sisters simply because they were always kind to him. Thus, each May, when his two daughters arrived for the summer, he insisted that they visit the nuns even though they did not want to. This is how the future Sister Barbara Marie got to know the sisters.[13]

In 1936, a year after graduating from high school, she decided to follow her father into the Catholic Church. "Once I became a Catholic," she notes, "it was only natural for me to gravitate towards the

Sisters of the Holy Family."[14] In 1940 she traveled to New Orleans to enter the convent, and in 1947 she was sent back home to teach music at Sacred Heart. In 1955 she became the first indigenous principal of the school. Four years later, she was reassigned to the United States, where she taught in various black Catholic high schools and later served as the congregation's first general councilor. In 1966 the Daughters of Charity invited her to become the first African American faculty member at St. Joseph High, their previously all-white New Orleans secondary school. She accepted their offer and in so doing played a historic role in desegregating the Catholic school system in southern Louisiana. Three years later she left St. Joseph to return to graduate school, where she eventually earned a Ph.D. in geography from the University of Cincinnati. When in retirement at the motherhouse, Sister Barbara Marie, while recalling her long, impressive career, noted that she was especially proud of the fact that in 1954, her last year as a classroom teacher in Stann Creek, the graduating students of Sacred Heart "had more distinctions [on government examinations] than all the rest of the students combined throughout the country of Belize."[15]

Mary Eleanor Gillett was another native Belizean who joined the congregation. Born in the capital city, she was educated by the Mercy Sisters at Holy Redeemer School. While doing her practice teaching at Holy Redeemer, Sister Mary Florence Aguet of the Holy Family Sisters came twice to visit the school: "Although I didn't talk with her," recalls Gillett, "I was impressed by her. I thought that if she [a black woman] could become a sister, then maybe I could also."[16] Impressed by books about Saint Thérèse of Lisieux, Gillett toyed with the idea of entering a cloistered Carmelite convent, but the thought of never seeing her family again caused her to reconsider. She did not think about joining the Holy Family Sisters, however, since she knew little about them. In 1934 she went to see a Jesuit priest to discuss her options concerning a religious vocation. Although she had spent much of her life with the Mercy Sisters and had taken nursing courses with the Pallottines, and therefore was most familiar with these two congregations, she realized that they were beyond consideration because they did not accept blacks.

Her Jesuit adviser suggested that it would be best for her to enter a black congregation and informed her that there were only three: the Oblates of Providence in Baltimore, the Franciscan Handmaidens of the Most Pure Heart of Mary in New York, and the Holy Family Sisters. Since he knew nothing about the first two but was familiar with the third due to their long history of working with the Jesuits in Stann Creek, he recommended that she enter their community. She did so in 1935. In 1947, Sister Eleanor was assigned to Stann Creek with Sister Barbara Marie. She taught at Sacred Heart and played a major role in establishing Austin High School. She was reassigned to the United States in 1965, where she served until her death on June 18, 2007.[17]

Sister Rebecca Carlos Castillo, a Garifuna from Stann Creek, was never a student of the Holy Family Sisters. Nevertheless, her pious parents took her to mass at Sacred Heart Church every Friday and Sunday. Thus, she came to know the local Holy Family community and was impressed by their spirituality. Later she became more familiar with their congregational charism while working with the sisters at Sacred Heart School. "They edified me," she recalls, "and influenced my vocation to live like them as a Holy Family Sister."[18] She eventually entered the congregation and was assigned to teach in Dangriga (Stann Creek) from 1969 to 1972 and from 1973 to 1977. After working in the United States for almost a quarter century, Sister Rebecca was again assigned to her hometown where she served at Delille Academy from 2001 to 2007.[19]

The lives of Sisters Barbara Marie, Eleanor, and Rebecca illustrate how many young Belizean black women with a penchant for religious life, for a variety of reasons, gravitated toward and eventually joined the African American Holy Family Congregation, even though they had not been educated by these sisters. As one would expect, however, the bulk of the sisters' native vocations came from young women whom they had taught at Stann Creek. Sisters Esther Marie Estero, Veronica Ruth Lambey, and Joan Flores fit into this category.

Born in 1920 and raised in Stann Creek, Estero attended Sacred Heart, where she came to admire the black Holy Family nuns who so skillfully instructed her. Sister Marie Louise Goodman, who taught at the school from 1912 to 1936, especially impressed her. Many years later at the age of twenty-four, inspired primarily by the piety of her mother, Estero felt a calling to the religious life. There was never a question of which congregation she would join. She chose the one that had educated her in her formative years.[20]

Lambey, a Garifuna, attended both Sacred Heart and Austin High School. In December 1959, after graduating from the latter, she entered the congregation. Although a religious now for over forty years, she, like Sister Esther Marie, has never been assigned by her religious superiors to teach in Belize. Instead, both sisters have used their teaching skills exclusively in educating black young people in the United States.[21]

Joan Flores's father was an elementary-school instructor who taught in schools throughout Belize. Two years after Austin High School was opened, he was assigned to a school in the Stann Creek Valley. Consequently, Joan was enrolled at Austin. While there, she joined the Sodality of Our Lady and was active in various religious activities at Sacred Heart Parish. Impressed by Sister Eleanor, who was the moderator of the Sodality, and by several of the other sisters, she decided to enter the convent after graduating in 1959. In 1966, Sister Joan returned to Stann Creek, where for eleven of the next twelve years she taught at Sacred Heart, Holy Ghost, and Holy Angels schools. She was reassigned to the United States in 1978 and since then has taught in several elementary schools in southern Louisiana.[22]

The above seven Holy Family Sisters are representative of the fifty nuns who entered the congregation in the twentieth century from Belize (British Honduras), and in particular the thirty-eight who joined prior to 1960. Almost half of the overall number returned at least for part of their teaching careers to their native country, where they joined the African American nuns assigned there in the crucial work of educating local black youth. These native sisters, however, did much more. They played an invaluable role in the important process of transforming the Catholic Church in Belize into one that is indigenous rather than foreign. Yet these sisters also spent part of their careers working in the United States along with the more than 50 percent of the Belizean Holy Family Sisters who were never assigned to teach in their native country. Thus, one can say that the Holy Family Sisters who came north from Belize (British Honduras) and constituted a substantial minority in the overall number of their congregation brought about an amalgamation of their rich Caribbean–Central American culture with the African American culture of their co-religious. Thus, they, along with the African American sisters who returned to the United States after serving in Belize, helped in the transformation of their congregation from a regionally oriented institution into one that was able to think and act more internationally. Such a transformation—which, as will soon be shown, would not be completed without some mistakes and pain—enabled the Holy Family Congregation to meet the challenges emanating from Pope John XXIII's call for *aggiornamento* (an updating of the church), a call that led to the Second Vatican Council.

But what about the sisters' contributions to the creation of a native clergy? The first of their former students to become a priest was ordained in 1931, but he served in the United States rather than in Belize. By the end of the century, however, eight more of the sisters' pupils had been ordained.[23] One of these, Father Philip Marin, a graduate of Sacred Heart Primary School who was ordained in 1934, was the first Garifuna to enter the priesthood. In 1948 he became pastor of Sacred Heart Church, while another of the sisters' former students, Richard Francis, became assistant pastor. With their appointments, Sacred Heart changed from a Jesuit mission to the first diocesan parish in Belizean history.[24] Another of the sisters' students, Osmond P. Martin, became the first native Belizean bishop in 1982, when he was named vicar apostolic of Belize and Belmopan.[25]

From the above, therefore, one can only conclude that as far as religious vocations go, the sisters' mission was extremely successful. The Holy Family Congregation provided an institutional community for black Belizean women who heard a call to religious life. Whereas these women, at least until the 1950s, were ineligible for admission to most Catholic religious congregations solely because of their race, they were not only welcomed into the ranks of the Holy Family Sisters but, equally important, found therein an environment where, for the most part, they could fit in with relative ease and make the most of their teaching and leadership skills. Moreover, the Holy Family Sisters' role in the transition of the foreign-dominated institutional Catholic Church in Belize to one that was more indigenous cannot be underestimated. The fact that this transition coincided with the birth of a movement for independence from Britain gives it additional significance. This struggle for independence soon spawned a popular-based nationalism that had not previously existed in the country. The masses as well as the elite class took pride in a church that, like the country itself, was breaking free of foreign influence.

The future for the Holy Family Sisters in British Honduras seemed brighter than ever as they entered the 1960s. Testimonies from Sisters Mary Bertille Hazeur and Mary Adrian Johnson typify the optimism and sense of fulfillment felt by the sisters who served in the British colony in the two decades prior to the Second Vatican Council. Sister Mary Bertille, a native of Mobile, Alabama, was assigned to the Stann Creek District in 1946. She taught at Sacred Heart and later in the 1950s at Holy Angels in Pomona. Although she experienced some culture shock upon her arrival—"the children were much poorer than those we worked with in the United States"—she quickly adjusted and came to cherish her missionary experience as one of the most satisfying periods of her life.[26] At first the students at Holy Angels were all Spanish-speaking, she recalls, but they learned English quickly. Later, Caribs enrolled and the sisters wound up teaching students of three cultures together—Indian, Spanish, and Garifuna: "Everybody cooperated. I never saw students so interested in studying; they worked so hard. The parents were so interested in the students and the people were so happy to have the sisters [in Pomona]. Many of our students went on to become teachers, and some [became] sisters."[27]

Sister Mary Adrian, a native of Lafayette, Louisiana, who served in British Honduras from 1952 to 1959, was just as positive:

> I expected a different culture [in British Honduras] and it was. The kids went barefoot to school. They would often walk five or ten miles before going to school to get plantain from the farm for the family. But they were anxious to learn; we had no trouble motivating them. I taught all types of students—Carib, Spanish, and even Chinese. Most of the Caribs became teachers, and they were excellent. I especially remember one boy. He was a "real boy," a holy terror, but he was brilliant. We had a vocation club. Six or eight joined, but only two became

sisters. Both are still in the congregation. One of them [Sister Veronica Ruth Lambey] is currently studying Biblical theology in Rome. She's a graduate of Austin High and is working on her Ph.D. In the summer time, Sister Barbara Marie [Francis] and I would take the students to a nearby river and we would swim. We would spend the whole day in that river. I loved [my time in British Honduras]; I loved every minute of it.[28]

Looking back on her life, Sister Mary Adrian contends that she had been especially privileged because God gave her two distinct vocations—one to religious life and the other as a missionary. Both Sister Mary Adrian and Sister Mary Bertille expressed regrets that they were "so old." If they were only younger, they said, they would have liked nothing better than to go back and labor in Belize again.[29]

Sister Carolyn Leslie, from Belize City, served in Stann Creek from 1949 to 1951 and again from 1955 to 1963. Her recollections make it clear that the sisters' value to the people and their church extended beyond their primary charism of teaching:

> We took care of the maintenance of the church; we did the washing and ironing and made the [communion] hosts.[30] We visited the sick and students in their homes when we had the time. The sisters came up to the United States more or less regularly and when they did, they would collect [second-hand] clothing and money and bring them back [for the poor of Stann Creek].... The priests and the sisters complemented each other well. Priests had to do the sacramental and administrative work, so the sisters were the ones who met with the people. Whatever you could do, you did.[31]

If the missionary nuns' success tempted them to rest on their laurels, however, they would have had little time to do so, for in 1959, Pope John XXIII announced that he planned to convene an ecumenical council in 1962. It would be the first such council in ninety-two years, and, as noted earlier, its purpose would be *aggiornamento,* the updating of the church so that it would be better able to meet the challenges of the modern world. The Second Vatican Council would shake religious orders and congregations to their very core. In doing so, it would create not only new opportunities but also new problems, and the transformation process would cause much pain. This would be especially true for female religious, and the Holy Family Congregation would be no exception.

The end of tranquility in British Honduras actually preceded Vatican II, however, for on October 31, 1961, Hattie, one of the worst hurricanes in Belizean history, slammed into the colony's Caribbean coast with Category 5 force.³² Over 275 people were killed and more than ten times that number were left homeless. Seventy-five percent of Belize City was destroyed when it was battered by a fifteen-foot tidal wave that submerged the city for several hours under ten feet of water. Small towns and villages all along the coast were wiped out. So bad was the destruction that the government of Mayor George Price issued a decree calling for the building of a new capital forty-four miles inland, on higher terrain. But Stann Creek, by this time the second largest city in British Honduras and the center of the colony's citrus industry, was hit the hardest. About fifty of its residents were killed and 90 percent of its property was destroyed, along with the district's entire citrus crop. Only four buildings survived relatively unscathed: a police station, Sacred Heart Church and its adjoining school, and the sisters' convent. The Holy Family Sisters distinguished themselves during this time of crisis by feeding, clothing, and housing those who had not been so fortunate; and, according to a notation in the sisters' New Orleans archives, they also assisted government officials by "making paper money and distributing it among the people."³³ Hurricane Hattie was only the first of many crises that the Holy Family Sisters would have to face in the last four decades of the twentieth century, but it was definitely the most harrowing.

Part II

The Post-Vatican II Years

CHAPTER 5

CHANGES IN THE 1950S THROUGH THE EARLY 1970S

As with all Catholic orders and congregations, new problems would face the Holy Family Sisters in the post–Vatican II era. But before this issue is addressed, it is necessary to look at how the Second Vatican Council changed the lives of American nuns in general. Vatican II (1962–1965) profoundly affected all female religious congregations by challenging them to break from their traditional isolationist convent culture. Ever since the Middle Ages and especially since the Council of Trent in the mid-sixteenth century, religious women were expected to live a contemplative, cloistered life.[1] The Vatican did not officially recognize active female religious who did not conform to this role until 1900, when Leo XIII issued his papal bull, *Conditae a Christo*. But while this bull granted the same status to active and contemplative congregations, it also obligated all female religious to restrict themselves to at least a semi-cloistered way of living that severely constrained their contact with those beyond their convent walls.[2] Transplanted congregations of European nuns and U.S. "home-grown" communities of sisters, especially those laboring on the frontier, were sometimes able to negotiate their way around cloister restrictions due to the special nature of their ministry.

This exception ended, however, in 1918, due to the promulgation by Rome of a new Code of Canon Law that made enclosure restrictions the norm, thereby fostering a "cloister mentality" among active female religious communities. As historian Amy Koehlinger explains,

Required to report their compliance with canon law to authorities in Rome every five years, many superiors of women's congregations from the 1920s through the 1950s rigidly enforced restrictions on sisters' physical movements, access to media and public meetings, and contact with family members, lay people, and even other religious. In a curious juxtaposition, during the first half of the twentieth century when papal encyclicals and American bishops were calling Catholics toward engagement with an ever-broader program of social action, sisters were increasingly required to limit the scope of their ministries to adhere to norms of enclosure.[3]

This "cloister mentality," adds Koehlinger, especially burdened those female religious who worked with "non-Catholics and communities of color beyond Catholic enclaves," forcing them to live "with constant tension between the unencumbered movement that such apostolates required and the concrete limitations that canon law placed on them."[4]

Historian Patricia Byrne notes that even sisters who taught in parochial schools avoided as much as possible the social and ministerial aspects of parish life. They were in the parish, she aptly asserts, but not of it.[5] Lora Ann Quiñonez and Mary Daniel Turner further emphasize Byrne's contention by pointing out that before Vatican II, it "would have been unthinkable" for female religious to take part in any type of public discourse.[6]

The seeds of change that would later bear fruit were actually planted in the 1950s, when some church leaders concluded that the isolation of convent life had instilled a lack of sophistication in nuns that impeded their ability to play an effective role in the increasingly complex modern world. Based on this judgment, Pope Pius XII urged all female congregations to update their customs and ministries so as to take into account the charism of their founders along with the needs of contemporary times. He further proposed that they make arrangements to ensure that their members were as well educated as their secular counterparts and that they wear habits that were practical and therefore did not impede their ministry.[7] To achieve these reforms, Pius urged the various religious congregations to work together cooperatively; and, to best facilitate this approach, he summoned religious superiors to Rome for a series of international congresses on reform that were held between 1950 and 1952.[8] As Koehlinger notes, these congresses introduced religious superiors to the collaborative process, thereby undermining the culture of isolation and competition between different congregations that had existed at least since 1918.[9]

Just prior to Vatican II, Archbishop Giovanni Montini of Milan took Pius XII's request a step further, urging sisters to replace their cloistered way of life with one that was more active. Several years later, Montini would repeat this call during the Council, after he had been elected Pope Paul VI.[10] Finally, in his highly influential book, *The Nun in the World*, published in an English edition in the early months of the Council, Cardinal Leon Joseph Suenens of Brussels argued that cloistered life was the primary obstacle to the apostolic advancement of sisters. Consequently, if nuns were to be relevant in contemporary society, then enclosure and all that it entailed must give way to new structures.[11]

In response to the church's call for renewal, beginning in the 1950s American sisters established a network of collaborative conferences that changed the nature of U.S. female religious life. Probably the most influential was the Sister Formation Conference (SFC), which was created by Sister Mary Emil Penet and others in 1954. As Mary Schneider aptly puts it in the subtitle of her study on the SFC, it was a catalyst for change.[12] The Conference encouraged communities of religious sisters to have their members complete their bachelor degrees before sending them into the classroom and to change their semi-cloistered way of life to make it more appropriate for addressing the needs of the modern world. It did this by supporting research projects and setting up regional and national conferences and workshops, where sisters from diverse communities could come together and discuss topics of an intellectual, spiritual, and cultural nature. It also kept religious sisters throughout the country abreast of its activities through the monthly *Sister Formation Bulletin*. Indeed, because of the SFC, thousands of U.S. sisters from diverse communities that in the past had had little if any contact now came to know each other and to feel a universal bond as Catholic religious. They learned how to work and plan together across congregational lines and find solutions to common problems. This cooperation in turn equipped many sisters with the educational tools, sophistication, and enthusiasm needed to face the challenges of Vatican II. Angelyn Dries sums up the importance of the SFC when she states that it helped sisters to create "a new paradigm as they answered questions about [their] identity."[13]

Another important organization that was established during this time of change was the Leadership Conference of Women Religious. Because the Vatican wanted major female religious superiors in each country to work together in bringing religious life into the modern world, the National Sisters Committee (NSC) was formed in 1952. Four years later, the Vatican's Congregation for Religious called for a more formal national organization, and in response the sisters in the NSC restructured as the Conference of Major Superiors of Women (CMSW), which received canonical approval in 1959. In 1971 the CMSW changed its name again, this time to the Leadership Conference of Women Religious (LCWR).[14] The CMSW/LCWR was the official sisters' voice in touch with Rome, which gave it unique authority and prestige. Its purpose was to enable superiors of the various pontifical female congregations in the United States "to collaboratively carry out their service of leadership to further the mission of the Gospel in today's world."[15] It developed educational programs ranging from weekend workshops to summer-long institutes. Proceedings of its meetings were published and circulated in convents throughout the country, thereby enabling sisters of its member congregations to keep up to date with its business. In short, the LCWR gave the leadership of female religious congregations and orders in the United States a unity and sense of solidarity that they had never experienced before. The LCWR dovetailed well with the SFC to transform American sisters into a more aggressive body. However, this transformation did not always sit well with Vatican and U.S. episcopal authorities.

The Second Vatican Council, more than the SFC or LCWR, was undoubtedly the decisive factor when it came to the redefining of religious life for female congregations. As Mary Ewens contends, "few groups in the church responded to the decrees of the Second Vatican

Council with the alacrity shown by American sisters."[16] Along with many other general reforms, the Council added a significant new dimension to mission philosophy when it stated that change must especially take into account the cultural, social, and economic circumstances of the people in the country where the missionaries are working.[17] Even prior to the Council, however, sisters were already in the process of gaining awareness of global problems by studying Pope John XXIII's *Mater et Magistra* (1961) and *Pacem in Terris* (1963), while also trying to comply with his 1961 clarion call for all U.S. religious orders and congregations to send 10 percent of their personnel to the Latin American missions. Soon the sisters would also be studying *Gaudium et Spes* (*The Church in the Modern World*), the Council's summons to an increase in Christian social activism, as well as Paul VI's social encyclical, *Populorum Progressio* (1967). The call by the Latin American bishops at their Medellín Conference (1968) to commit the church without reservation to the poor and oppressed also had a profound effect on female religious, especially because many of them had already been assigned to Latin America following the pope's 1961 request.[18]

In 1966, after the Council had ended, the Vatican issued *Ecclesiae Sanctae*, directing all religious congregations to convene a general chapter within the next three years in order to put renewal into effect. It also called for the revision of religious constitutions. As a result, sisters were soon deeply involved in research on the original charism of their communities and their congregational histories. Study and discussion groups were formed, but the transformational process did not proceed without conflict. Many sisters were unwilling to accept the changes that their communities decided to implement and therefore left the religious life. For the majority who stayed, however, the new constitutions meant a radical change in their lives and ministry. By the end of the 1960s, more sisters than ever before were pursuing bachelor's and graduate degrees. They were studying not only elementary and secondary education but theology, psychology, sociology, political science, law, history, and the humanities as well. Most of these women were attending Catholic colleges or universities, but many were matriculating at secular institutions.[19]

A substantial number moved from traditional teaching and nursing roles to take up professions that filled contemporary needs. Some involved themselves in parish ministry, while others became lawyers, social workers, retreat directors, psychologists, physicians, and college professors. For these new roles, many moved out of their traditional convents and into apartments, often in poverty-stricken neighborhoods where they resided with one or two other nuns. Finding their traditional habits an impediment to their work, congregations now either modified them or replaced them with modest secular attire. As Byrne notes, loss of cloister meant social interchange with those people whom the sisters served, something that was unheard of in the pre–Vatican II church.[20] Moreover, service to the poor in the United States, coupled with that in the mission fields, caused most sisters to reevaluate their outlook on both their church and their country as well as on the relationship between the rich and the poor. As Quiñonez and Turner state so appropriately, the command to female religious to update their constitutions certainly had important political ramifications. Sisters now involved themselves "in public discourse and dissent" as they began to champion "the cause of the excluded."[21] Influenced by the Vatican Council's new emphasis on ecumenism, they also cooperated with those of other faiths in their attempt to make "God's kingdom of justice" a reality on earth.

When it came to implementing the decrees of the Second Vatican Council, the Sisters of the Holy Family, like the other black religious congregations, experienced less change than most other female religious communities. The fact that they were African Americans totally committed to serving poor black people had ensured that they would never be a wealthy congregation. Indeed, the history of these sisters at least up to the early twentieth century is one of barely surviving financially—a history of perpetually doing without many of the basic necessities of life. Likewise, from their origin in the antebellum South, they had ministered for over a century to the poorest of the poor. Consequently, since they had already dedicated themselves to the Vatican II–Medellín call for a "preferential option for the poor," they did not have to make the drastic changes required of many predominantly white congregations. They were, at least in many respects, already there, although they would have to do some reforming in order to fulfill the Council's call for religious to adjust to "the signs of the times."

Moreover, as a black religious community based in segregated New Orleans, they had always suffered from the racial bigotry and prejudice that was commonplace in their society and within the local church. As a result, in their earliest years they had come to the conclusion that the best way to survive and flourish was by adhering to the original charism of their foundress. They began as a small New Orleans community devoted to teaching poor black youth and ministering to the needs of the indigent African American elderly. As they expanded into other regions, they never deviated from this ministry. As a result, they did not have to "rediscover" their roots. Like other female religious congregations, after Vatican II they rewrote their constitutions; but they continued almost exclusively to be a teaching community, which also ministered to needy older people.

Within that role, however, they searched for innovations that exemplified the spirit of the Council and tried to incorporate them into their work. This was certainly the case in their Belize mission. They would make their share of mistakes and in so doing would be forced to confront their own biases. In the long run, however, they would move beyond their comfort zone, devising innovative, nontraditional ways of teaching the poor and serving the elderly. They would become quite proficient in heeding the call of Vatican II to read the signs of the times, and in so doing, they would become even more valuable to the people whom they served.

Although, as stated above, virtually all female religious congregations in the United States prior to the creation of the SFC and LCWR had had little contact with each other, this was especially true when it came to black congregations. Segregation laws and customs in the South, where the Holy Family Sisters and the Oblates of Providence were based, were partly responsible for the isolation of African American sisters from white congregations in their locale. The prejudiced attitudes of many southern bishops and leaders of white religious communities were also a factor. Indeed, many prelates, pastors, and principals of Catholic schools justified their lack of initiative on questions of racial justice with the excuse that, since Catholics were a minority in the South and were viewed with suspicion by the Protestant majority, it was prudent for the church to avoid challenging the racial status quo. Thus, the creation of the LCWR and the SFC was particularly valuable for the Holy Family and Oblate Sisters because of the racially inclusive nature and practices of these conferences.

In her report to the Holy Family Sisters summarizing the congregation's accomplishments from 1958 to 1964, Mother Marie Anselm Duffel notes the participation of her religious community in the SFC: "In line with the thinking of His Holiness, Pope Pius XII, the Sisters of the Holy Family . . . have joined with other communities in the Sister Formation Program," in order to instill a deeper formation of piety and asceticism in our sisters and a better understanding of the work and spirit of our congregation.[22]

Inspired by a talk given at Catholic University, Duffel and the Holy Family community decided in 1959 to establish DeLisle Junior College in New Orleans as part of its juniorate and formation program.[23] All credits earned there were recognized by both Xavier University and Loyola University in New Orleans and by "any college that was affiliated with Catholic University of America."[24] This meant that after finishing their studies at DeLisle, sisters could transfer to any of the above institutions to complete their bachelor's degrees.[25] Mother Marie Anselm notes that an impressive number did so. Indeed, by 1964, fifty Holy Family Sisters had earned "basic [presumably bachelor's] degrees," while an additional fifteen had completed their master's and two their doctoral degrees. Fifteen more were studying full-time in Catholic colleges and universities throughout the United States.[26] DeLisle was terminated as a junior college in 1967,[27] in part since by that time it was no longer difficult for sisters to enroll in other local Catholic institutions of higher learning. However, in her 1964–1970 Report to the Congregation, Duffel indicates that many of the courses it had offered—notably those in theology, spirituality, the religious vows, scripture studies, liturgy, and art appreciation—had been integrated into the formation program.[28]

In no small part because of their affiliation with the SFC, and to a lesser degree the LCWR, by 1964 Holy Family Sisters had matriculated at Marymount College, the College of St. Teresa in Minnesota,[29] the College of Mount St. Joseph in Ohio, Seton Hill College in Pennsylvania, Cardinal Stritch College in Wisconsin, St. Louis University,

Catholic University, and Loyola and Xavier Universities in New Orleans.[30] As part of formation, sisters were also taking classes, including a course on the documents of Vatican II, at Notre Dame Seminary in New Orleans.[31] An intercongregational program was also developed in which Holy Family Sisters in formation participated with their counterparts from other New Orleans communities. These included novices and junior sisters from the Mount Carmel Congregation, the Sisters of St. Joseph, the Eucharistic Dominicans, the Dominicans, and the Poor Clares. Program activities included workshops conducted by Father Thomas Dubay, a Marist from Notre Dame Seminary, First Sunday retreats, Bible study and discussion, plays on spiritual subjects, and liturgical services.[32]

The congregation also realized that there was a need for ongoing formation for all of its members, and thus it initiated for perpetually professed sisters an annual renewal program aimed at deepening the spiritual and apostolic dimensions of their lives.[33] While novices and junior sisters were not permitted to participate in national workshops and seminars sponsored by the SFC, directresses of formation did take part.[34] They also attended canon law seminars and workshops that were conducted over five summers by Jesuit professors.[35]

In short, because of the SFC, CMSW/LCWR, and Vatican II, the Holy Family Sisters had educational opportunities that had not been previously available to them. As a result they, as a community, were better prepared than ever before to teach at both the elementary and high-school levels in both the United States and Belize. A few would even teach at the college level. Moreover, by studying at Catholic colleges and universities throughout the country, most of which were run by predominantly white religious congregations, the Holy Family Sisters were able to develop relationships with other religious communities and broaden their perspectives as vowed female religious.

A few northern schools actually began their contacts with the Holy Family Sisters prior to the creation of the SFC/LCWR. Cardinal Stritch College is a case in point. In 1951, Mother Bartholomew, superior general of the Franciscan Sisters, invited the Holy Family Congregation to send two of its sisters each semester to matriculate at its Milwaukee college. She did so, notes Sister Coletta Dunn, because she saw this as a way for her religious congregation to reach out to the Holy Family community, whose members "had difficulty in their own city due to segregation." Holy Family Sisters at Stritch "were treated as guests" at our motherhouse, says Dunn. Room and board were given free of charge. "Payment was in terms of their lasting gratitude to us. Even in recent years we are kept in touch with graduates [from the Holy Family Congregation] who [still] remember us."[36] The matriculation of Holy Family Sisters at Cardinal Stritch continued until the mid-1960s and to a lesser degree until as late as 1980.[37]

There were other changes in the Holy Family community that were initiated at least in part by SFC and LCWR programs and reinforced and expanded by the reform mentality of the Second Vatican Council. Sisters, if they chose to do so, were now permitted to return to their "baptismal names." Some titles of authority were dropped; "Mistress" was changed to "directress," and "Mother" was no longer used for local leaders. Only the superior general of the congregation retained this title, and by 1998 it too had been abolished. Modifications in the habit were gradually made. Beginning in the 1970s, sisters living in very hot climates were permitted to wear white or tan habits in place of black. More emphasis was placed on scripture study, the liturgy of the Eucharist, church history, and the history and charism of the congregation. The Little Office of the Blessed Virgin Mary was replaced by the Liturgy of the Hours. Sisters were allowed more personal responsibility for some aspects of their prayer life, such as meditation and spiritual reading.[38]

Holy Family Sisters who were assigned to Dangriga (Stann Creek) applied what they learned from the LCWR and SFC to their work there.[39] Later, from the mid-1970s onward, one or two Holy Family Sisters, along with representatives from the Mercy Congregation, the Jesuits, and diocesan clergy serving in Belize, attended conferences for religious men and women that were held annually in different Caribbean countries. They listened to speakers, and took part in workshops and sessions on formation and a variety of other topics. Among those who were sent to such conferences were Sisters Clare of Assisi Pierre, Joan Flores, Rebecca Carlos Castillo, and Jean Martínez. When they returned to Belize, they participated with various other religious groups in the diocese and shared what they had learned at the conferences.[40] A few sisters also ventured to Guatemala to attend summer scripture classes, but these trips were discontinued after only a few years due perhaps to the ever-increasing violence that permeated that nation from the 1970s onward.[41] Following Vatican II some of the sisters expanded their apostolate by accompanying the Jesuits of Sacred Heart Parish to rural villages, where they catechized the young and assisted the priests in whatever ways were needed.[42]

Under the direction of Mother Marie Anselm Duffel, and following the directives of Vatican II, an extensive self-study was undertaken from 1966 to 1968 aimed at spiritual and apostolic renewal within the congregation. The study resulted in a Special Chapter in 1968–1969. Changes were introduced, legislated, and implemented by the community and in 1970 they became part of the sisters' Interim Constitutions and Directives, which were submitted to Rome and finally approved by the Vatican in 1983.[43] These constitutional reforms affected the entire Holy Family Congregation and in this respect influenced the way in which the missionary sisters in Dangriga served and lived. There were, however, no specific reforms in the Constitutions and Directives aimed exclusively at or particularly to the mission in Dangriga.[44]

The National Black Sisters' Conference (NBSC) was another organization that helped shape the Holy Family Sisters in the post–Vatican II period, albeit not nearly as much as did the SFC or LCWR. Founded in August 1968, it grew out of the Civil Rights Movement and the sense of black identity and pride promoted by such African American figures as Martin Luther King, Jr., and Malcolm X. The NBSC was the brainchild of a young Pittsburgh Sister of Mercy, Martin de Porres (Patricia) Grey, who in April 1968 had been the only female religious to attend the first Black Catholic Clergy Caucus. She left that meeting convinced that African American religious sisters, like their male clergy counterparts, should have an organization that would address the need for the Catholic Church to become more relevant to black people and more concerned with the evils of racism that permeated both the church and secular society.

With the backing of Grey's superior general and the endorsement of the CMSW, Mount Mercy College (now Carlow University) in Pittsburgh hosted the inaugural meeting in August 1968. One hundred fifty-five sisters from seventy-nine different communities attended, and prominent black scholars gave lectures on such topics as black identity and issues of race. Officers and an ad hoc board of directors were elected. At the 1969 meeting in Ohio at the University of Dayton, the NBSC became more formalized: a committee was chosen to draw up a constitution, which was approved by the general membership by the end of the year, and new officers were elected along with a board to replace the ad hoc board. A position paper was drawn up that specified the goals of the Conference. In the following year the Conference meeting was held in Indiana at the University of Notre Dame, and it has met annually in August ever since.[45] M. Shawn Copeland, writing almost three decades after the formation of the NBSC, aptly notes its importance:

> By making visible and uniting black women vowed religious, and especially those black members of predominantly white religious congregations, the Conference reshaped public perception of Catholic sisters both within the church, the black Catholic community, and the black community at large. In a most proactive way, the NBSC promoted and advocated an "image" of the black Catholic sister and her mission in terms of liberation.[46]

Copeland points out that although it tried to distance itself from "pejorative political and polemical connotations," in its "impulse and style, plans and projects," there is no denying that the NBSC was "foundationally political."[47]

Holy Family Sisters, especially some of the younger ones, were very active in the NBSC. "Our sisters attended the conferences," says Sister Sylvia Thibodeaux, "and we were among the first sisters on board."[48] Sister Mary Judith Therese Barial was one of the twenty-one sisters chosen at the second annual meeting at the University of Dayton in 1969 to draft the Conference's position paper, which was then debated and ratified.[49] She was also involved in the pre-convention planning conference in February 1970, which was hosted by the Holy Family Sisters at their motherhouse in New Orleans.[50] In 1971 the Conference produced its *Practicability Study*, "an attempt to search out the ingredients and the means to attract to religious life, to form, and to support black Catholic sisters who would be effective agents in the liberation of their people."[51] Sister Sylvia Thibodeaux was one of the sixteen black women and men chosen for its directional committee.[52] She was also a driving force in convincing the NBSC staff to give high priority to the development of a plan to strengthen and maintain parochial schools in predominantly black areas at a time when many bishops were closing or merging inner-city schools.

The result of these efforts was Project DESIGN (Development of Educational Services in the Growing Nation). Through this project the Conference organized an all-black staff of professional educational consultants who developed a curriculum that was best suited for African American schools, implemented programs designed to create "parental involvement in the total educational process of the school," and provided in-service training for school administrators, teachers, and students.[53] Some of the other early Holy Family participants in the NBSC were Sisters Marie de Montfort Breaux, Mary Adrian Johnson, and Eva Regina Martin.[54]

From its inception, young black sisters from predominantly white congregations dominated the NBSC. Soon many older and some younger members of the Holy Family Congregation—and the other two traditionally black congregations as well—began to resent what they viewed as these sisters' overly invasive and aggressive attitudes. They thought that the NBSC had taken on a "quasi-congregational-like character" and interfered in the internal affairs of their community.[55] They also came to believe that Conference leaders lacked the discernment that comes from experience and were too simplistic in their militant approach to racial injustice.[56] Many young Holy Family Sisters, however, did not agree with this assessment and became frustrated at what they saw as the lack of support for the Conference among their own leadership. Consequently, some tension developed within the congregation, which possibly was a factor in the decision of some sisters to leave the convent. Reflecting four decades after the founding of the NBSC, Sister Sylvia Thibodeaux puts her congregation's relationship with the Conference in its proper perspective: "We came from the South; we were comfortable with ourselves as African Americans. NBSC was established for sisters in non-black communities, sisters who needed support and acceptance. The organization helped the Sisters of the Holy Family individually and we in turn contributed. It was a mutually giving situation."[57]

When all is said and done, however, there is no denying that the NBSC—together with the National Black Catholic Clergy Caucus, the National Black Lay Catholic Caucus, and the National Office for Black Catholics—forced U.S. Catholic leaders to reexamine the institutional church's insensitivity not only to African Americans but also in particular to Catholic African Americans. Because it was successful in doing this, the NBSC had a positive effect on many of the younger Holy Family Sisters, some of whom would later become leaders of their congregation. Indeed, this is especially true for Sister Sylvia Thibodeaux, who has had a long, continuous association with the NBSC and who served as Holy Family superior general from 1998 to 2006. "The National Black Sisters' Council gave me meaning," she says. "It gave me a place, a comfort zone, as I grew as a sister. I found a lot of support [in the NBSC], especially in [matters of] black consciousness."[58]

One of the reforms of the Vatican II era that especially benefited the sisters in Dangriga was the modification of the habit. The issue of clothing was always a major problem for the Holy Family Sisters in Belize. Prior to the 1960s, the hot, humid climate of British Honduras posed serious difficulties for the sisters in large part because their rule required them to wear a heavy, multilayered black habit with starched head, neck, and shoulder linen. Indeed, it would be hard to find clothing less suitable for muggy, bug-infested Belize. It is not surprising, therefore, that over their first sixty years as missionaries, a substantial number of sisters were forced to return to the United States, either temporarily or permanently, due to extreme exhaustion or poor health. Obviously this impeded the effectiveness of their mission work, exacerbated their financial difficulties, and, as we have seen, led to conflict with Bishop Hopkins. Yet, since the rule of the Holy Family Sisters was specific when it came to dress, the congregation made no attempt to deviate from the norm. The missionary sisters would simply have to live with the discomforts that their habit imposed on them. All this would change, however, as a result of Pius XII's call in the 1950s for reform and Vatican II's call in the 1960s for *aggiornamento*.

Mother Henriette Delille. *All gallery photographs are courtesy of the Archives of the Sisters of the Holy Family.*

Left to right, Sisters Mary Inez Soler, Mary Gertrude Miller, Mary Bernadette Elback, Mary Helena Plaisance, Mary Charles Hernández, and Mary Eusebia Birmingham, 1907

Left to right, Mother Mary Rita Mather and Sisters Mary Philip Goodman, Mary Francis Borgia Hart, Mary Edmond Ogaldez, and Mary Inez Soler, 1912

Garifuna homes and children, early 1930s

Corpus Christi Procession in front of Sacred Heart Convent and Church, 1933

Barefoot altar boys

Sacred Heart Convent, burned down on January 26, 1942

Sacred Heart Church, burned down on January 26, 1942

The sisters' new convent, 1955

Father Philip Marin, graduate of Sacred Heart School, first Garifuna ordained to the priesthood, 1934, pastor of Sacred Heart Parish

Flower girls in procession on Front Street, early 1950s

First row, left to right, Sisters Mary Delphine Townsend, Mary Eleanor Gillett, Mary Henriette Lazare, and Mary Lorene Le Blanc; back row, Sisters Marie de Montfort Breaux, Mary Elma (David) Olivera, and Mary Elaine Vavasseur, early 1960s

Sacred Heart School on Front Street, 1964

Sisters return from New Orleans wearing the modified habit

Sisters Marie Yvette Ozene, Mary Jude Thadine Gremillion, Joan Flores, and Mary Rita Austin Méndez wading in their new white habits, 1966

Bishop Osmund Martin, Sister Gabriella Guidry, and Father Alvin Dixon, S.V.D. Bishop Martin, the first native Belizean bishop, was a graduate of Sacred Heart School

First row, left to right, Sisters Mary Joseph Ann Gillett, Mary Jude Thadine Gremillion, Marie Yvette Ozene, and Joan Flores; back row, Sisters Mary Rita Austin Méndez, Dorothy Marie Stuart, Mary Jacinta Blanchard, Mary Henriette Lazare, Mary Vincent Ferrer Gill, and Mary Eleanor Gillett

One-hundred-year anniversary celebration of the Holy Family Congregation in Belize

Ms. Sylvia Flores, former mayor of Dangriga and Speaker of the Belize Legislature; a student at Sacred Heart and Holy Ghost School and a Holy Family lay associate

Since so many other female congregations, in compliance with the proposals of the papacy and Vatican II, either modified or discarded their habit altogether, it would seem that the sisters would have no problem in doing the same. This was not the case, however. In the early decades of their history, the Holy Family community had had to fight against the bigotry of bishops and local white female congregations for the right to wear a nun's habit. Thus, it was a symbol of their legitimacy; it was proof that they were "real sisters."[59] There was no question, therefore, of their opting for the course taken by so many other U.S. female congregations. Thus, they would not discard their religious garb altogether. They decided instead on a modified habit that was based on simplicity and suitability to their needs, modern conditions, and the demands of hygiene, yet would continue to be a visible and recognizable sign of their corporate identity as Sisters of the Holy Family. As time went on, the sisters in Belize were permitted to replace their black habit with either a light tan or white one, since these colors were more appropriate for the tropics. Needless to say, this lighter, more adaptable habit was a welcome relief for the sisters in hot, humid Dangriga (Stann Creek), since it helped to make their work less burdensome and therefore more productive.

By the late 1960s, the Sisters of the Holy Family and the Belizean Catholic Church faced financial and staffing problems at Austin High School that were severe enough to threaten the very existence of the school. Since its opening in 1953, Austin High had proven to be an enormous success—but that was its problem. Over the years the number of matriculating students had grown so rapidly that the school's facilities had become grossly inadequate. Furthermore, enrollment was projected to grow even larger in the future. A bigger building was needed, but neither the sisters nor the bishop and his Jesuit Order had the funds necessary to pay for its construction.

A second problem was the lack of sisters available to staff Austin High School. In the 1950s, when female religious communities were blessed with an abundance of religious vocations,[60] the Holy Family Congregation had agreed to expand its education commitment in the Stann Creek District by opening not only Austin High but another primary school as well. In 1964 they added another primary school. Thus, between 1952 and 1964, the New Orleans–based community's responsibilities in Belize had increased fourfold. Yet at the same time the sisters were significantly extending their operations in the United States.[61]

Partly due to the reforms of Vatican II, however, by the mid-1960s female religious congregations no longer refused to accept black candidates. Although this was a positive development in the Catholic Church, it would soon negatively affect black congregations such as the Holy Family Sisters. African American and Belizean women who heard a call to religious life now had more options, which drained the pool of potential candidates for all-black congregations.[62] Moreover, following the Second Vatican Council, there had been an unexpected and drastic decline in religious vocations in wealthy, industrialized nations such as the United States, the effects of which were becoming apparent by the mid- to late 1960s. Radical changes in religious life resulting from the Council's call for *aggiornamento* caused tensions and divisions in religious communities, and, as a consequence, many women left their congregations and returned to secular life. Although the Holy Family Sisters were probably hit less hard than predominantly white religious congregations, they nevertheless suffered substantial losses.

Simply stated, then, by the late 1960s the sisters were overextended in British Honduras. They were not the only ones in the country, however, who were facing problems when it came to education. A Methodist school and an Anglican high school, called Stann Creek College, had also been opened in Dangriga, and, as with Austin High, by the late 1960s financial and staffing problems were forcing their administrators to consider closing them. New, creative ideas were needed by all three religious denominations if secondary education were to continue and expand in the Stann Creek District. Due in great part to the thaw in Catholic-Protestant tensions that was a by-product of Vatican II, such ideas were now possible. Consequently, a novel experiment that would have been out of the question in the pre–Vatican II era was now proposed. It is explained in a March 1968 letter from Jesuit Father William P. Thro to Mother Marie Anselm Duffel, the superior general in New Orleans. Thro begins his letter by noting that he is writing at the suggestion of Sister Mary Henriette Lazare, the principal of Austin High School. He then explains:

> For some time now, at least a year and a half, the Bishop [Robert Hodapp] and I and others of the Fathers here have been discussing the future prospects of Austin High School. Because of very limited funds we have little hope of building an adequate facility for an increased student enrollment (not to mention the present enrollment). We could not now, nor in the future, possibly pay an adequate staff, if we had to hire the entire staff. This consideration looms large in our thinking. And, I might add for emphasis, we have no desire to give up a project that I for one and the Bishop for another and your Sisters here think of as one having lasting and far-reaching value for the community and the country.[63]

Thro now gets to the heart of the matter:

> The idea of forming a new, combined school with the Protestants in town who have a secondary school running in about the same financial and academic condition as ours is a natural development of the whole ecumenical approach to cooperation with them. The Anglican Bishop is much in favour of a united effort and one aspect that he finds attractive is the possibility of having our Sisters as part of the staff. He, honestly and sincerely I believe, thinks they would lend a special note of religious dedication to their work as well as a deeper and more spiritual interest in the students than lay people could normally have. The Methodists too, as well as lay people who have been consulted all seem to favour the project.[64]

After noting that he had discussed with Sister Mary Elaine Vavasseur, the superior of the local Holy Family convent, the possibility of joining the schools and that she enthusiastically supported the move, Thro asserts that his proposal was not only in keeping with the spirit of Vatican II but also promised a plethora of positive benefits for the church:

Besides the trend in the Church toward ecumenical cooperation there would be the pressure to work together for the purpose of achieving the best in educational advantages possible for our children. We would stand a much better chance to receive government assistance in building and equipment. We would get to know non-Catholics more appreciatively and I do believe we would have a better and more widespread influence in the local community.[65]

Thro next makes it clear that he was not so naïve as to think that his proposal would be the panacea that would erase all prejudices between local Catholics and Protestants, while also eradicating all the financial problems entailed in maintaining a secondary school in Dangriga. Nonetheless, he was sure that it would prove to be a good start and over time would pay dividends.[66]

As for the administrative organization of the ecumenical school, Thro notes that all parties envisioned a joint venture. A Board of Governors consisting of Catholics, Anglicans, and Methodists would be responsible for hiring a principal and staff, but all three religious denominations would be consulted before any decisions were made. It had already been decided that heads of the three religions involved or their representatives would meet during the following week with Belizean officials to determine the government's willingness to provide a suitable site and adequate funds for a new building. All parties involved, however, agreed that there was no need to wait until the building was in place before implementing their plans. In the meantime, Austin High School and the Anglicans' Stann Creek College could pool their buildings, library resources, furniture, and equipment. It was hoped that the Holy Family Congregation would provide three sisters for the school. Indeed, if all went according to plan, Thro saw no reason why the ecumenical school could not be up and running by September 1969.[67]

The Jesuit's timeline proved overly optimistic. Two letters from September 1971, the first from Jesuit Father Howard Oliver and the second from Sister Mary Cecilia Higinio, principal of Austin High, to George Price, now premier of Belize, called on the government to "give the project of the new high school the highest priority"[68] and indicated that meetings between local school officials and governmental educational officials were still in the planning stage.[69] A third letter, in October, from Father Oliver to Minister of Education E. P. York invited the latter to a meeting on the evening of October 29 with the "committee for the Stann Creek Ecumenical High School." It listed the names of the ten-person committee, which included those of the directors of the Anglican, Methodist, and Catholic "missions" in Dangriga (Stann Creek) as well as the principals of the three denominational schools involved in the consolidation process.[70] The result of these efforts, appropriately enough, was called "Ecumenical High School." However, it would not become a reality until 1974.[71]

At that time it was decided, with the approval of Bishop Hodapp, the sisters, and the Jesuits,[72] that the Anglican principal of Stann Creek College would serve as principal. It was also agreed that Sister Joseph Ellen Cavalier would be in charge of creating a religious training program for the school,[73] whose student population was mostly Catholic.[74] A staff list for the 1978–1979 academic year includes Sister Ellen Joseph as a teacher of the English language and literature and Sister Jennie Jones as a teacher of religious studies.[75]

In 1990, when the school was in its fifteenth year of operation, it had a staff of forty-three people drawn from a wide variety of countries and backgrounds. Along with local personnel, the staff included people from the United States, Guyana, and England. The national government financed 65 percent of its expenses, while the other 35 percent was generated by tuition, scholarships, and an annual fundraising drive.[76] In addition to their usual teaching loads, which included Bible study, the Holy Family faculty members conducted an annual day of recollection for each grade.[77] Unfortunately, by 1990 the school was badly overcrowded, and the students' academic performance suffered as a result.[78]

When Sister Judith Therese Barial relinquished her faculty position at Ecumenical following the 1989–1990 academic year so that she could work full-time on the development of the Christian Youth Enrichment program,[79] only two sisters still taught at the high school, Sisters Clare of Assisi Pierre and Hortensia Maria Flowers. By 1995, however, they had been reassigned to other duties and, as Sister Hortensia stated in a letter to a congregation member in New Orleans, "assignments of Sisters to Ecumenical [was now] a thing of the past."[80]

Twice per month, however, Sister Hortensia and Sister Andria Marie Donald accompanied the two parish priests at Sacred Heart to Ecumenical to assist them with the religion program there.[81]

There were several reasons for the sisters' withdrawal from the high school. First, as will be discussed in chapter 7, the Holy Family Congregation had by the second half of the 1990s established Delille Academy, a new type of high school in Dangriga, and had to assign nuns to its faculty. Thus, it was more difficult to spare sisters for Ecumenical, especially since very few new recruits were entering the congregation. Second, the retirement age for teachers in Belize was fifty-five,[82] and by 1995 most members of the Holy Family Congregation were over that age. And third, as will later be discussed, by the 1990s the sisters in Dangriga had expanded their apostolate into non-teaching fields that kept some of them from the classroom.

Today, Ecumenical High School is still thriving, and large numbers of graduates from the elementary schools that the sisters had founded matriculate there. Even though no sister has served on the faculty for over a decade, the legacy of the sisters still remains primarily as a result of Christian youth groups that Sister Clare had established during her tenure there.[83]

The creation of Ecumenical High School was a radical venture in Christian ecumenism.[84] Although the idea for such a school probably originated with Father Thro or with the Anglican mission director of Dangriga,[85] the Belize Holy Family community and the sisters' governing council in New Orleans were ardent supporters of the project from its inception. The Holy Family Congregation likewise played a major role in the long process of transforming the plan from an idea to concrete reality. Thus, it can be said with certainty that the creation of Ecumenical High is a vivid case study of how the Holy Family Sisters, together with the help of the Jesuits, adapted to the spirit of the Second Vatican Council's call for *aggiornamento*. Both read the signs of the times and in so doing earned the right to be called pioneers in the field of interdenominational ecumenism.

CHAPTER 6

Problems over Language and Inculturation

The issue of inculturation would prove to be one of the most painful challenges that the Holy Family Congregation would face in the post–Vatican II years.[1] Mistakes would be made that would threaten the harmony of the Holy Family community in Dangriga, but in the end the sisters would learn to read the signs of the times and transform their approach to their mission apostolate, making it more vibrant and productive. In order to fully understand this challenge, however, it should prove helpful to begin with a brief overview of the Belizean struggles for independence from Great Britain and for social justice.

British Honduras did not formally become a Crown colony until 1862, although the British had dominated the area throughout the nineteenth century. The colonial government soon created a socioeconomic structure that guaranteed to lumber companies a cheap source of labor. The Belize Estate and Produce Company (BEC), for instance, was granted ownership of about a third of the colony's territory, and it refused to sell or lease any of its land for agricultural use. Much of the underclass had no option other than to work as loggers for the BEC at very low wages. Salaries throughout the nineteenth century and well into the twentieth ranged from about twelve to fifteen dollars per month. Moreover, through a series of unjust company practices that robbed workers of what little they earned, most were forced into constant debt and therefore obligated to remain with the logging company. Those who tried to leave their jobs before fulfilling the terms of their contracts or before paying off their debts were subject to imprisonment. The Great Depression, coupled with a destructive hurricane in 1931, only made the plight of Belizean workers and their families worse. Less global demand for Belizean lumber and other products meant massive unemployment, which brought many people close to starvation.

In 1934 a group of about 18,000 desperate men, calling themselves the Unemployed Brigade, marched to the governor's office demanding employment. When the governor responded by offering only eighty jobs, and these at twenty-five cents per day, the leader of the marchers, Antonio Soberanis Gómez, formed the Labor and Unemployed Association (LUA), which began picketing the businesses of wealthy merchants with a call for a national boycott of their products. Through such methods Soberanis was able to get dockworkers in Stann Creek (Dangriga) a raise from eight cents per hour to twenty-five. When picketing at the BEC sawmill in Belize City resulted in violence, however, Soberanis was arrested and imprisoned for five weeks. With its leader in jail, the LUA split into two rival factions and, as the government had hoped, lost much of its effectiveness. A new organization was needed, and, in 1939, Soberanis formed the General Workers Union (GWU), which rapidly grew in membership over the next decade.

Economic hardship eased somewhat during World War II, when large numbers of Belizean workers emigrated to the United States, the U.S. Canal Zone, and England, where the war effort had caused a scarcity of labor. When the war ended, however, these jobs were terminated and the Belizean émigrés returned home, thereby creating even greater unemployment in the British colony. Despite such economic hardship, on December 31, 1949, the governor of British Honduras decided to devalue the Belizean dollar, even though the colony's legislative body had opposed such a move. In response to the governor's decree, a People's Committee was formed in early January that soon developed into the People's United Party (PUP), a political organization whose main goal was independence from Britain. When one of its leaders, George Price, was chosen to head the GWU in

1952, the two organizations merged, thereby creating a powerful nationalistic movement.

When citrus factory workers in the Stann Creek District went on strike in October 1952, the PUP-GWU leadership decided to take advantage of the situation and called for a general strike. Although the strike, which lasted forty-nine days, did not achieve all of its goals, it did raise the popularity of the PUP throughout the colony. The party was able to pressure the government into granting universal adult suffrage; and on April 28, 1954, in the first-ever general elections in British Honduras, the PUP won eight of the nine contested seats. From that time until December 1984, the PUP dominated Belizean politics and won every general election.

In 1961, following Price's acquittal by a jury on questionable charges of sedition, his party won all eighteen seats in the Belizean House of Representatives. With this victory, Price, who now controlled the PUP, was able to force the British government in London to agree to accept the new Belizean Constitution, which went into effect on January 1, 1964, and which granted the colony full self-government. Price next dedicated himself to nation building. He designed a new flag and composed a national anthem for Belize as well as a national prayer. Since the creation of the PUP, its leaders had refused to use the name British Honduras, choosing instead to refer to their nation as Belize. In 1973, Britain finally capitulated to the PUP's demand and officially recognized Belize as the name of the nation. On September 21, 1981, Price and his party finally prevailed, when the British granted the tiny nation full independence.

The young middle-class Creoles, who in the 1950s had formed the PUP, were all graduates of the prestigious Jesuit-run St. John's College (high school) in Belize City. Its head, George Price, had studied for the priesthood and throughout his life attended daily mass. Influenced by the ideals of Catholic social justice, the PUP leadership intentionally tried to instill a feeling of nationalistic unity and cultural pride in the various ethnic peoples of British Honduras. They succeeded, and this reawakened pride only intensified with the various triumphs of the party.[2]

This nationalistic struggle affected the people of Stann Creek just as it did those of the country's five other districts. Following the lead of the PUP, they were able to get the national government to officially change the name of their city from the English-imposed Stann Creek to Dangriga, its Garifuna name, in 1974.[3] Likewise, the majority of the district, who had long been called Caribs by outsiders, began to refer to themselves exclusively as Garifuna, their indigenous name. In 1977 the government declared that henceforth November 19, which had previously been known as "Carib Settlement Day," would now be called "Garifuna Settlement Day" and be celebrated as a national holiday throughout Belize.

No mention is made in the documents found in the archives of the Holy Family Congregation of the injustices perpetrated upon the people of Belize by agro-export companies or of the collaboration of these companies with the British government. Indeed, prior to the 1980s very little can be found in the archives concerning socioeconomic or political issues in Belize. This gap is not surprising. Nuns, at least in the pre–Vatican II era, were expected to avoid involvement in secular affairs. As noted earlier, they were to live a semi-cloistered life, "being in the parish but not of it." Consequently, it is impossible to know if the missionary sisters in Dangriga were fully aware of the social injustice that existed in Belize and, if they were, how they analyzed the situation.

What we do know, however, is that the Garifuna members of the Holy Family community were at least by the 1970s not immune to the newly found pride in their heritage. This is made clear in a March 1974 letter from Bishop Hodapp to the congregation's superior general in New Orleans. The bishop begins his correspondence by noting that he had just returned from a visit with the sisters in Dangriga, where, at their request, he had a long, informal discussion with them. Next he states the reason for his letter: "In the course of the meeting, the Sisters spoke to me openly of their apostolate, their hopes and disappointments, their frustrations and ambitions. They are worried about the future of the mission because the number of Sisters assigned to it seems to be decreasing. They also feel that the urgency and importance of their work is not fully understood or appreciated."[4] The bishop continues by pointing out that over the years Belize had contributed "a considerable number of [religious] vocations" to the Holy Family Congregation, but that now the members of the Dangriga convent were worried that the source of these vocations would dry up if the governing council in New Orleans continued with their recent policy of decreasing the number of sisters assigned to the Stann Creek District. He notes that, far from reducing their mission efforts in Belize, the sisters who were working there actually wanted to expand their commitment to the region.[5]

Hodapp next turns to the issue of nationalism and the growing sense of ethnic awareness among the Garifuna nuns: "I notice that especially among the younger, local sisters there is growing interest in the welfare of their own people and an increased desire to work among them. To some extent, this may be the result of the growing spirit of nationalism and I think it is a good thing."[6] He closes with a plea to the U.S. sisters to "develop an interest in" and an "appreciation of" the missionary endeavors of their co-workers in Dangriga and to favorably consider the requests made by them.[7]

This letter is significant in that it shows that Bishop Hodapp was fully cognizant of the spirit of nationalism and ethnic pride that was growing among the Belizean members of the Holy Family community. It also clearly demonstrates that he realized that this was a positive development, one that needed to be encouraged especially because it greatly motivated the Belizean sisters to expand their ministry to the people of the Stann Creek District. He further realized, however, that this awakened nationalistic fervor was responsible for the frustration and resentment that was stirring within the Belizean sisters, who were coming to think that their fellow nuns in the United States misunderstood and undervalued their ministry in Dangriga. Indeed, this was the major reason why Hodapp felt compelled to write a frank letter to the superior general in New Orleans, advising her and her governing counsel to pay more attention to the dynamics at play in Belize.

With the benefit of hindsight, it is now clear that Bishop Hodapp's letter provides its readers with a premonition of the crisis over inculturation that was about to befall the Holy Family Congregation. In early 1978, eight Garifuna sisters were members of the Holy Family Congregation, three of whom were assigned to Belize.[8] In February, during a day of recollection, these three proposed that all the sisters in the community henceforth say the "Our Father" and "Hail Mary" together in the local dialect. Up to this time, communal prayers in the congregation's houses had been in English. Well aware that Vatican II had emphasized the importance of cultural sensitivity, the sisters in the Dangriga convent unanimously agreed to acquiesce to the indigenous sisters' request. Soon the whole community was saying one and occasionally two decades of the rosary in Garifuna. The vast majority of the communal prayers, however, remained in English.

This arrangement seems to have worked well until the end of summer of the same year, when three members of the Dangriga house were transferred back to the United States and replaced by Sisters Jennie Jones, Germaine Henry, and the local superior, Sienna Marie Braxton. All three women were North Americans and none had previously served in Belize. Moreover, none had been informed of the agreement previously made by the local community concerning communal prayer in the indigenous language.

Shortly after the three sisters' arrival in Dangriga, Sister Sienna wrote the following to Mother Tekakwitha Vega, the congregation's superior in New Orleans:

> I think we are well settled now. Trying to create a proper spirit of religious living, sharing and being responsible etc. among the sisters will be a real challenge for me!
>
> I stopped the sisters from praying in Carrib [sic] today. They respected my decision, . . . but they are not satisfied with it. So I need to know what is your thinking on this. Is it something the house could decide on? That's mainly what I want to know because some are in favor of it and some are not. So, just want to know if it is permissible if the majority of sisters are in favor of it. Until we hear from you I asked them not to pray in Carrib.[9]

From her letter, it is apparent that Sister Sienna, as the convent's new superior, felt responsible for creating "a proper spirit of religious living." Since Holy Family nuns everywhere had always prayed in English, she was unsure whether the rules of the congregation permitted sisters to pray communally in another language. Thus, without discussing the question with the more seasoned members of the Dangriga house, she forbade the use of Garifuna in communal prayer. It is also obvious that she knew little or nothing of the local culture and the ramifications that her decision would have on the Dangriga convent and on the Garifuna people at large. When some sisters were "not satisfied" with her decision, however, she took the proper step of writing to Mother Tekakwitha, who, displaying more developed leadership skills, responded by inviting every sister in the Dangriga community to personally send her opinion on this issue to her. Once the letters were all received, she would submit them to the congregation's general council for deliberation and a collaborative final decision.[10] Had Sister Sienna earlier responded in this more Vatican II-like, collaborative way on the local level, she might have avoided or at least mitigated the tension that resulted from her unilateral ruling.

At any rate, over the next month Mother Tekakwitha received seven letters from the Dangriga community. One sister, Mary Elyswith López, who was a Garifuna, did not respond or, if she did, there is no record of her letter in the Holy Family archives. The seven letters sent to Mother Tekakwitha, together with the general council's decision and Sister Sienna's subsequent correspondence, provide a valuable case study of the pain and difficulty that most religious congregations experienced in the process of transforming themselves in accordance with the spirit of Vatican II.

The letters from the three newly arrived U.S. sisters were short and almost exact in their similarity. Sister Sienna comments as follows:

> I'm totally against saying some of our community prayers in Carib. It is not our native language and we do not teach in Carib. . . . Even if such a permission was granted everyone would not answer the prayers [in] Carib. This would create a division in the prayers which would soon create a division in other areas. . . . We all speak English, and we are an English speaking community. . . . Community prayers are for all not just two or three.[11]

Sister Germaine agrees:

> I do not feel that Community prayers should be said in Carib. Since I do not understand the language, it has no meaning to me and prayers become merely a rattling off of unfamiliar sounds. I feel that the sisters can say their private prayers in

Carib. I am not condemning the language. I just don't like saying prayers this way.[12]

Sister Jennie Jones is also of the same mind:

> I am not in favor of saying Community Prayers in Carib. I enjoy the Carib songs that are sung during mass and the other Carib services and celebrations. I feel however, that Community Prayers should be prayed in the language that is familiar to *all* in the house. Even after memorizing (which would take me a long time) the Hail Mary, Our Father and Glory Be, it would no longer be a prayer for me but an effort to pronounce and say words that are unfamiliar to me.
>
> Mother, please understand, I think that the Carib language is very beautiful in itself and I enjoy learning how to exchange greetings. But in the light of Community Prayer as a common bond uniting us to one another in Christ, I feel that we must be united first in one voice understandable to all.[13]

The commonalities in the above three letters are revealing. First, all three writers only use the English term, Carib, while ignoring Garifuna, the name preferred by the indigenous people of the region. Indeed, they seem totally unmindful of the fact that cultural sensitivities are involved in the issue. At the same time, however, they are all convinced that the American sisters would face hardships and difficulties if they were "forced" to recite prayers in the Garifuna tongue. Second, all three sisters are emphatic in pointing out that the language of the congregation is English, not Garifuna. Third, they all predict that if Garifuna communal prayer were allowed, unity in the convent would be undermined and replaced with division. Finally, all three sisters seem oblivious to the significant fact that the vast majority of communal prayers would have continued to be recited in English. And Sister Jennie's letter reveals another important point that merits mention. In an attempt to bolster her case for the prohibition of community prayer in Garifuna, she notes that hymns and prayers in this dialect were already standard fare at Sunday mass and at other public church services in Dangriga. As will soon be seen, the Garifuna sisters would cite this same point to show that it was the moment for the Holy Family Congregation to read the signs of the times and adjust to them.

The other two U.S. sisters assigned to the Holy Family convent in Dangriga, John Mary Jackson and Joseph Ellen Cavalier, were veteran missionaries. Both had taught in the district from 1971 to 1974 and were at the midpoint of a second three-year commitment when the controversy over the use of Garifuna arose. Their experience and familiarity with the local people and culture are apparent in their approach to the language controversy. In her letter to Mother Tekakwitha, Sister John Mary states that she supported the agreement that the Dangriga sisters made at their February day of recollection—that is, that a limited number of communal prayers be recited by the entire convent in Garifuna. She added, however, that she would not favor having a greater percentage of prayers in the native language "because it would impose a hardship on the new sisters."[14] A quarter-century later, in a telephone conversation with the author, Sister John Mary was more specific. She pointed out that the Garifuna sisters never asked that all prayers or even more prayers be said in their language; and therefore it made no sense to her at the time, nor did it later, why their limited request created such a furor in the congregation.[15]

Sister Joseph Ellen Cavalier in her short letter to the mother superior was the only one of the North American nuns who broached the important issue of cultural sensitivity: "I am in favor of saying part of this prayer [the rosary] in Garifuna, especially if such proves spiritually beneficial to our Garifuna sisters. I know this will demand from the rest of us a concerted effort to learn the Garifuna, but such will be worthwhile, for it will tell our Garifuna sisters that we wish to participate in their cultural expression."[16] Like Sister John Mary, Sister Joseph Ellen avoided using the word Carib in her letter, preferring Garifuna instead. This preference contrasts sharply with that of the three newly arrived U.S. sisters who, by their exclusive use of Carib, demonstrate that they were unaware of the cultural significance involved in one's choice of words.

Two Garifuna sisters responded to Mother Tekakwitha's request, and both their letters display a passion and desperation not found in the correspondence of the other letter writers. Sister Jean Martínez's three-page letter was easily the longest and most detailed of the seven sent to the mother superior, and it was almost exclusively concerned with issues of cultural sensitivity and national pride. Although she made no mention of the Second Vatican Council, she indirectly referred to it when she stated emphatically that Garifuna was the language of the majority of the people of Dangriga, and "[i]t was the spirit of the universal Church that people pray in their language and culture."[17] She also pointed out that in Dangriga, mass had been celebrated in Garifuna "for several years" and that ever since the Charity Sisters had come to the district, communion and funeral services had likewise been in the native tongue.[18]

Connecting the issue of nationalism to the convent's language controversy, Sister Jean contended that by reciting some prayers in Garifuna the Holy Family community would be showing its solidarity with the people of Dangriga while also displaying "sensitivity to . . . a small country struggling to become a nation."[19] On the other hand, Sister Jean continues, if the general council decided that Garifuna should be prohibited, then the consequences for the Holy Family Sisters would be dire. Garifuna sisters would find themselves unable to "pray deeply" with a community that rejected their culture. Moreover, the "cultural snobbery" that had already permeated the community over the issue of language would expand to further include issues of food and even casual conversation. Sisters would be alienated from the people whom they claimed to serve, and the Holy Family congregation would "be deliberately guilty of thwarting the progress of Belize towards national unity." Finally, if such prayer were forbidden, it would discourage "Garifuna vocations in and to the Holy Family community."[20]

To support her contentions, Sister Jean included a copy of a letter sent by Sister Stephen Franco, a Pallottine missionary and member of the Belizean Conscientization Committee, to all the priests and religious men and women of Belize:

> Belize is going through a crucial moment in its national development. Because of this it is important for people who are working in the Belizean Church to have an understanding of Belize, an appreciation and respect of her History, Cultural Heritage and Distinctive Personality of her people.

If we are aware of the above, we may be better prepared to nourish the development of a mature Belizean Church capable of relating to her flock and aware of the challenge to take a definitive stand on issues of National Development.[21]

The letter goes on to announce "a series of talks aimed at bringing about a process of conscientization in Belize; that is, an awareness of the problems and a sensitivity that will urge us all to action." The speakers listed, mostly priests and nuns, were drawn from all the orders and congregations working in Belize. A diocesan priest was also included, and Sister Jean was the speaker representing the Holy Family Congregation.[22] This letter is significant because it demonstrates that members of the Catholic missionary community in Belize were well aware at this time of the challenges facing the church as a result of national development and cultural sensitivities.

Sister Evelyn Estrada's letter displays a sense of indignation not found in the other six letters: "My annoyance at this injustice, lack of respect and acceptance of other cultures such as ours by too many in our community interferes with the harmony of good order and peace. Please [Mother Tekakwitha] try to see my side of the story, or put yourself in my place."[23] She continues by accusing Sister Sienna of presenting the language issue to Mother Tekakwitha in a way that was "quite misleading, in fact . . . untrue," adding that the local superior should have engaged in dialogue with the Dangriga community before writing the mother superior for advice.[24]

After explaining that the entire convent, Garifuna and North American as well, had agreed before the arrival of the new nuns to say a decade or two of the rosary in the local language, Sister Evelyn asserts that no Garifuna sister ever intended to create tension in the community by asking to pray in her own language, for to do so would have been uncharitable.[25] Next, she appeals to the spirit of the Second Vatican Council to support her case:

> The church has sanctioned the use of the vernacular. Inculturalization is now a big and positive issue in the church, giving us hope and a sense of worth. . . . The Constitution on the Sacred Liturgy explicitly allows and fosters adaptation according to the

genius and the talents of the various nations and races. It goes on to say: that one of the most pressing needs of man (modern) is to be able to worship God in his own cultural pattern.[26]

Sister Evelyn concludes her letter by contending that when one "race" accepted and respected the "first language and culture of other races," it creates in the latter a sense of worth and a positive self-image; and, moreover, it contributes to cultural preservation and "an appreciation of individual differences."[27]

After a review of all seven of the above letters, several significant points are apparent: First, the language issue had initially been discussed by the entire Dangriga community, and the sisters—including the local superior—had unanimously agreed that some communal prayers should be said in Garifuna. All agreed, however, that the vast majority of the convent's common prayer should remain in English. Second, there did not seem to be a problem until the three newly assigned U.S. nuns arrived, and these sisters were the only members of the Dangriga house to object to the recitation of some communal prayers in Garifuna. These U.S. nuns had never served in Belize prior to their 1978 assignments; indeed, none of them had any prior missionary experience whatsoever. Moreover, all three women had little if any understanding of Garifuna history and culture and no concept of how important it was for missionaries to practice cultural sensitivity. Third, the two U.S. nuns in the convent who did have prior missionary experience in Dangriga sided with the Garifuna sisters. Fourth, local priests and the Sisters of Charity of Nazareth, who had been working in Dangriga since 1974, had already incorporated Garifuna hymns and prayers in the mass and other public liturgical services. Moreover, members of all the religious communities in Belize were beginning talks on how to be more sensitive to native culture in their ministries. Thus, missionary awareness of the need for cultural sensitivity was not a novel concept in Belize when it became an issue at the Holy Family convent. Fifth, Sister Sienna, even though she had been in Belize for only a few days, forbade communal praying in Garifuna without allowing her sisters to discuss the matter. Such a noncollaborative act was not in keeping with the spirit of Vatican II, or by any stretch of the imagination could it be considered wise leadership policy. And finally, four of the seven sisters who responded to Mother

Tekakwitha's request for letters favored keeping a limited amount of the communal prayers in Garifuna. Thus, the majority of the convent disagreed with Sister Sienna's decree. Indeed, this majority is actually larger, since Sister Elyswith López, a Garifuna who either did not write a letter or whose letter has been lost, was a staunch supporter of prayer in the native language.

In light of the above, one would assume that Mother Tekakwitha and the general council would almost certainly rule in favor of the majority view and thereby allow the Dangriga house to continue the recitation of a few communal prayers in Garifuna. Nevertheless, the council upheld the earlier decision of Sister Sienna with the following decree:

> The Church dropped Latin because she recognized the importance of praying in a language understood by all. All the Sisters in Dangriga speak and understand English; therefore, this is the language to be used in community prayers. In view of the growing nationalism among the Caribs, it was suggested that some minor activities could be selected to introduce the Sisters to the language, e.g., grace before meals, greetings, etc. Everyone is not capable of learning a second language and this should be borne in mind. The general consensus was that the Dangriga Community should pray in English.[28]

Mother Tekakwitha's letter to the sisters in Dangriga attempts to soften the council's decision and is therefore worth repeating here at least in part:

> After discussing the issue, the general council concludes that all community prayers are to be recited in English. The council notes, however, that Carib is the language spoken by the majority of the people in Dangriga. The council is aware of some of the cultural differences and the growing spirit of legitimate pride among Caribs. Establishing identity is good and necessary. The council acknowledges and respects the cultural differences and in so doing, urges the local community to acquaint themselves with the language, the history, [and] the tradition of the people whom they serve.[29]

Mother Tekakwitha next pleads with the Dangriga convent to come together "with one heart and one spirit [and] speak the language of love, a language freed from all narrowness of spirit and bonds of selfishness, a language open and ready to serve the needs of the people of God in Dangriga."[30]

The general council's decision, however, ironically produced exactly what it was intended to prevent. Instead of preserving unity and harmony among the sisters, it caused bitterness and division. One can only wonder why Mother Tekakwitha and the general council did not realize that this would be the end result of their decision. Perhaps this can be partly attributed to the fact that four of the six members of the council were North Americans with no missionary experience or service in Dangriga. Two council members were Belizean Creoles with service in Dangriga, but only prior to 1964—in other words, long before Garifuna culture became a burning issue in the Belizean Holy Family community. Mother Tekakwitha was likewise a Belizean Creole, but she had never served in Dangriga. (It must also be noted that, although the Garifuna and Creole are both black peoples, they have never had any sense of commonality or shared culture.)[31] In summary, then, it seems safe to assume that neither Mother Tekakwitha nor any of the six council members fully understood the dynamics of Garifuna cultural pride that was blossoming in the 1970s.[32] Consequently, they were unaware of the ramifications that their decision would have on the Garifuna sisters in the Holy Family community.

In a letter written in 1978 by Sister Sienna to Mother Tekakwitha just before Christmas, the former describes how the unity of her convent had degenerated:

> Srs. Ellswyth [sic] and Jean have a much better spirit and presence [towards the community] since you spoke to Sr. Ellswyth, and since the community dialogued with them. Sr. Jean is trying, but not because of my efforts. Sr. Joseph Ellen is the one who was able to get through to her after our community dialogue. You see, Sr. Jean claimed that her behavior of separation from us was [due] to my not letting them pray in Carib. She feels that I have rejected her language, food, and culture. . . . [B]ut I really can't help her. . . . Sister is very moody. . . . She seems to be bitter . . . to me.

> [Sister Elyswith's] behavior just might be different with another group of sisters. She does not relate at all to Srs. Germaine and Jenny. There is very little interaction or communication with them. I think Sr. Ellswyth separated herself from the community because of those two.... The quality of the presence of Sr. Ellswyth and Sr. Jean when bodily with us was nil. Their silence and body language expressed a feeling of not wanting to be with us.... I will try to work with Sr. Ellswyth. I have been getting her to do things that involve her in community projects in the house, and she has been cooperating nicely, but Sr. Jean doesn't respond to me too well so I can't ask her to do anything.[33]

By February 1979, the situation had only deteriorated further, as another letter from Sister Sienna to the mother superior makes clear:

> I had another conference with Srs. Jean and Ellswyth [sic] on February 13th. At that time I advised them to write and inform you of their plans. I think you should know that both sisters are making definite plans to leave our community at the end of the school year....
>
> You may know already that Sr. Jean plans to start her own community here, which is [supposed] to be dependent on, or attached to [the] Holy Family Sisters here (for financial support I'm sure). She has been looking for a house. Now, I got all this information from the lay people. Half the town knows they are leaving; they have been talking their business foolishly to the lay people and they tell us. If you need facts concerning Sr. Jean's leaving you can write Bishop Hodapp. She has been conferring with him....
>
> I think it was a big mistake to have all those sisters here together. There are no big outward acts of not getting along. But what has happened is that they stay out of each [other's] way. I want you to know we do not have real community here, and there is nothing I can do about it. Sr. Germaine and Sr. Ellswith, no communication, they do not relate in any way, just no interaction. Sr. Jenny and Sr. Ellswyth, the same thing, they simply give each other the mutual respect that is [due]. One reason why

Sr. Ellswyth is leaving is that she said she will always be meeting up with them. They simply DO NOT MIX!! AND I CANNOT FORCE THEM! You know this has caused the other sisters in the house to feel a little tense. And their relationship with Sr. Jean is the same as it is with Sr. Ellswyth.[34]

A letter from Sister Jennie to Mother Tekakwitha, written in late March, confirms the tense state of convent life in Dangriga: "Our house is pretty calm right now. Although Sisters Jean and Elyswith don't say much more than good morning and good evening and I only see them for meals and prayers, the atmosphere is a little better. I've learned to live above all of that anyway."[35]

From these three letters, then, it is clear that the Dangriga convent was divided and that this division had a negative effect on all of the sisters. It should be noted, however, that in the 1970s, due to the strains resulting from the Second Vatican Council's call for change, most religious communities underwent some degree of polarization. Thus, what happened to the Holy Family Sisters in Dangriga was more the norm than something out of the ordinary. It is also evident from the above-mentioned letters that the lay people of Dangriga were well aware of the turbulent situation and what caused it, and this, too, could only have had a negative effect on the sisters' relationship with those to whom they ministered. At any rate, at the end of the year, tensions finally eased when Sisters Jean and Elyswith left the Holy Family community in hopes of establishing an indigenous-based religious house. Later, when their efforts did not succeed, Sister Jean petitioned to reenter the Holy Family Congregation and her request was granted. After working for several years in the United States, she was reassigned to Dangriga in 1998 and served there until 2004. Although Elyswith López did not reenter the congregation, she eventually taught in a lay role at Sacred Heart School and served as its principal from 1992 to 1997.

In reflecting today on the language controversy, we can see that four factors need to be taken into consideration in order to make sense of what happened. First, prior to the 1970s it was the general rule among female religious congregations that their mission convents conform in all things concerning communal life with motherhouse customs and traditions. By 1978, however, many congregations had abandoned this practice. Nevertheless, it could have been a factor in the Holy Family leadership team's decision to disallow the use of the Garifuna language in communal prayer.

The second factor is fear of the unknown. The years following Vatican II were a time of change and uncertainty, not only for the Holy Family Sisters but also for all religious orders and congregations. Many traditions that had never been questioned prior to the Second Vatican Council had already been discarded by the late 1970s. Understandably, this caused a sense of insecurity in some religious. And now a handful of Garifuna sisters, who had always joined the rest of the Holy Family community in praying in English, claimed to be dissatisfied and asked for change. If their request was granted, would the Garifuna minority next demand more? Would a concession on this matter open the door for further concessions that might threaten the traditional stability of the congregation? These were the questions that worried that segment of the congregation who did not fully comprehend the nationalistic and cultural pride that had arisen in the second half of the twentieth century in Belize.

Fear of the unknown was compounded by a third factor, the seldom-mentioned social stratification that permeated the Holy Family community from its inception and, according to Sister Sylvia Thibodeaux, lasted through most of the twentieth century.[36] Prior to the acceptance into the congregation of the ex-slave Chloe Preval in 1869, all community members were light-skinned, Creole *gens de couleur libre*. The dominant white society considered them inferior but placed them far above darker-skinned African Americans in the New Orleans social order. Consequently, they were allowed "privileges" that were denied former slaves and their descendants. Even though the sisters ministered to African American slaves, most of the nuns, at least up until 1869, accepted the supposed inferiority of these darker-skinned people. This is why, when Preval sought to enter into the congregation, the majority of sisters voted to reject her. This, in turn, caused a minority to split from the other nuns and form another convent that welcomed Preval.

But even after this division was healed and a significant number of dark-skinned women joined the congregation, Holy Family leaders found that when it came to negotiating with members of the dominant class—whether they were church personnel or secular—light-skinned sisters were treated more favorably than their darker counterparts. No doubt this helps to explain why only two of the seventeen Holy Family mothers superior—the brilliantly gifted Austin Jones and the current superior, Eva Regina Martin—had darker skin pigmentation. In general, then, the powers that be in New Orleans favored those women with lighter, Caucasian features, and, since the Holy Family Sisters needed these "favors" in order to succeed in their apostolate to those people of African descent, an unequal, two-tiered social hierarchy developed in the congregation. Lighter-skinned sisters not only received privileged treatment but, what is more, they came to expect it.

When the sisters entered British Honduras in 1898, they found a stratified social system that was remarkably similar to that of New Orleans. White descendants of Europeans were at the top of the social pyramid. Below them were the Creoles, people of mixed European and African ancestry; and below them were the Caribs (Garifuna) and Maya. The Creoles were treated better by the dominant European class than were the Garifuna, and as a consequence they came to view the latter as inferior. In 1872 the government of British Honduras had gone so far as to establish reservations for the Garifuna.[37] They were prevented from owning their own land and were treated as squatters and nothing more than a source of cheap labor.[38] As William Setzekorn noted, in more recent decades efforts have been made to better integrate the Garifuna into Belizean life, but even as late as the 1970s "the urban Creole still hesitate[d] to accept this strange [Garifuna] Negro who speaks an Indian language-form and retains Indian cultural traits."[39]

It is not surprising, then, that some American Holy Family missionary sisters subconsciously merged the stratified social mentality of New Orleans into that which they found in Belize. Furthermore, most Creole Belizean women who entered the congregation retained, again perhaps subconsciously, the prejudices of their ethnic group, including the assumption that the Garifuna culture was "foreign" and that the language of the Garifuna people was a pidgin tongue inferior to the English spoken by North Americans, the British, and Belizean Creole society. This attitude at least partly explains why Creoles on the governing council in New Orleans were unable to empathize with their Garifuna counterparts when it came to the communal prayer controversy.

The fourth factor in understanding the congregation's conduct in the language controversy can be attributed to ignorance of what the church was asking of its missionaries in the post–Vatican II era. Few Holy Family sisters had traveled outside of Belize. They had taught Belizean students for eighty years in the same way that they had taught African Americans in the United States. Like virtually all sisters before Vatican II, they had lived a semi-cloistered existence, being "in the parish but not of it," and this way of life was only beginning to change for the congregation by 1978. Moreover, few of the Holy Family sisters had the sophistication by the late 1970s to understand the nuances of the missionary process of inculturation. Consequently, sisters were sent to Belize without any cultural sensitivity training or any instruction in the history or anthropology of the region. In retrospect, it seems that their leadership made a decision in good faith that proved highly flawed.

After Sisters Jean and Elyswith left the Dangriga community, tensions in the convent eased. According to Sister Carolyn Leslie, archivist of the congregation, the issue never resurfaced. Yet, she adds, "although I have no proof, I feel that [our] Garifuna Sisters were disappointed."[40] Indeed, while researching this study, the author wrote to the seven sisters who three decades earlier had sent letters to Mother Tekakwitha, stating their opinions on the language controversy. Only three responded, leading the author to speculate that the other four sisters—Jennie Jones, Germaine Henry, Jean Martínez, and Evelyn Estrada—thought that it was better not to reopen the matter. The two U.S. sisters who had favored allowing prayers in Garifuna replied by remarking that they still feel today as they did at the time of the controversy and that they have never understood why such a modest request by the Garifuna sisters caused such a furor.[41] Although she was suffering from terminal cancer, Sister Sienna Marie Braxton wrote a short, six-line letter, implying that at the time she did not fully understand "what was going on." Her last sentence is worth quoting: "At this [the present] time I would have handled [the situation] differently and allowed [the sisters] to pray in their Native Language."[42]

One further question must be addressed before the issue of inculturation can be put to rest. In her 1978 letter to Mother Tekakwitha Vega, Sister Jean Martínez warned that if the general council forbade communal prayer in the indigenous language, then Garifuna religious vocations to the Holy Family Congregation would decline. Has history proven her correct?

Records indicate that after 1978 no Garifuna has taken final vows as a Holy Family Sister. Two or three did enter the community, but none stayed more than a short time.[43] It would be ludicrous to claim that the lack of religious vocations can be attributed solely or even primarily to the 1978 prohibition of communal prayer in Garifuna. Indeed, there is little doubt that the primary responsibility lies with the changes that took place in the social fabric of Belize in the latter quarter of the twentieth century. It was at this time that large numbers of Garifuna left Belize for the United States in pursuit of better jobs. It was not uncommon for these Garifuna to leave their children behind for a grandparent or other relative to care for in their absence. Not surprisingly, these separations contributed to a breakdown in the traditional Belizean family structure, a breakdown that was compounded by the introduction of widespread drug use, gang culture, and permissive sexual mores in Belizean society.

Nevertheless, there is some evidence to suggest that the prohibition of communal prayer in Garifuna might have been at least a minor factor. Although it is true that vocations to almost all female religious congregations in the United States and Europe consistently dropped from the late 1970s to the present, this was not the case in most of the developing world. In Latin America as a whole, female religious vocations increased by 9 percent from 1972 to 2001.[44] In the Central American neighboring countries of Belize the increase was far more dramatic. In El Salvador the number of sisters increased from 705 in 1972 to 1,542 in 2001, a 118.7 percent increase. In Guatemala, during the same time span, the number increased from 1,018 to 2,070, a 103 percent growth rate, while in Honduras the increase went from 277 sisters to 561, a 102.5 percent rise. Likewise, in Nicaragua the number rose from 484 to 977, a growth rate of 101.5 percent. Only in Costa Rica did the number of female religious remain static, with an increase of only one sister (887 to 888).[45] Belize, on the other hand, experienced a significant reduction in the number of female religious during this time period, decreasing from ninety-nine in 1972 to eighty-four in 2001, a decline of about 15 percent.[46]

Moreover, when Sister Sylvia Thibodeaux was sent in 1973 by the Holy Family Congregation to establish an indigenous female congregation in Benin, Nigeria, her efforts proved so successful that today the community, the Sisters of the Sacred Heart of Jesus, have approximately one hundred members. Yet, when, as superior of the Holy Family congregation, she attempted in the early years of the twenty-first century to use the Nigerian model to create a similar independent indigenous congregation in Belize, she failed.[47]

It is also telling that in the latter quarter of the twentieth century, two Garifuna women who decided to enter religious life chose to bypass the Holy Family community and instead affiliate with the predominantly white Sisters of Charity of Nazareth. Indeed, in response to the author's query, one of these nuns, Sister Barbara Flores, agreed to discuss the reasons for her decision. She began her correspondence by noting that although Holy Family Sisters had not educated her, she has known and respected them since 1973: "My close and direct contact with them has been as friend and colleague. I have worked with Holy Family Sisters on the same teaching faculty, collaborated with them as Parish youth moderators and served together on a pastoral team for Sacred [Heart] Parish in Stann Creek District."[48]

Sister Barbara was likewise well aware of the "huge and significant" contributions that the New Orleans–based congregation had made to both the nation of Belize and its people:

> One cannot begin to list all of the services they rendered so tirelessly to the people of Sacred Heart Parish in the Stann Creek District. Their many contributions and dedicated service include education on elementary and secondary levels, [work as] parish youth/young adult moderators, counselors, pastoral ministers and spiritual leaders. In formal and informal ways the Holy Family Sisters mentored many generations of lay educators. These services have been rendered to generations of families in the town of Dangriga.[49]

Indeed, so impressed with these hard-working sisters was she that when she heard the call to religious life, she considered entering their congregation. This intention changed, however, when she came to know the Sisters of Charity, who impressed her for many reasons, but especially for their commitment to inculturation when it came to lay liturgical practices:

> I was attracted to their outgoing attitude, hospitality, simplicity, spirit of joy, openness, reverence for cultures, progressive thinking and a spirituality relevant to and connected with the times.
>
> I met and worked closely with the Sisters of Charity prior to entering the Congregation. We designed a two-year Lay Ministry Training Program for Sacred Heart Parish which was subsequently used as a model for Lay Ministry Training in the Diocese of Belize. Integral to the curricula of the program were Vatican 2 teachings on the value of human cultures and the call for inculturation in the Church. As a result songs, prayer services, communion and burial services were translated into the primary languages of the people of the area, which were Garifuna and Maya.
>
> With regard to liturgical celebrations the people of the parish were encouraged to use their particular cultural instruments in the Church. Consequently the Garifuna drums, [and] the Mayan harp, guitar and marimba were integrated into liturgical worship.... The people were encouraged to practice reading of the Bible in the vernacular. For the lay people of the area this was a totally new experience of Church but especially a new appreciation of themselves as peoples with a rich cultural heritage. It gave all a greater sense of dignity as persons. It was a new discovery of self and a new way of being, which opened up new understandings of God.
>
> All of these actions taken under the leadership of the Sisters of Charity and encouraged by the Jesuit pastor were indicative of their reverencing of cultures and their commitment to integrate the best of the external cultural traditions into the life of the Catholic Church. Many participants in the program expressed gratitude for this new and positive attitude of the Church toward the cultures of the people.[50]

From the above, then, it is obvious that although Sister Barbara had great respect for the Holy Family community and held their decades of service to the people of Dangriga in high esteem, she nevertheless chose to enter the Sisters of Charity due in large part to the fact that they integrated their ministry into the culture of the people whom they served.

In summary, then, the 1970s were a time of trial and error for all female religious orders and congregations. Following centuries of separation or quasi-separation from the world, sisters were expected to make wholesale changes in their traditional way of life and conform to an abstract blueprint for modernization outlined by Vatican II. But change had to be effected in the concrete realities of the sisters' daily lives with no model to imitate. Even with the best of intentions, this change could result in tension, stress, and mistakes. Much was asked of the female congregations, and virtually all of them experienced pain and conflict in their process of transformation. The Holy Family Sisters were no exception. In many ways they underwent less pain and insecurity than did most of their female religious counterparts. Yet due at least in part to their perpetual lack of financial security and to the racial prejudice that they encountered through most of their history, they were never in a position to develop the international sophistication that was required for a smooth inculturation process in their mission apostolate. Nevertheless, it must be conceded that the pain and division that resulted from the Garifuna prayer issue cannot be totally attributed to the congregation's insularity. Congregational leaders made unfortunate errors of judgment that could have been avoided had they paid more attention to the views of the sisters in Dangriga who had had missionary experience.

CHAPTER 7

MISSION EXPERIENCES OF THREE HOLY FAMILY SISTERS

In early 1980, Mother Tekakwitha Vega traveled to Dangriga to evaluate the Holy Family missionary community; and in a March 6 letter, following her return to New Orleans, she sent the sisters an assessment of what she had observed. She praised the sisters for the "conscientious performance" of their duties, their "fidelity to community prayer," and the "wholesome" nature of their interpersonal relationships.[1] Thus, from Mother Tekakwitha's comments, the division in the Dangriga house over the issue of communal prayer had dissipated at least to the point where it was no longer seen as a major problem. However, she did have one criticism, which she thought merited immediate attention: "As dedicated missionaries involved in the work of service to the Church and the building of Christ's kingdom, and in accord with the spirit and charism of our Congregation, there is need to be more available to the people of Dangriga. Loving care of the poor and needy must be given. The people need to know that you care and are concerned about them."[2] In other words, in keeping with the call of Vatican II for inculturation, Mother Tekakwitha was telling the Dangriga religious community that it was no longer acceptable to be "in the parish but not of it."[3] The case studies of Sisters Clare of Assisi Pierre, Lucia Carl, and Judith Barial persuasively demonstrate that in the 1980s and 1990s the sisters in Dangriga took her suggestion to heart. In so doing, they redirected the missionary community so that it integrated itself into the culture of those whom they served.

Sister Clare

When Sister Clare of Assisi Pierre arrived in Dangriga in 1981 to teach at Ecumenical High School, she knew virtually nothing about Belize or the culture of its people.[4] When she returned to the United States a decade later, however, she was a changed person as a result of her mission experience. Her story is especially valuable in that it reveals the ways in which the Holy Family Congregation in the 1980s overcame its earlier missteps concerning inculturation and adjusted to the challenges of Belizean nationalism, Garifuna cultural awakening, and the Second Vatican Council.

While reflecting on her time in Belize, Sister Clare notes how unready she was for her new assignment:

> I was totally unprepared for what I encountered in this ministry. I didn't know a thing about Belize. I had never even been out of the [United States]. I couldn't understand the language and I thought the area looked like the Old West. The houses were [on stilts] off the ground and the people would make fires under them. This worried me and when I mentioned to the other sisters that I thought this [created a fire hazard], they calmed my fear by asking me how many burnt houses I had seen. [None.] I saw kids in bare feet and I was struck by how limited their educational opportunities were. Those who couldn't make the grade cut-off [on the Belize National Selection Examination] couldn't go on to high school. But I also saw that these were happy people.[5]

Although Sister Clare taught a full load of four classes at Ecumenical High School, she soon became involved in pastoral ministry as well.

> We [sisters] were all prepared to be classroom educators; pastoral ministry was not something we did, so this was a whole new career that I learned there. Our pastoral team consisted of two Holy Family Sisters, two priests, and two sisters from another community [Sisters of Charity of Nazareth, one of whom was Sister Barbara Flores]. We were responsible for those in

town as well as those in seventeen villages. We did a lot of leadership training. We trained catechists and prepared people for the sacraments. We lived very close to [the people]. We slept on floors and ate things you don't even want to think about eating. We immersed ourselves in the culture. I learned a lot about how church and community could work together. You could be with the people where they were. You weren't coming [to the missions] to work for them, but to work with them and we developed lifelong friends there. [Pastoral ministry] made me grow tremendously as a person. My experience gave me a much deeper understanding of what church means, what God means, what ministry means. It gave me an understanding of the conditions that people live in, who are outside my own little world, the one I had lived in so long. [It taught me that] church can be church in a different setting. Ours is a sacramental church and many of the people in Belize only get to see a priest once or twice a year. So I learned that church had to be done in different ways. So I'm now very comfortable with doing things differently.[6]

Sister Clare was emphatic in contending that the Belizean community's work in pastoral ministry also benefited the members of the Holy Family Congregation back in the United States, who before the 1980s had no idea of what everyday life was like for the people of Dangriga:

> The charism of the missions helped the whole congregation grow in their understanding of what the missions are all about. When we would come home, we would bring photos of the people and places we visited in our pastoral work. We would tell the [U.S.] sisters stories of the situations we encountered. And the sisters would tell us that they hadn't had a clue of how Belizean people looked or lived except for the [Belizean] sisters in the community, who didn't look any different than the rest of us.[7]

Sister Clare was convinced that immersing herself in the culture of the Garifuna helped her to be more effective not only in her pastoral work in Belize but also in her teaching at Ecumenical High and back in the United States. Prior to going to Belize, she had planned to begin work on a master's degree in religious education. When she returned home, she was granted permission to pursue such a degree at Loyola University in New Orleans. While in class, she frequently found herself relating her pastoral ministry experiences in Belize to the subject matter that was being studied, and her fellow students in the master's program seemed genuinely interested in hearing about how "church" looked in another setting.[8]

SISTER LUCIA

In 1987, Bishop Osmond Martin made an appeal to Mother Rose de Lima Hazeur, asking her to consider sending an additional sister to Dangriga to work full-time with the elderly. Due to changing socioeconomic circumstances in Belize, there was a dire need for such a ministry, and Mother Rose readily agreed to the bishop's request.[9] Care for the aged had been a part of the congregation's original charism, and Bishop Martin's request provided the sisters with an opportunity to plant and nurture this part of their calling on Belizean soil. Sister Lucia Carl, who had spent several years doing pastoral work with the elderly at Lafon Nursing Home in New Orleans, was chosen for this assignment.[10] Her six-year ministry in Belize provides another case study of how the Holy Family Sisters adjusted to the spirit of Vatican II by expanding their ministry in Dangriga to meet the needs of the time.

In a letter to Father James Short, pastor of Sacred Heart Parish, Mother Rose notes that Sister Lucia enjoyed "relatively good health" and therefore should without much trouble "be able to visit the homes of the elderly . . . to identify their needs in terms of food, medication, and hospitalization and to distribute Communion to shut-ins."[11] In what was typical of the Holy Family commitment to service, she then adds: "There may be other areas in which Sister Lucia can serve. . . . I suggest that you discuss these with her and that you draw up a program to guide her."[12]

Father Short's first task for Sister Lucia when she arrived in Belize was for her to take a census of the Catholic population of Dangriga.

He reasoned that such work would not only help her to become familiar with the area, but it would also give her an excellent opportunity to experience the culture of the common people and to see firsthand what life was like for them. He reasoned correctly, for as Sister Lucia notes in an essay she later wrote, by going from house to house she met and talked with people of different religious faiths, hearing personally about their lives and problems. She further remarked that the ones who most touched her heart were the elderly women: "I learned to greatly admire the grannies most of all. They have an enviable resiliency. They seemingly feel obligated to care for (anywhere from three to ten) grandchildren, and this with little or no resources, unless their children send support money from the U.S. where they have gone to seek jobs, or if the grannies sell fruits or vegetables or baked bread daily."[13] As she immersed herself in her ministry to the elderly, her admiration for "the grannies" grew even more:

> In my daily walks around town, I began to learn of more needy families and their situations, which included lots of children. I discovered bit by bit the physical conditions and specific needs of the elderly. Many of these also had grandkids living with them, whose mothers and/or fathers were around but not supporting their own kids.[14]

She also encountered many elderly women in poor health who lived alone. This part of her ministry was crucial, since there were no health facilities in the region to care for the indigent elderly. She came to realize that in the latter decades of the twentieth century, it had become common for many young adults to migrate to the United States, leaving their parents in Belize to fend for themselves. These people were poor and often very lonely. Thus, Sister Lucia would visit them daily, talking to and praying with them or, as she put it, "just be[ing] with them."[15] She would find out if they needed anything—medicine, bed linen, food—and then she would try to obtain it for them. Sometimes shops and pharmacies would donate what was needed, but when they did not, she would somehow find enough money.[16]

Sister Clare of Assisi remembers one case in particular, which illustrates Sister Lucia's commitment to the aged. Sister Lucia encountered an ailing, elderly woman who had absolutely no one to care for her. She knew about a woman who had a shed in her yard, and she saw to it that it was cleaned up and made habitable. The shed became the old woman's home, and Sister Lucia organized the neighbors to make meals for this formerly neglected woman and to routinely look in on her to make sure that she was comfortable.[17]

Because of Sister Lucia's efforts, the Dangriga Holy Family community began a "little bread and butter ministry."[18] The sisters would break up large sacks of beans and rice into one-pound bags. Sister Lucia would then deliver the bags, together with milk or other staples, on her daily visits. Eventually the laity was brought into this ministry and organized a St. Vincent de Paul Society, which made the sisters' convent its base of operations. As Sister Clare of Assisi noted, "Sister Lucia was able to do a lot with the little we had." But the most valuable part of her ministry was "just being there with so many lonely people who were otherwise totally neglected."[19] The ministry to the elderly also provided a way for the sisters in the Dangriga community to develop a fuller understanding of the culture of those whom they served.

Before concluding this narration on the missionary work of Sister Lucia, one important point needs to be mentioned. The late 1980s and early 1990s were times when the Dangriga Holy Family community was desperately strapped financially, due to the fact that several of the sisters had given up salaried faculty positions at Ecumenical High School for work in the unpaid Christian Youth Enrichment (CYE) program. This is why the $500 per month that Father Short had agreed to pay Sister Lucia in a 1987 letter to Mother Rose de Lima Hazeur was crucial to the Dangriga convent's well-being. Yet after only four payments had been made, no more money was forthcoming from the pastor. Although Short's letter to Hazeur is no longer extant, a 1992 letter from Father Frank Schmidt to Sister Clare admits that the Jesuits had been remiss in paying Sister Lucia what had been promised.[20] A second letter from Schmidt notes exactly how delinquent the Jesuits were: "Here is the final payment on Lucia's back pay that I promised. This brings it to $26,000 for the fifty-two months the Jesuits were responsible. Once again I'm sorry for all the pain and anguish some of 'us' caused you, Lucia, and your community. I hope belated justice and recognition of the original injustice can help heal the wounds."[21] Suffice it to say, history demonstrates that the Jesuits of Dangriga were not alone among clergy who reneged on promises of monetary compensation to the sisters for their services. But at least in this case the Jesuits did eventually render "belated justice."

When Sister Lucia was reassigned to the United States, a Jamaican nun, Sister Andria Marie Donald, replaced her.[22] She too read the signs of the times and consequently by 1994 had expanded her apostolate by adding a ministry to the immigrant Mayan Indian settlement at Red Bank, about fifty miles south of Dangriga. Accompanied by a Belizean laywoman who had lived in El Salvador and was fluent in Spanish, Sister Andria visited the Mayan community on Monday and Thursday afternoons. Sister Lisa Langlois had begun this ministry in 1994, during her one-year stay in Dangriga. Since the Indians were desperately poor, the sisters took money from their own allowances to buy seeds for the Mayan peasant farmers. As a result, the Indians were able to grow subsistence crops for their community. The nuns also offered religious instruction to the Indian children and prepared some of them for the sacrament of Confirmation.[23]

Sister Judith

Due to the shrinking number of vocations, the Holy Family Congregation was forced to reduce the number of sisters assigned to Belize in the 1980s to six and then to five. Yet, as has been seen, despite this reduction in personnel, the sisters expanded their apostolate to include pastoral ministry as well as ministry to the elderly. But that was not all. Following the Second Vatican Council's dictum to read the signs of the times, the sisters also expanded their educational efforts in a new, nontraditional direction, in which Sister Judith Therese Barial, who arrived in Dangriga with Sister Lucia in 1987, was the driving force.

Sister Judith, who was assigned to Belize in order to teach at Ecumenical High, claims that from the moment she first set eyes on the country, she fell in love with it:

> I'm from a small town on the Mississippi Gulf Coast, so when I came to Belize I thought it was wonderful because I like small-town life. I loved the culture, the language, the drumming. I tried to learn the language and be part of the culture. I was especially impressed with the elderly. They had great faith and dedication to the church. A short time after I got to Dangriga, I found out that my father had been diagnosed with cancer. Sister Clare had started a charismatic prayer group and, although the people had never met my father and had only known me for a little while, they began praying for him. Those people there, well, they just get into your life.[24]

Almost immediately after her arrival, Sister Judith had a chance encounter with a group of teenagers, which caused her to see the need for another kind of educational ministry:

> In the first week I got there [Dangriga], I went with another sister [Sister Theresa Sue Joseph] to visit this young woman who was very, very sick. When we got [to her house], sitting on the steps were these teenagers. I'm a high school teacher, so I was drawn to them and began speaking with them. I asked them what their names were, what school they went to, and what grade they were in. There were two of the girls, both thirteen years old, who, when I asked these questions, just dropped their heads. I asked them what was wrong and they said that they were not in school. They said that they had not been able to pass the test [the Belize National Selection Examination] that was required to go on to high school. So I asked them, can you take it again, and they said yes, in another year. So I said, would you like me to tutor you?[25]

The next week, Sister Judith met with the two girls after finishing her workday at Ecumenical High School, and she began working with them, one on one. But the word got out, and the next week about six to eight additional girls showed up. Sister Judith decided that it would be better to teach them all on Saturdays, and she did so for about a year. But more teenage girls continued to turn up, and by the end of the school year, her class had grown to twenty. When the next academic term began, Sister Judith expanded her tutoring to twice a week, adding Thursdays to the schedule. But the students begged for more. "Sister," they asked, "why can't we have school every day?" Consequently, in September 1989 she initiated the Christian Youth Enrichment (CYE) program, an outreach for girls between the ages of fourteen and eighteen who were not in regular school.[26]

CYE offered evening classes on Mondays through Fridays from 3:00 to 5:00 p.m. at the Sacred Heart Parish Center. In September 1990 it became an all-day program with instruction for first-year participants in the morning and second-year students in the afternoon.[27] It consisted of academic classes, along with instruction in sewing, cooking, and dance,[28] but it was unstructured so that students could work at their own pace.[29] Sister Judith did most of the instruction, teaching English language, literature, mathematics, sewing, and Christian living. Sylvia Flores, the mayor of Dangriga, taught Spanish, while Sister Hortensia Flowers, Russell García, and other instructors from Ecumenical High taught Belizean history, music, and science, among other classes. The program was tuition-free and all teachers served without pay. It was financed by donations from the Holy Family Sisters in New Orleans as well as by other friends of the congregation in England and various parts of the United States.[30] In its first year, twenty-five girls were enrolled.[31] Because most of the girls were poor and unemployed, long-term plans were drawn up for a sewing cooperative, where students would contract to make uniforms for the local primary schools, thereby allowing them to become self-supporting.[32]

After about five months of operation, it was obvious that Sister Judith could not physically continue to run the CYE program while also teaching full-time at Ecumenical. Thus, she asked Mother Rose de Lima, the congregation's superior general, to allow her to give up her teaching assignment at the high school, even though this would deprive the Belize convent of one full-time teaching salary. Realizing the value of the CYE program for the youth of Dangriga, Mother Rose granted Sister Judith's request and informed Ecumenical's principal that she would not be returning to the high school after the current term ended.[33] There were five sisters in the Dangriga convent at the time, and they all agreed to make do with one less salary rather than ask the financially strapped motherhouse in New Orleans to support them.[34]

A 1990 grant application seeking $4,000 for the CYE sheds light on exactly why the Holy Family Sisters thought that their program was important. After pointing out that Belize was one of the most economically deprived countries in the Caribbean, Sister Judith explains that the nation's poverty had both negative moral and physical consequences for Belizean teens:

> Approximately 80% of this nation's youth do not complete high school either because of finances, poor scores on the highly competitive national examination, or inability to sustain the rigorous course load designed for the academically gifted. In the entire Stann Creek District, of which Dangriga is the chief town, there is only one high school with the capacity of educating about 500 students, about one-third of the potential student population. There are no alternative educational institutions such as vocational or technical schools in the district.[35]

Young females who did not complete at least two years of high school, Sister Judith continued, had almost no chance of obtaining employment. Moreover, since there were no recreational facilities and few church-sponsored programs for youth in Dangriga, young girls had too much time on their hands and many became sexually active. As a consequence, many became mothers before they reached the age of fifteen, some as young as twelve. The CYE program gave a second chance to those girls who had not previously been able to pursue their education beyond the elementary grades. It combined traditional academic instruction, classes in Christian living, and training in a variety of trades that would help students find meaningful employment in the future. Sister Judith noted that during the program's first year, thirteen of the fifteen regular students participated in GROWTH, a four-month project sponsored by CARE International, which teaches good business practices and offers start-up loans to participants.[36] Indeed, since so many young Dangrigans were interested in the program, the sisters planned to expand it and therefore were applying for additional funds that would enable them to do so. According to the grant application:

> In September of 1990, the program will operate all day, with classes for first-year students in the morning and second-year students in the afternoon. Our basic current needs are funds for uniforms for the thirty students and space funds: rent and utilities.
>
> We are presently using one room of the parish center for our late afternoon classes. However, it will be almost impossible for us to be assured of this room on a permanent basis all day. There[fore], we are seeking funds to rent space until we can actually build our center for the cooperative.[37]

Sister Judith concludes the grant application by summarizing the objectives of the program: to prepare youth for taking the stiff national examinations, to teach them a trade, to encourage self-esteem, and to prepare them to face the moral problems of their time and culture.[38] From the above, then, we can see that from its inception the CYE program was meant to be pragmatic; that is, its objective was to ensure a productive future for young girls who otherwise would have little or no chance of finding suitable employment in Belize and could well sink into hopelessness and poverty. Finally, with its nontraditional educational methodology—students working at their own pace in a somewhat informal academic setting—the program also represented another example of how the Holy Family Sisters introduced innovative methods into the Belizean educational system.

In 1991 a cooperative education program was added to the curriculum, whereby students were placed in business settings in order to receive on-the-job training. For the traditionally oriented Belizean educational system, this was a much-needed change that integrated academic study and classroom theory with experience at the work site.[39]

Realizing that a building was needed to ensure the permanence and continuity of the CYE program, the Holy Family community in Dangriga formed a building committee consisting of a "Search Executive, the pastor [of Sacred Heart Parish], two representatives of the

Civic Community, the parish council president, a contractor and two Sisters of the Holy Family."[40] The contractor drew up blueprints and did a cost analysis, free of charge.[41] He estimated that it would take $400,000 to complete the project. Sisters Clare and Judith then wrote a joint letter to Bishop Osmond Martin asking him to allocate diocesan property for the new school and seeking his permission to solicit funds from both within and outside the diocese to pay for it.[42]

The number of CYE students grew rapidly, and soon boys began to ask for admittance. The first one was accepted in 1993, and in the following year several other boys joined him.[43] By the 1994–1995 academic year, school enrollment had grown to thirty-seven, and typing, journalism, and computer classes were added to the curriculum.[44] Three teachers with master's degrees, one with a bachelor's degree, another with an associate's degree, and a retired nurse now assisted Sister Judith. Three additional instructors—a cook, a carpenter, and a dancing instructor—also joined the staff, thereby expanding the trade-school dimension of the program.[45] A community garden was also begun, which was meant to enable interested students to "experience the pleasures of growing their own vegetables."[46]

With the CYE rapidly expanding, Sister Judith realized that the volunteer teachers could not be expected to continue without some monetary compensation from the state. She therefore petitioned the government for help in paying teachers' salaries. When it seemed that her request was about to be granted, national elections took place and a new party came to power.[47] It soon became clear that state financial help would not be coming in the near future, so Sister Judith decided to send a second petition to the government, this time asking for accreditation. Students in the CYE program were doing high school–level work, for which after two years they received a certificate. But, as Sister Judith notes, "the certificate wasn't really worth anything," because the Ministry of Education did not grant the students official high school credits for their work.[48] Consequently, heeding the suggestion of the government's Officer for Continuing Education, Sister Judith petitioned state authorities, asking that the CYE program be granted accreditation as a junior secondary school.[49] Her request was approved in 1996, retroactive to September 1995, because the evaluation process had been initiated at that time.[50] Delille Junior Academy was chosen as the name of what was now the only Catholic secondary school in the southern region of Belize.

A major problem remained, however. Teachers still worked without salaries, and few lay teachers could afford to work for more than a short time without pay. Moreover, by 1997, the Holy Family sisters in Dangriga had resigned from their salaried faculty positions at Ecumenical High School in order to devote their full time to the CYE program and Delille Junior Academy. This meant that the sisters no longer had a steady source of income. Correspondence from Sister Theresa Sue Joseph, who was involved in ministry to the elderly, to Sister Sylvia Thibodeaux, the newly elected superior general, explains the community's hardship and uncertainty.

> I'm writing this letter to express some concerns. The first and greatest concern is our financial situation. I don't know if you are aware that our monthly income is $1,500, which is equivalent to $750 U.S. Out of this all utilities—electricity, gas, water, telephone, etc.—must be paid and food bought. We are now waiting for the end of the month so we can make [buy] groceries. There are some repairs, including repairs on the truck, that need attention but we're unable to do them at this time or at any time in the foreseeable future. . . .
>
> At the present time we have less than $100 left in the bank. The sisters are holding their breath hoping that there are no outstanding checks, otherwise, we are in trouble.[51]

Sister Theresa Sue goes on to explain that the Dangriga convent is in dire need of a computer but cannot afford to buy one, and that the local sisters' community cannot pay for a round-trip airline ticket to New Orleans so that she may attend an important Congregational Assembly.[52] She adds that no assistance can be expected from Sacred Heart Parish:

> We cannot ask the parish for help because it is in worse shape than we are. Last Sunday there was a notice in the bulletin to all parish employees stating that effective October 1st their jobs may have to be terminated because there is no money to pay them. When I was here before [1970–1972, 1980–1990], every-

thing that needed to be done at the convent was done by the men working in the parish workshop. But all that has changed. We are now responsible for our own maintenance.[53]

And in a letter written a short time earlier to Mother Mary de Chantal St. Julien, Sister Judith likewise discusses the Dangriga convent's monetary problems:

> Speaking of finances . . . We have exhausted the money left in the checking account from the time when we were all drawing government salaries. For two years now, we have not had anyone receiving a salary. We are living from donations that I receive from St. Mary's CSMC, my family, friends, mission clubs from various schools and some of our Sisters. . . . St. Mary's Faculty House [in New Orleans] paid our grocery bill for several months. Father Siebert, our pastor, gave us BZ$900 after the Parish Bazaar.
>
> We have a minimal school fee [at Delille Junior Academy] of $350 per year, which includes registration, book rental, yearbook and a monthly fee of $25. Actually only about 1/3 of the students can afford to pay.[54]

But Sister Judith explains that there may be a long-term solution:

> I am ready again to apply for [government] Grant-Aid. But I was told that we must first have a four-year program to qualify. . . . I have spoken at length with Mr. Fabian Cayetano, the Education Officer of the Stann Creek District and his Assistant, Mr. Oscar Reyes. They are very supportive of my vision for the school. I've also shared these ideas with Mr. Reuben Gordon, Education Officer of Continuing Education, who was instrumental in helping us get the accreditation. He encourages us to try for the 4-year program and Grant-Aid.[55]

Thus, since only teachers at four-year institutions were eligible for government salaries, Sister Judith was asking Mother Mary de Chantal to permit her to take Delille Junior Academy to a higher level by petitioning the state to allow it to become a four-year high school. Permission was granted; and in 1998, the same year that the sisters celebrated one hundred years of service in Belize, Delille became a four-year institution.[56] In 1999 the Ministry of Education issued a grant sufficient to cover most of the salaries of ten full-time teachers.[57] This meant that, along with providing teachers with compensation for their labors, the Dangriga convent's financial woes were mitigated substantially since several sisters were on the Delille Academy faculty.

A letter from Sister Judith to two sisters at the New Orleans motherhouse sums up the status of Delille Academy, as it made ready to enter the twenty-first century. It also shows how much she had accomplished and what still needed to be done:

> Let me try to bring you up to date to what is happening at Delille Academy. Last school year, we ran out of space in our facilities [in] the downstairs floor of the convent. We sought permission to use a government house about a block away. With the help of our Speaker of the House, Honorable Sylvia Flores, we received permission and [were] able to make a full-sized classroom and a smaller classroom from the structure.
>
> In anticipation of an increased enrollment, we requested and got permission to enclose the bottom floor for additional classrooms. . . . The building materials were donated by the local community. . . . [T]hree classrooms packed with students calls for some ventilation. So we put out an appeal to our parishioners of Sacred Heart for ventilation and paint. Several have donated fans [or] money for fans. The Bishop was visiting the Sunday that we put out the appeal. He has since donated the paint. . . .
>
> We hope that these facilities will be temporary; that we will soon have our own building. But we have to take one small step at a time with government assistance. We have just received confirmation that the government will pay 70% of our teachers' salaries and the tuition of all of our students except the preparatory class. . . . We are awaiting the computers to be installed that were awarded to us through the Basic Needs Trust Fund, approved last June.[58]

However, years of hard work, long hours, and stress had exhausted Sister Judith, so much so that, as she herself later stated, she was burned out.[59] It was decided that she be reassigned to the United States. Sister Jean Martínez, the Garifuna nun who had played such a large role in the language controversy of 1978 and who had later served as assistant principal at Delille Academy, replaced her as principal in 2001. At that time, the Delille student population had grown to 154 and its faculty to seventeen, four of whom were Holy Family Sisters.[60]

It should be noted that while Sister Judith was transforming the Belizean education system, Belize and its people were likewise transforming her. Indeed, she was well aware of this and remarked on it when describing her mission experience to the author in 2003: "There were five sisters in our house and a real sense of togetherness. Sister Clare [the local superior] made us feel at home. Our prayer life was very strong and we took a lot of trips together to the cayes. We had wonderful retreats, with a lot of sharing. I'm a very shy person and tend to be a loner, but the other sisters brought me out."[61] But what most changed her was working with the girls in the CYE program. More than anything else, they helped her to overcome her shyness and develop self-confidence:

> The girls I was working with weren't highly intellectual. They were just ordinary girls that I was reaching out to and they and their parents were very, very grateful. I became a part of them in a way I have never been a part of anybody else except my family. I felt so loved and so blessed. I just received so much, being in that mission for fourteen years. The last years were hard because I kind of burned out, but there was still that deep inner joy of being there and being a part of those people. Right now I have the sound of those [Garifuna] drums on my computer. Those drums got into my bones and I can't get rid of them. They allow me to be more open. I just feel freer, more myself, and nothing makes me feel inhibited anymore. It was a wonderful spiritual and social experience for me. It was the highlight of my religious life. I'm so much more open to people now than I was before. [After] working with all the kids there,

there's nobody now that I would turn away. A young man [from one of our schools in New Orleans] came to our house while we were on vacation and stole everything, but I took him back into school. I sit on the discipline committee here at our school [St. Mary's Academy in New Orleans], and [my Belize experience] makes me more compassionate.[62]

In summing up what the mission experience meant for her, Sister Lucia, Sister Judith, and the other sisters who lived with them during their years in the Dangriga community, Sister Clare spoke for all when she notes:

> We all had our separate personalities and talents, and we didn't feel constrained, so we could blossom. We could grow as we were. We dreamed together; we started talking about what we could do, what services we could give here. We were teachers and as such we got good salaries, but then we asked permission for sisters to not teach at all, which meant that there was a nice hefty salary we wouldn't have, but we knew we could make it and nobody was hungry, nobody was sick, or whatever. We just did some wonderful things together, and it was because we entered into where we were. We were willing to learn; we were not the teachers. Those of us who were there when I was there, we're just different women [now] because of that. The Belizean people are a proud people, who are very loyal to their culture. But once you win their trust then they are very open. I do know that being invited by the Lord to share in another culture is one of the greatest gifts ever given.[63]

With these elegant words, Sister Clare expressed how, following the mistakes made in 1978 over communal prayer in the Garifuna language, the Sisters of the Holy Family nevertheless learned how to read the signs of the times and to apply the dictums of the Second Vatican Council to their mission experiences in Belize.

CHAPTER 8

WITHDRAWAL FROM BELIZE

Due to the shortage of new vocations, by the early 1990s the number of Holy Family Sisters assigned to Belize had been reduced from five to four, yet their workload had expanded to include pastoral and youth ministry, daily ministry to the aged, and programs for nontraditional students in the CYE program. One sister still served as principal at Sacred Heart School. All other teaching and administrative positions, however, not only at Sacred Heart but at the other elementary schools that the sisters had previously established were now in the hands of lay people, most of whom were graduates of the congregation's pupil-teacher training center. One sister was working full-time in ministry to the elderly, and another had relinquished her position at Ecumenical High School in order to give her full attention to the CYE. In 1990, Sisters Hortensia and Clare were the only Holy Family members still teaching at Ecumenical, but by the end of 1992 both had been reassigned to the United States and henceforth no more sisters served as full-time faculty at the school. In short, it was obvious that the sisters in Belize had overextended themselves. If they were to avoid burning themselves out, they would have to streamline their workload, retaining what was most valuable to the people of Dangriga and eliminating what was least important or what could be done by others.

With this in mind, the four sisters in Dangriga began a process of discernment in the latter months of 1991, which included prayer, in-house reading and discussion of Pope John Paul II's mission documents, in-house dialogue relating to personal experiences and observations, and discussion with the local lay community. The latter included a questionnaire that the sisters drew up and distributed to Dangriga residents ranging in age from "teenager" to "over 50 years old."[1] Sister Clare also conducted interviews with a group of sixth-standard students from Sacred Heart School,[2] a second group from Ecumenical High, and six selected adults. The latter included two men and a woman who were listed as teachers at Ecumenical High, a woman who was described as a "nurse, parent, and lay minister," another woman listed as "a teacher, parent, and leader of Garifuna culture," and a man who was described as a "teacher, parish council president, and leader of Garifuna culture."[3]

When the discernment process was concluded and results from the questionnaire and interviews were recorded and analyzed, the Dangriga sisters sent a ten-page document to the motherhouse in New Orleans. It began with the following "Statement of Purpose":

> In his encyclical, *Apostolic Letter to the Religious of Latin America,* Pope John Paul II stressed the necessity of the presence of religious communities in developing nations. His Holiness praised missionaries, past and present, for their evangelizing efforts . . . [and] stated that religious communities must continue to spread the Good News throughout the world and now, more that ever, [their] presence . . . in Third World countries is crucial.
>
> In view of the Church's stress on the need for Religious Institutes to serve the people in developing nations, we are submitting to you this paper. Its purpose is to inform you of what we have assessed, with the help of the Church here, to be the needs of the people in this area. We pray that this information will serve the people of Belize in accordance with the mandate of Pope John Paul II.[4]

The sisters next included a paragraph that briefly encapsulated all that they had achieved in their ninety-plus years in Dangriga. Highlighted were the schools they had formed, including the Pupil-Teacher Training Center, and the vocations they had fostered not only in their own community but to the priesthood as well.[5] Next came the crux of the matter. How should the sisters approach their mission commitment with fewer sisters available for work in a Belize that no longer resembled the country served by earlier generations of Holy Family nuns?

> Our numerical presence is diminished to four but the imperative of our call continues into the nineties. The Belize of 1991 is quite different from our foresisters' experience. . . .
> With the advent of Belize's independence just a decade ago and because of close Belizean-U.S. ties via intermigration there is an increasing bombardment . . . of First World materialism and hedonism. Traditional values and morals are steadily being replaced by warped ideals, especially among the young adults and the youth. . . . Hence the inculturation and acculturation[6] of the present set clear imperatives for us Sisters of the Holy Family as followers of the prime Missionary Jesus and our own . . . Mother Henriette.
> It was with this mind and heart that the four of us decided to act. The course of action was to discern where Sisters of the Holy Family have been, are now and should go in this mission in Belize.[7]

The sisters enclosed a copy of their questionnaire with their letter. It opened with the question: "Do you believe that the Sisters of the Holy Family have a future role to play in the Church of Belize?" Three choices were given: Yes, No, and I'm Not Sure. Next came the question: "If you answered Yes above, in which areas of ministry below do you think the Sisters should concentrate?" Fourteen choices covering various subdivisions of education, parish ministry, and the social apostolate were listed, along with instructions for those filling out the questionnaire to choose only the three that they considered the most important.

In the letter sent to the New Orleans community, there is no indication of how the Dangriga interviewees answered the first question. Sister Clare of Assisi, however, in an interview with the author, stated that to the best of her recollection all respondents answered Yes, the sisters had a future role to play in Belize.⁸ The large number of responses to the second question provide further evidence that this was probably the case. Of the fourteen categories listed in the second question, top priority was given by respondents to "coordinators of church-related group" (57 percent of all respondents), "teachers of regular subjects in schools" (47 percent), and "religion coordinators in Catholic schools" (41 percent). The next three highest categories were the establishment of "a temporary shelter for neglected/abused children" (40 percent), "working with abused/neglected children" (38 percent), and "working with the elderly poor" (26 percent). The Dangriga sisters concluded their letter with a suggestion to the governing council in New Orleans that it allow any sister who heard a call to work in Belize to do so. It also proposed that all missionary sisters, prior to their arrival in Belize, complete an orientation course that familiarized them with the culture of the region.⁹

This letter/questionnaire is significant for several reasons. First, even though the nuns in Dangriga understood that the motherhouse in New Orleans was finding it ever more difficult to spare sisters for assignment to Belize, they nevertheless believed that the congregation's missionary presence there was of the utmost importance and therefore should be given very high priority. Second, they realized that, because of this dwindling supply of sisters, they would have to streamline their apostolate in Dangriga and concentrate on what was considered most vital. Third, they had learned from the congregation's long experience in Belize that on-the-job mission training could prove deleterious to the success of their efforts. Thus, it was essential that Holy Family Sisters, like all missionaries, have a basic understanding of the culture they were about to enter before being sent into the field. Fourth, they realized that missionaries, regardless of how overextended they might be in their ministry, must nonetheless find time to study and discuss as a community the latest church mission documents. Finally, and perhaps most important, they had learned that missionaries must enter into dialogue with the people whom they had come to serve. Consequently, the sisters in Dangriga were careful to consult with the local people before making any decisions concerning the future of their ministry, and these people told them that they were needed the most in pastoral work, Catholic education, and care for the elderly and neglected youth. In short, the sisters had come a long way since the governing council's unfortunate decision in 1978 to prohibit communal prayer in the Garifuna language.

The sisters' letter/questionnaire notwithstanding, by 1994 it was apparent to the Holy Family leadership in New Orleans that there were no longer enough nuns to fully maintain the congregation's traditional commitment to the church in Belize. The sisters, however, could not walk away from a people whom they had served so valiantly for almost a century. A middle way was sought, and, consequently, a proposal was drawn up and submitted to the community at its Ninth General Chapter. It called for the Holy Family Sisters to assist the bishop of Belize in establishing an independent, indigenous religious foundation of sisters who could carry on and possibly expand the New Orleans–based community's apostolate in Dangriga. The proposal was discussed, voted upon, and passed.[10]

It is ironic that the Holy Family Congregation was now suggesting a course of action that Bishop Hopkins had tried to implement in the early years of the twentieth century, when he recommended that a novitiate be established in Punta Gorda for Garifuna and black Creole girls who would form a second branch of the Holy Family Sisters, but one that would be under his jurisdiction rather than that of the mother superior in New Orleans.[11] At that time the sisters had tenaciously opposed his proposal, but by the 1990s the situation had changed dramatically, and now an indigenous community seemed the only reasonable course.[12]

In October 1994, Mother de Chantal St. Julien sent Sister Sylvia Thibodeaux to Belize to inform Bishop Martin of the General Chapter's proposal for an indigenous community. She returned to New Orleans with word that he was interested in the concept. Mother de Chantal followed with a letter to the bishop in December, in which she was careful to point out that the Holy Family Sisters only intended to be co-founders of the indigenous community and that it would not be set up as a province or any type of extension of the New Orleans–based congregation. She proposed that the ordinary of Belize also be a co-founder and that he be responsible for overseeing the drafting of a constitution for the foundation and for presiding over its elections for General Chapters. He would also have the right over alienation of its property and the power to suppress the community if he saw fit.[13] In other words, the Holy Family Sisters would play a major role in establishing the new religious institute, but the bishop of Belize would hold primary power over it.

The Holy Family Congregation would be responsible for providing personnel and instructional materials related to formation. It would be expected to work with and render financial assistance to the foundation until the Holy Family leadership, the bishop, and the pioneer members of the new institute all agreed that it was stable enough to function independently. It would work cooperatively with the bishop to determine the kind of spirituality that was best suited for the native sisters. Learning from the mistakes made in 1978 concerning communal prayer in the Garifuna language, Mother de Chantal pledged that her congregation would "be respectful of the uniqueness of the various cultures present in the new foundation" and in no way show any preference or imply that one culture was superior to another. On the contrary, the sisters' formation staff would work with the bishop to instill within the community a spirituality that was "respectful of the richness of the varieties of Belizean cultures."[14]

This proposal for a new, independent community was modeled on the Holy Family Congregation's establishment twenty-one years earlier of the indigenous Sisters of the Sacred Heart in Benin, Nigeria. It was there that Sister Sylvia Thibodeaux labored for eighteen years in an attempt to form a native religious order out of women from several Nigerian tribes, some of whom had traditionally been hostile to each other. So successful was her effort that by 1993 the foundation had over seventy-five members and ten novices.[15] With this venture in mind, and with Bishop Martin's interest in a similar community for his diocese, Mother de Chantal asked Archbishop Patrick Ekpu of Benin, during his visit to New Orleans in July 1995, to take a few days to travel to Belize to share his views with Bishop Martin on the development and importance of an indigenous community. Ekpu did so, and upon his return to New Orleans he related to Sister Sylvia what he had discussed with the Belizean bishop and what were the latter's concerns. Sister Sylvia then drew up a summary of his report for her congregation.

A few points from this report are worth noting. Ekpu made it clear to Bishop Martin that success in creating a religious institute hinged on having strong women, who were secure in their own vocations, involved in the formation process. They also had to be open to learning from other cultures and not impose their own congregation's spirituality on their indigenous charges. Instead, they must "be willing to let the new family evolve its own spirit." They must also be patient and not easily discouraged, since molding a new religious foundation will always be "a slow and long process."[16] Finally, Archbishop Ekpu assured Bishop Martin that if a successful indigenous congregation became a reality, it would be a great blessing for the church in Belize in that the sisters would go a long way in countering the negative effects of having so few priests in his diocese.[17]

Although Ekpu reported that Martin seemed open to the possibility of creating an indigenous foundation, he also noted that the Belizean bishop's primary concern was the financial commitment of his diocese. The Belizean Catholic Church was quite poor, and Martin thought that it did not have the means to finance the creation of a religious foundation. Although the Holy Family Sisters had pledged to help pay for the project, they had not specified how much money they were willing to invest or what they expected the Belizean church to contribute.[18] The bishop's anxiety over finances would, in the long run, prove to be an important factor in his eventual decision to suspend the project indefinitely.

Following Archbishop Ekpu's sanguine report, Mother de Chantal asked Sister Sylvia to chair a meeting on September 28, 1995, of the Belizean members of the congregation in order to update them "on the progress made thus far on establishing an indigenous community." They were also to elect one of their number to spearhead the project. Sister Jean Martínez received the most votes, and her selection was approved by Mother de Chantal shortly thereafter.[19] Sister Jean, as noted earlier, had played a leading role in the late 1970s in advocating the incorporation of Garifuna culture into the Dangriga Holy Family community.[20] She had also tried, but failed, to create a native religious community at the time.[21] In that attempt, however, she had not had the support of the Holy Family Congregation. This time, she did.

Following a second visit to Belize by Sister Sylvia—this time in 1998—to update Bishop Martin on the congregation's progress concerning the indigenous foundation, the bishop drew up a statement of his own thoughts and sent it to the sisters in New Orleans.[22] He noted that he favored the creation of an indigenous group and that it was time to identify qualified personnel to help him in the preparation stage. He contended that the charism of the new community should be such that it kept in mind the signs of the time; that is, that it should concern itself above all with the spiritual formation of the laity as well as with issues of peace and justice. But more specifically, it should devote itself to the needs of Belizean youth, following in the direction set forth by Sister Judith Barial, who had established Delille Academy.[23]

Bishop Martin's last point is a significant one. Later, in 2001, Sister Jean Martínez replaced Sister Judith Barial as principal of Delille Academy. Sister Judith was immensely popular in Dangriga. A pioneer in practical education, she had proven herself an indefatigable champion of Delille Academy and its students. She was also greatly admired by Bishop Martin, who had once been a student at Sacred Heart School and therefore knew that little opportunity had existed for youth in the Stann Creek District prior to the creation of Delille. When Sister Jean was appointed principal, she had the unenviable task of replacing her extremely popular predecessor. Her leadership as principal would be judged by how well it measured up to that of Sister Judith, and it did not take long for some faculty members and parents to claim that Sister Jean had deviated from the blueprint that Sister Judith had put in place for Delille Academy, a charge that to this day Sister Jean strongly denies.[24] Complaints about Sister Jean reached Bishop Martin, who found them credible. The bishop's concern—whether justified or not—that Sister Jean was attempting to deviate from Delille Academy's philosophy placed her in a negative light in his eyes. These concerns would certainly color his attitude toward Sister Jean when she undertook her commission to begin the spade work needed to form an indigenous religious foundation.[25]

In May 2003, Sister Jean wrote a letter to Said Musa, the prime minister of Belize. She begins with great exuberance:

> For more than 24 years, I have thought and talked, and for more than 43 years I have prayed, longed, hoped and waited for an indigenous religious community of women to be established in Belize.
>
> In more recent times, I have this great desire to request a parcel of land from you and your government as the future home of this home-grown religious community of women and maybe men for Belize.²⁶

After specifying exactly how many acres of land the sisters would need and where she would like it to be located (in the vicinity of Salvapan or Maya Mopan near Belmopan), she informs the prime minister that she had "verbal approval from Bishop Martin."²⁷

A few months after writing to Musa, Sister Jean met with Bishop Martin. In her written report of their meeting she states that the bishop told her that the idea of founding an indigenous religious community was "excellent." But when she informed him that she had been invited to visit the mayor's office in Belmopan to discuss a suitable site, he suggested that before dealing with issues of land, she should first read about the lives of female founders of religious communities, review church documents on religious life, and collect documentation on the charisms of the six congregations of nuns currently working in Belize, so that she could determine what was best for the foundation. And furthermore, while doing this, she should also observe the youth of Sacred Heart Parish in order to determine what their preferences were concerning liturgical practices and issues of Catholic social justice. He cautioned that only after she had gathered all of this information and thoroughly digested and analyzed it, should she begin to deal with the more tangible work that was involved in establishing an indigenous community.²⁸

Sister Jean then notes that she told the bishop that she thought the land issue was too important to put off; it was something concrete that she could work on while she was gathering and studying the data that he had mentioned. Sister Jean concludes her report by stating that Bishop Martin left the decision about the land up to her, but when she asked him if she could state that he supported the indigenous project, "he said clearly that he is *'verbally'* supportive" but would not "put anything on paper."[29] Sister Jean did not see a problem with the bishop's reluctance to state his support in writing, because, in 1979, when she first attempted to create an indigenous community, Bishop Hodapp had also given verbal rather than written support.[30]

In hindsight, it is apparent that Bishop Martin's words were meant as a veiled warning; he wanted Sister Jean to move more slowly in her approach to the indigenous project. He was concerned about the wisdom of acquiring land for a community that was not yet even in the embryonic stage of development. If the attempt to create an indigenous congregation proved unsuccessful, then his poverty-stricken diocese could be held legally responsible for the cost of whatever property had been purchased. That Sister Jean did not pick up on Martin's fears is understandable. The bishop could have been clearer in expressing his apprehensions. She certainly cannot be faulted for missing the meaning of his words when they were stated in such a vague manner.

Beginning in October 2003, Sister Jean embarked on a four-month visitation of sixteen primary and secondary schools throughout Belize, speaking to over four thousand students about religious life and her indigenous dream. She adds in her report on these visitations that in November she went to Belmopan to meet with the mayor concerning the acquisition of land, and that in December she returned to the capital city where she met with the valuation officer, who gave her a form to sign concerning the lease of land.[31] Both of these actions were taken without first obtaining the approval of Bishop Martin. Later, in defense of her conduct, she remarked that she did not think that she needed to consult directly with the bishop over matters of real estate, since when she had earlier met with him she had gotten the impression that he had left such issues totally in her hands.[32]

On December 23, the diocesan canon lawyer, Father Lazarus Augustine, met with Sister Jean at the request of Bishop Martin to counsel her on her formation plans. Martínez's recollection of the meeting is as follows:

> I gave Father Augustine a copy of the report on the visit with Bishop Martin in September that I had sent to [the] Bishop

and Sister Sylvia Thibodeaux. . . . Father Augustine asked if I had done the research on charism of the different [female religious] communities in Belize as Bishop Martin suggested. I told Father that I had started. I had spent more time on the familiarization segment—speaking to students—over 3,000. I also told Father that I had gone to see the location of the site.[33]

Father Augustine expressed interest in the project, and his willingness to review the charism material when I send them [*sic*] to him. . . . However, I have not yet sent Father Augustine the material.[34]

Suffice it to say, Sister Jean again seems to have missed the message that Bishop Martin's canon lawyer was attempting to convey to her: Go slowly and adhere to the procedures that the bishop had outlined.

Following Sister Jean's meeting with Father Augustine, Bishop Martin decided to suspend the indigenous project indefinitely. He initiated a meeting with Sister Sylvia, who was now congregational leader, to express his "concerns about Sr. Jean Martínez's ministry in the diocese of Belize."[35] Sister Clare, who was a member of the leadership team, was asked to keep minutes of the meeting. In her straightforward report, she quotes the bishop verbatim, point by point, and in doing so clearly illustrates Martin's frustration with Sister Jean.

She begins by listing Martin's "concerns," the most pertinent of which follow:

- Although Sr. Jean was granted permission by her community to pursue the possibility of establishing an indigenous community, she did not seek the approbation of the Local Ordinary.
- "When Sr. Jean visited me she did not ask my thoughts or approval of her plans. She simply stated them. I listened with courteous attention."
- "There is no congruence between the call to found a community and the personality of Sr. Jean."
- "Sr. Jean asked me nothing about acquiring property. I do not wish to be responsible for it."
- "Why did no one consult me about changing the philosophy of Delille Academy?"[36]

Sister Clare next lists Sister Sylvia's response to the bishop's "concerns":

- Sr. Jean was told more than once that approval of the Local Ordinary, Bishop O. P. Martin, must be obtained before attempting any mention or activity regarding establishing an indigenous community.
- The Sisters of the Holy Family will claim any property acquired by Sr. Jean.[37]
- We will abide by any and all of your [Bishop Martin's] directives.[38]

On February 27, 2004, Sister Sylvia wrote a letter to Bishop Martin, which seems to have ended any immediate plans for an indigenous institute in Belize: "As soon as I hear from you, Bishop, I will direct Sister Jean to cease all activities related to establishing a religious community in your diocese."[39] With the indigenous project no longer active, Sister Jean applied for and obtained a teaching position at Muffles College, the Mercy Sisters' high school in Orange Walk Town, outside of the Stann Creek District. After teaching there for a short time, she was reassigned in early 2007 to New Orleans.[40]

Why did the attempt to create an indigenous female religious foundation in Belize fail, especially when both Bishop Martin and the Holy Family Congregation had initially backed the project with great enthusiasm? Indeed, why did such a plan not even get beyond the embryonic stage, when a similar Holy Family project had succeeded so spectacularly in Nigeria? The answer seems clear. First, from the time that the establishment of an indigenous foundation was initially proposed, Bishop Martin was deeply concerned that his poverty-stricken diocese might be saddled with real estate and other costs that it simply could not afford. Sister Jean Martínez, perhaps due to her enthusiasm, misread the bishop's warnings to move forward slowly in her task and took upon herself the initiative for acquiring property, obviously not realizing the ramifications of her action. On the other hand, the bishop's warnings seem to have always been vague. Had he expressed his misgivings to Sister Jean in a more direct way, perhaps much of the miscommunication and misunderstanding between the sister and the bishop would have been avoided.

Second, Sister Jean ignored the wise advice of Archbishop Ekpu of Nigeria, who had warned that the creation and molding of a new community was always a slow and long process that required great patience. Although she was counseled by her congregation and by Bishop Martin to take the time to become familiar with the charisms of other missionary congregations in Belize and to read the biographies of their founders before moving on to more concrete work, in her enthusiasm she either disregarded their counsel or at least relegated it to a place of secondary importance. And third, accusations that Sister Jean was attempting to change the philosophy of Delille Academy predisposed Bishop Martin to distrust the nun who had been chosen by her community to spearhead the indigenous project. While Sister Jean denies those accusations, their validity is beside the point; it seems fair to say that they played an important role in the bishop's negativity toward her.

Misunderstandings between Sister Jean and Bishop Martin aside, it should be noted that by the beginning of the twenty-first century, Belize was no longer the fertile ground for religious vocations that it had been in the past. A breakdown in traditional family values in the latter quarter of the previous century, coupled with a gang culture and the widespread use of illegal drugs that were introduced to the country by Belizean youth returning from the United States, drastically reduced the pool of suitable candidates for religious life.[41] Indeed, since the late 1970s no more than three or four Belizean women had entered the Holy Family Congregation as postulants, and none of them had persevered to final vows. Thus, the breakdown in family values in Belize no doubt played a part in causing the Holy Family leadership by the late 1990s to conclude that the cost in money, time, and energy was too high a price to pay when the likelihood for building a successful indigenous religious community was so minimal. Therefore, they abandoned or at least suspended, albeit reluctantly, their plans.

Following Sister Jean's tenure as principal of Delille Academy, all subsequent principals at the school were lay people.[42] At her request, Sister Judith Barial returned to Dangriga in August 2004. According to a letter sent by Sister Sylvia Thibodeaux, the congregation's superior, to the principal of Delille Academy and copied to Bishop Martin, she was "to teach two subjects" and also "assist the present leadership in realizing the original spirit and philosophy of the school."[43] A letter from Bishop Martin to Sister Sylvia declares that her "decision to send back Sr. Judith is an excellent one. I am already hearing good news about her welcomed presence."[44] Her reassignment to Dangriga also meant that the Holy Family Congregation intended to make Delille Academy the focal point of its now limited ministry in Belize. The fact that Sister Judith was not named principal, but rather was sent to "assist the present [lay] leadership in realizing the original spirit and philosophy of the school" is also significant. It clearly points out that the congregational leaders understood that there was little hope that the sisters' physical presence in Belize could last much longer, due to the shortage of Holy Family personnel. The congregation hoped to gradually replace its sisters with lay people who would be trained by the sisters and thus would have the leadership experience needed to continue the teaching mission carried out by the Holy Family Congregation for the last century.

In 2003, just prior to Sister Judith's return, the U.S. Army Reserve Engineer Command, through its New Horizons humanitarian aid program and with help from the Belize Defense Force, constructed six concrete school buildings for Delille Academy.[45] Sister Judith had earlier applied for this help, but the project had been postponed due to U.S. military intervention in the Middle East following the terrorist acts of September 11, 2001.[46] As a result of these new, state-of-the-art buildings, Delille was now able to expand its student population significantly, and by the 2004–2005 academic year enrollment had grown to 420.[47] The salaried staff had also increased to twenty-one full-time and three part-time teachers.[48]

The school was thriving, but Sister Judith was not content. By October 2004, she was again applying for grant money—this time from the Archdiocese of New Orleans' Mission Cooperative Plan—in order to bolster the school's vocational trade program. In a letter to the director she asked for a grant of $2,500 to purchase electrical and hand tools for "construction technology" instruction. In her application she explains why vocational training was important for Delille students: "About 25% of our graduates go immediately into higher education. . . . So 75% . . . need to be immediately ready for the job market." For this reason, "this year (2004) we are initiating and renewing programs that will give our students marketable skills."[49] She further notes that courses were currently being taught or were in the planning stage in sewing, practical and theoretical electricity, and cabinet-making and household carpentry repairs. Since tourism was an important component of the Belizean economy, courses were also being offered in hospitality, restaurant culinary arts, and visual arts and woodcrafts aimed at the tourist market. A practical biology course was being taught on a working farm, so that students could learn "first hand about grafting, seeding, composting and using local untapped resources." Already seventy-five students were in the construction technology program, seventy-five in culinary arts, seventy in biology, twenty-five in electricity, and thirty-five each in sewing, woodcrafts, and visual arts. And now Sister Judith gets to the point: Since "these courses are expensive, especially in the initial stages," and "we are working with the minimum of tools and equipment in each area," Delille Academy needs financial help from outside sources in order to carry on its mission.[50]

Because of health problems, Sister Judith was eventually forced to return to New Orleans. By 2008, due to the lack of new religious vocations and to a plethora of unforeseen expenses resulting from Hurricane Katrina, which destroyed or heavily damaged almost all of the Holy Family Congregation's buildings in New Orleans, no religious sister could be spared for faculty or staff positions at Delille Academy. Sister Rebecca Carlos Castillo, a Garifuna, who was allowed to remain in Dangriga in order to care for her ailing brother and sister, was the last Holy Family Sister assigned on a full-time basis to Belize. Due to her own illness, however, she was forced to return to New Orleans in August 2008. By this time, the sisters had trained enough lay teachers, both women and men, so that Delille Academy could continue to thrive in the manner that Sister Judith and her congregation had envisioned when it was founded. Clearly, Delille Academy has proven to be a flourishing missionary venture, created and molded in accordance with the spirit of Vatican II. The Holy Family Sisters, reading the signs of the times, had fashioned a school in which they replaced the British educational system (education for the elite few) that was standard in Belize up to that time, with an American system (education for the many). So successful was it, and so crucial to the economic well-being of many Belizean youth, that it became a model for the country's educational system, which has opened vocational schools similar to Delille Academy in other districts.

Two more points need to be made before closing this chapter. First, in 1998, after the sisters and people of Dangriga had celebrated the centennial of the congregation's presence in Belize, the Associates of the Sisters of the Holy Family was formed. This was an organization of lay people, both male and female, who had been taught by the sisters and who wanted to live out in their lay state the spirituality and charism of Mother Henriette Delille and the Holy Family Congregation. The concept of lay associates developed as a result of the Second Vatican Council's call for the renewal of religious congregations to include collaboration with the laity. Some female religious communities initiated associate relationships in the 1970s and 1980s, and by the mid-1990s over two hundred congregations had associate programs in place with a combined membership of over 14,500.[51] Those wishing to join the Holy Family Associates in Belize had to go through a short period of training, in which they learned how to pray the Liturgy of the Hours and became familiar with the history, spirituality, charism, and ministries of the Holy Family Congregation. Following this training, they made a formal commitment, renewable on an annual basis,[52] in front of family, friends, vowed sisters, and previously committed Associates to live out the values of the congregation for one year.

In 2008 the Associates celebrated their first ten years of existence. At that time there were thirty-two members in Dangriga, twenty-three of whom were active. Associates met every second Monday of the month, attended mass together, and organized activities that were in keeping with the Holy Family charism. In an effort to mark their ten-year anniversary, members raised funds for the construction of the Henriette Delille Spiritual Life Center. According to Associate member and former mayor of Dangriga Sylvia Flores, the center was meant to be a tribute to the Holy Family Congregation and a symbol of its enduring legacy to the people of Dangriga. Flores adds that it also stood as a hope that someday the sisters will be able to return to Belize.[53] In 2010 the Associates initiated a campaign aimed at raising funds for a chapel at Delille Academy.

Second, even though the New Orleans–based congregation was no longer able to spare sisters for full-time missionary work, it had no intention of fully severing its ties with Belize. Since the sisters had some free time in the summer, the congregation decided that it could spare a small number for a few weeks between the spring and fall academic terms. Thus, in July 2008, Sisters Josita Marie Ogaldez, Hortensia Maria Flowers, Andria Marie Donald, and Theresa Sue Joseph[54] were sent to conduct a two-week catechetical program in Independence and Red Bank, rural villages located about fifty or so miles south of Dangriga. In a report on the program, Sister Josita states that it was quite challenging but also rewarding. In Independence, where the four sisters spent their first week, they taught children who were from relatively well-off families. Like their parents, most were bilingual, which enabled the sisters to communicate in English without any problem. The children did not attend a Catholic school, since there was none in the area. Therefore, there was a need for Bible classes and instruction on the basics of the faith, especially on understanding the sacraments. "The students were cooperative and appreciative and eager to learn," says Ogaldez. Some parents who came to observe were pleased with the sisters and wished, as did the children, that the nuns could stay longer than a week.[55]

Their second week was spent in Red Bank Village and was more taxing. Red Bank was a Q'eqchi Indian community, where the people were very poor and spoke very little English, so communication was a challenge for the four sisters. Nevertheless, they were able to overcome the language barrier and put their basic points across to the students. Although the people were Catholic, many of the village children attended a summer program at the Faith Assembly of God School. Consequently, only about twenty-two to twenty-four attended the sisters' program. The four sisters made sure that there was always time to talk to the parents: "I invited parents to come inside the church to see what their children were learning. I took time to listen to the parents and their complaints about not having doctors in the area to check on them and their children. I tried to give them hope and courage by praying with them."[56] Sister Josita was pleasantly surprised to discover that two of her nieces and a nephew, whom she had not seen since they were children, were now grown up and living in the village. "They are my Q'eqchi family," she remarks.[57] She concludes her report by stating that the Red Bank catechetical program was one of "the most challenging ministries" that she had ever experienced, due to the poverty and primitive conditions found in the area.[58]

The Holy Family summertime work in the rural villages of Belize signifies that even when the nuns were only able to provide four sisters for two weeks, they were still willing to expand their missionary efforts, this time catechizing Q'eqchi Indians—many of whom did not speak English—in a region of Belize where they had not previously served. In so doing, they were again reading the signs of the times in true Vatican II fashion.

Conclusion

When one reviews the history of the Holy Family Congregation from its founding in 1842 until 1897, when Bishop Di Pietro invited the sisters to send missionaries to British Honduras, one can only wonder why the vicar apostolic decided to ask this particular religious community for help and, even more so, why they agreed to his request. No African American Catholics had ever been missionaries before. Throughout much of the nineteenth century, the New Orleans–based community, battered by racial discrimination both from within the church and from civil society, had been poverty-stricken and on the verge of extinction. Its membership had only recently grown to more than a handful of sisters, and, with this increase in numbers, it had taken on additional teaching assignments in other regions of Louisiana and in other states as well. Moreover, these African American nuns knew almost nothing about the culture of British Honduras and even less about the so-called black Caribs whom they were supposed to serve. Indeed, they did not even realize when they began their assignment in Stann Creek that the children whom they were to instruct understood almost no English, and that the same was true for most of their parents. To put it bluntly, it seemed highly probable that the sisters would fail in Belize, since they did not have the wealth, cross-cultural experience, or numbers available for a successful missionary venture. Could Bishop Di Pietro not find any other congregation willing to take on this challenge and therefore had no alternative other than to ask these black sisters for help? This may be so, but on the other hand, perhaps he saw something special in their dedication and tenacity, with little support from church or state, in their five decades of working with the poorest of the poor in New Orleans.

As for Mother Austin and her congregation, what caused them to respond positively to Bishop Di Pietro's request? They had to realize that the odds for success in British Honduras were stacked against them, and failure would only add fuel to the fire for those in the Catholic power structure—and these were many—who claimed that there was no place in the church for a black religious congregation. But stacked odds aside, since their foundation the Holy Family Sisters had always overcome the seemingly insurmountable barriers they had been forced to climb due largely to their race and gender. Once again, the poorest of the poor desperately needed their services—but this time they were the Garifuna of Stann Creek, British Honduras. If it were God's will, the sisters must have reasoned, then their labors would prove fruitful in Central America just as they had in the inhospitable Jim Crow state of Louisiana. In other words, their lack of power and status had bred in them a selfless, total dependence on God, and this hope-filled simplicity enabled them to take a risk.

The Holy Family Congregation was not naïve, however, as they entered into their new missionary endeavor. They were realists who had survived because they had long ago learned how to negotiate with the white power structure, be it governmental or hierarchical, that viewed them as inferior. Consequently, they insisted that the bishop of Belize sign a written contract that listed in detail their rights and responsibilities as well as his. Only when he did so did they consent to send sisters to his diocese. This proved to be a wise move on the sisters' part; following Di Pietro's death, this contract enabled the congregation's mother superior in New Orleans to thwart the attempts of his successor to usurp her prerogatives and dictate how their community should be run in Belize.

Indeed, the New Orleans–based Sisters of Mercy were not so fortunate. They had come to Belize City in 1883 and within a few short years were running two primary schools and the colony's first secondary school. Their success resulted in part because they had been willing to invest $10,000 of their own money in property and buildings, since the poverty-stricken diocese of Belize did not have the funds to do so itself. Within a short time, however, Bishop Di Pietro had pressured the Mercy Motherhouse in Louisiana into granting him title to their land. Moreover, his episcopal successor, Bishop Hopkins, against the wishes of the sisters, was able to take control of the Mercy community in British Honduras and severed it from the Mercy Motherhouse in New Orleans. The Mercy Sisters were more numerous than their Holy Family counterparts, much better off financially, and, significantly, members of the dominant white race, but whereas the Holy Family Sisters managed to repel episcopal attempts to control them, the Mercy Congregation was unable to do so. Had the latter had the foresight to obtain a written contract stipulating the prerogatives of their motherhouse in New Orleans vis-à-vis those of the vicar apostolic, the outcome of their struggles with the bishops might have been different.

For their first seven decades in British Honduras, the Holy Family nuns conducted their missionary enterprise almost exactly as they carried out their work in the United States. Those assigned to Stann Creek lived a semi-cloistered convent life, just as did their Holy Family counterparts in the United States. Communal prayer was the same and, inasmuch as it was possible, so were the ways of convent life. Even the food served in the Dangriga house was basically what the sisters would have eaten if they had been in the United States. Those women chosen for mission work received no special training to prepare them for the culture they were about to enter. As a result, they knew little if anything about the nearly four-hundred-year history or the way of life of the Garifuna. They had no conception of the prejudices that other Belizeans held toward this unique people. If they even noticed that it was the custom of the Garifuna people to keep apart from other ethnic groups and rarely to marry outsiders, then the sisters would have had no idea why.

In the classroom the sisters taught in English. Even though this was not the native language of the vast majority of their students, they made little if any attempt to learn the dialect that the Garifuna spoke among themselves. They employed the same basic curriculum that they used in teaching African American students in the United States. The one exception was their model pupil-teacher training program, but this had initially been imposed on the sisters by British Honduran law and by the Jesuit priests of Sacred Heart Parish.

When the sisters traveled to other regions of the country they would stay, if possible, with the local sisters—the Mercy nuns or the Pallottines—and when sisters from these congregations traveled to Dangriga, they would likewise stay in the Holy Family convent. Aside from these trips, however, they had very little contact with other female congregations and virtually never collaborated with them when it came to matters of ministry. Indeed, it is probably not much of an exaggeration to say that for the most part in the pre–Vatican II period, the Holy Family Sisters in British Honduras were only missionaries in a geographical sense in that they conducted their apostolate in a way that was little different from how their counterparts in the United States conducted theirs. Sister Carolyn Leslie, who served in Dangriga from 1949 to 1951 and from 1955 to 1963, confirms this in her correspondence with the author: "Except for distance from homeland and family," she writes, "Dangriga did not seem to be any different from any other mission on which we served in the USA."[1] It should be pointed out, however, that in this respect the Holy Family Sisters were probably no different from many other U.S. female religious congregations—indeed, probably most—who were involved in missionary work in Latin America. After Vatican II, however, when the church urged missionaries to make inculturation a top priority, the Holy Family Sisters seemed slower than some other congregations in coming to an understanding of what this involved and why it was important.

In spite of whatever shortcomings they may have had, there is no denying that on the whole the Holy Family Congregation was remarkably successful in its mission work in British Honduras in the pre–Vatican II period. Its sisters educated generations of Garifuna and other Belizean children in their elementary schools in the Stann Creek District and also opened Austin High, the nation's first girls' high school outside of the city of Belize. In doing the latter, they were educational pioneers, and others soon followed their lead. The missionary sisters also produced an impressive number of sorely needed teachers through their Pupil-Teacher Training Center, and this enabled them to expand from one to four schools while never employing more than a small number of nuns as teachers. Indeed, the Pupil-Teacher Training Center was a major ingredient in their recipe for success. Without these lay teachers, they could never have met the educational needs of the rapidly growing population of the Stann Creek District.

The sisters were also remarkably successful in promoting native religious vocations to their congregation as well as to the priesthood. Fifty Belizean women, some Garifuna and some Creole, joined the Holy Family Sisters in the twentieth century. Thirty-eight of these did so prior to 1960. This number is especially impressive when one compares them to the Mercy Sisters, who produced only thirty-one Belizean vocations to their congregation in their first 116 years in Belize.[2] The Holy Family Sisters also provided elementary school training to nine boys who later became priests; eight of these would serve in Belize. One, the first Garifuna ever to be ordained, became in 1948 the first diocesan priest to serve as pastor of Sacred Heart Parish, thereby making this, at least for a short time, the first diocesan parish in the nation. (Jesuit missionaries had run all other churches prior to this.) Another of the sisters' students, Osmond Martin, who was ordained a priest in 1959, later in 1982 became the small nation's first native bishop and also its first black bishop. Thus, the sisters contributed to the creation of an indigenous leadership in the Belizean church.

So why did the sisters succeed in spite of the negatives mentioned above? Although it cannot be proven with concrete data, in all probability the black people to whom they ministered were able to better identify with them because they were of the same race. Indeed, one needs only recall Sister Eleanor Gillett and the profound effect that merely seeing a black missionary sister could have on a young Belizean woman. While a student at the Mercy Sisters' Holy Redeemer School in Belize City, Gillett saw a Holy Family Sister who had come for a visit. "Although I didn't talk to her," she remembers, "I was impressed by her. I thought that if she [a black woman] could become a sister, then maybe I could also."[3]

Coupled with racial identification is the fact that the Holy Family Congregation, a religious community that always had to struggle with barely enough resources to survive and who had to cope with racial prejudice, throughout its history had worked with the desperately poor and downtrodden. Consequently, the sisters, as a result of their past, were untroubled by a ministry to black people who were both poor and oppressed. Simply stated, they did not have to make as many adjustments as did the more diverse and prosperous white congregations who came to Belize.

As with all religious orders and congregations, the second half of the twentieth century, highlighted by the Second Vatican Council, brought new challenges as well as painful introspection for the Holy Family Sisters. The church's call for religious women to study and reflect on their history and return to the charism of their founders was probably less stressful for the New Orleans–based community than it was for congregations of other nuns because they had never deviated from the mission that Mother Henriette Delille had set for them. The challenge for the Holy Family Sisters was to continue to educate the poor and minister to the needs of the indigent elderly, while addressing the problems of the day with creative approaches that remained within their charism.

When one reviews the results of their efforts to do so in Belize in the post–Vatican II period, one can only conclude that they are truly impressive. With the help of the Jesuits, the Holy Family Sisters joined in the early 1970s with the Anglicans and Methodists in Dangriga to found a Catholic-Protestant ecumenical high school. In so doing they were in the vanguard when it came to ecumenism. Later, recognizing that young girls were unable to continue their education after elementary school due to low scores on standardized government tests, the sisters, following the lead of the gifted Sister Judith Barial, again read the signs of the times and opened a high school for Belizeans that emphasized practical vocational training. When it became clear to the sisters that teenage boys also needed this type of training, the school became coeducational. Considering the history of the British-oriented Belizean secondary educational system, with its unwillingness to go beyond the narrow confines of classical traditionalism, Delille Academy was certainly innovative. But innovation aside, what is more important is that the pragmatic vocational training introduced by the sisters to the newly independent country saved countless young women and men from a life of almost certain underemployment and despair. This, probably more so than its innovative nature, is why it became a model for the government to imitate in other districts in Belize.

In summary then, in the field of education, the contribution that the Holy Family Sisters made to Belize is impressive. When it comes to Dangriga, however, it is immense. At a ceremony honoring the sisters for one hundred years of service in the Stann Creek District, Sylvia Flores, a graduate of Sacred Heart School and the first female mayor of Dangriga, remarked: "The history of Catholic education in Dangriga and its environs is inextricably linked to the Sisters of the Holy Family.... Their story is our [the people of Dangriga's] story and their history our history."[4] Her words are no exaggeration.

The Holy Family Congregation was less successful, however, when it came to reading the signs of the times and adjusting to the Second Vatican Council's call for inculturation in missionary work. Mother Tekakwitha Vega, the order's general council in New Orleans, and Sister Sienna Braxton, the local superior in Belize, certainly misread the ethnic and nationalistic pride that had grown in Dangriga when they refused to allow the recitation of several communal prayers in the Garifuna language. Ironically, their decision caused the very division among the sisters that it was meant to avoid. It further aroused in the Garifuna sisters, either in Belize or in the United States, a feeling of betrayal. Although most attempted to suffer in silence, they concluded correctly that both they and their culture were being treated in a disparaging way.

The congregation, however, quickly learned from the language fiasco. Even as early as March 1980, only a few months after its unfortunate decision was rendered by the general council, Mother Tekakwitha was challenging the sisters in Belize "to be more available to the people of Dangriga," advising them that "the people need to know that you care and are concerned about them."[5] In other words, in keeping with the spirit of the Second Vatican Council, she was telling them that it was no longer acceptable to be "in the parish but not of it."

The mission experiences of Sisters Clare of Assisi Pierre, Lucia Carl, and Judith Barial demonstrate that the Holy Family Sisters took to heart Mother Tekakwitha's advice. In the 1980s the three emerged from the semi-cloistered, traditional convent life and redirected their missionary community in Belize so that it integrated itself into the culture of the Garifuna people. In so doing, they took care to hold to the original charism of their congregation, while developing creative ways to expand it and make it more relevant.

Sister Clare admits that when she was assigned to Dangriga to teach at Ecumenical High School, she knew nothing about Belize or its people. Like all of the missionary sisters in her congregation, she had been prepared for the classroom and nothing more. Although she continued to serve the youth of Dangriga as a high-school teacher, she became gradually more attracted to pastoral ministry. Soon she became part of a team that included members of other religious congregations. Such collaboration was something new for the Holy Family Sisters in Belize.[6] Indeed, "We immersed ourselves in the culture."[7] Sister Clare is convinced that by involving themselves in the everyday life of the people, the sisters developed into much more effective missionaries.

Sister Lucia Carl was assigned to Belize because Bishop Martin asked Mother Rose de Lima Hazeur to send an additional nun to work exclusively with the indigent elderly of Dangriga. Her ministry provides another example of how the Holy Family Congregation adjusted to the spirit of Vatican II by expanding its mission in Belize to meet the needs of the day. Sister Lucia spent most of her time visiting the homes of the desperately poor "grannies" of the region and, in so doing, learned of their poverty and lack of medical care. Soon she had the other sisters in Dangriga stuffing bags with food and medicines that she would deliver to them. She convinced parishioners at Sacred Heart Parish that a branch of the St. Vincent de Paul Society was needed, and soon the Holy Family convent was serving as its base of operations, something that would never have been allowed when the sisters were living a strictly semi-cloistered life. By visiting and listening to her "grannies," Sister Lucia came to understand some of the socioeconomic realities of the poverty-stricken nation of Belize. The migration to the United States of large numbers of job-seeking Belizeans had contributed to the breakdown of family life, the development of a violent gang culture, and a rise in drug addiction and in the number of unmarried young pregnant females, who, once they gave birth, were unable to properly care for their infants. Such an understanding enabled her and her fellow missionary sisters to perform their work more effectively, and they expanded their ministry to include desperately poor immigrant Mayan Indians who had settled south of Dangriga. Again, reading the signs of the times, they had now added to their missionary repertoire catechizing Indian children and using their own personal allowances to buy seeds for Mayan farmers.

Sister Judith Barial's story follows a similar pattern. Almost immediately after she arrived in Dangriga to teach at Ecumenical High School, she realized that something had to be done for out-of-school teenage girls. On her own she began an after-school outreach teaching program for them and convinced the other sisters in her convent and some of her fellow teachers at Ecumenical to volunteer their services without pay. When the number of girls attending the sessions snowballed, she petitioned Mother Rose de Lima in New Orleans to allow her to resign from Ecumenical High so that she could devote herself full-time to the program. Mother Rose, in the true spirit of Vatican II, granted her request, even though it meant that the Dangriga community would have to do without her teacher's salary. Within a few years, all the Holy Family Sisters in Dangriga had left their positions at Ecumenical, and with it their salaries, to teach without pay in Sister Judith's program, which she eventually transformed into a much-needed, fully accredited vocational high school.

By deciding as a community to give up their jobs and therefore their salaries at Ecumenical, the missionary sisters were doing more than simply shifting their teaching vocations to better serve the needs of the youth of Dangriga. They were also consciously abandoning the relatively comfortable life-style that they had enjoyed after the Jesuits built them a "state of the art" convent in 1947. They were deliberately trading their material security for poverty and the insecurity that accompanies it. In other words, they were opting to be more like the poor whom they served. But more than that, they were consciously choosing to hold onto, albeit to a lesser degree, the state of stressful poverty and uncertainty that the Holy Family missionaries in the first half of the twentieth century—and Mother Henriette Delille and her sisters in the nineteenth century—had experienced. They were reconnecting with their religious roots and the original charism of their founder.

But the sisters' inculturation did more than change their own lives and enable them to be more effective missionaries. It produced a domino effect, though in a less fully transformational way, in that it touched African Americans who had never had a Third World experience. As Sisters Clare and Judith point out, once the missionary sisters began to involve themselves in the lives and culture of the Garifuna, they would return to the United States with photos of the people and their way of life to show to the sisters and others and would share personal stories. They were now better able to devise a sophisticated analysis of the problems encountered in their mission work. Sister Clare notes that the non-missionary nuns were shocked at what they learned. Although the congregation had been working in Belize for almost a century, many of the U.S. sisters had still assumed that their Belizean counterparts had the same cultural preferences as they did. More significantly, they had not previously understood the depth of the poverty experienced by the Garifuna on a daily basis.

In a 2010 interview with the author, Sister Jean Martínez, the Garifuna nun who had left the Holy Family community in 1979 over the language controversy and later returned, remarks that much has changed in the last quarter-century. She states that today she is very comfortable as a Garifuna sister in the Holy Family Congregation. Indeed, by the end of the 1980s, the sisters as a whole had developed a much greater sensitivity toward her native culture:

> Those [sisters] who never personally went to Belize now know a good deal more about the Garifuna culture and respond positively to it. They are more aware [of the sensibilities] of the Garifuna sisters and are very accepting of us. We [the Garifuna sisters] cook our own foods and make our cassava bread [in the New Orleans Motherhouse]. We participate in cultural events with Garifuna communities in the United States. When the Garifuna community in New Orleans has a mass in our language [with our hymns and drums], some of the U.S. sisters attend. All of this is a big change. I now have good vibes when it comes to the American sisters' respect for our culture.[8]

When Sister Jean earned her master's degree in 2005 at the Institute for Black Catholic Studies at Xavier University in New Orleans, she wrote her thesis on Garifuna healing rites as an instrument for Catholic evangelization.[9] More recently she developed a practicum for Sacred Heart Parish in Dangriga in which twenty or more Garifuna parishioners will learn how to incorporate elements of the *dugu* and *chugu* Garifuna healing rituals into Catholic healing services.[10] The fact that Sister Jean has been permitted by the leadership of her congregation to research Garifuna healing rites so that they can be incorporated into Catholic ritual in Belize shows how far her religious community has come in regard to the concept of inculturation. Altogether, Sister Jean's words, along with her studies, serve as an example of how the returning missionaries were able to arouse intercultural awareness both within their religious community and among their African American students and friends.

In summary, then, it can be said with some certainty that the Holy Family Congregation—like all religious orders and congregations, whether female or male, who sent significant numbers of their members to the foreign missions in the post–Vatican II period—was transformed as a result of its missionary experience, as were all religious. Moreover, they in turn transformed others when they returned to the United States, teaching them not only about the unfortunate realities of the Third World but also about the dignity and beauty of foreign cultures.

Ironically, just as the sisters were branching out into more expansive ministries in Belize and immersing themselves in the lives of those who most needed their help, the ever-growing shortage of new religious vocations meant that fewer and fewer sisters could be spared for missionary work. By the latter months of 1991, only four sisters were still working in Dangriga. To prevent burnout, they had no recourse but to streamline their ministry, yet they hoped to do so without decreasing their most crucial services. Instead of deciding what to cut and what to retain on their own or with the help of the clergy, as they no doubt would have done in earlier times, they themselves drew up a questionnaire asking for input from the residents of Dangriga. The fact that they chose to involve the laity in such important decision making shows how far they had come in enveloping themselves in the inclusive spirit of Vatican II.

Streamlining their ministry in a more efficient manner, however, only postponed the inevitable. Due to the shortage of religious vocations, the Holy Family community in the United States could no longer spare sisters for mission work in Belize. Consequently, the congregation decided to work with the bishop of Belize in forming an indigenous religious community of women who could carry on their ministry to the people of Dangriga. When this effort failed, the sisters had no recourse but to close the mission they had run so well for 110 years. With the reassignment of Sister Rebecca Carlos Castillo in August 2008 to New Orleans, no Holy Family Sister remained in Belize. Their legacy lives on, however, through the Associates of the Sisters of the Holy Family, the organization that was formed in 1998 by lay women and men whose lives had been influenced by these missionary sisters and who therefore wanted to live in accordance with their charism. Its members, together with the schools staffed in large part by teachers whom the sisters had trained, serve as a visible reminder of the crucial role played by a tiny group of African American nuns in the history of Belize and the Garifuna people.

Before closing, one more point is worth making. Like the Holy Family Sisters, the Mercy and Pallottine Congregations have a long history in Belize and have contributed greatly to the success of the Catholic Church there and to the well-being of its people. Over the years the Mercy Sisters have expanded their ministry and by 1982 had twenty-four sisters serving in Belize City, Belmopan, Orange Walk, and Corozal. While still primarily committed to teaching, they have, like the Holy Family Sisters, expanded their ministry so that it now incorporates pastoral work and services for the sick and poor.[11] The Pallottine Sisters, who first came to British Honduras in 1913 to teach Maya students in Benque Viejo del Carmen, eventually expanded their operations to almost all of the districts of the nation. In 2008 twenty-two sisters were serving in education, health care, and pastoral ministry in the districts of Belize, Corozal, Cayo, Toledo, and Orange Walk. Like the Holy Family and Mercy Sisters, following the Second Vatican Council they have read the signs of the times and adjusted their apostolate accordingly. No one would contest the fact that all three congregations have made enormous contributions to the poverty-stricken country of Belize, its Catholic Church, and its people.

What makes the Holy Family Sisters' ministry in Belize stand out, however, is that whereas the Mercy and Pallottine Sisters usually had twenty or more nuns and a relatively sufficient source of funds at their disposal, the same was never true for the Holy Family community. The latter never had more than ten sisters working in Belize at one time; usually they had to make do with only six or seven sisters or even fewer. Moreover, they were always forced to work with very little money at their disposal. When one takes these liabilities into account, the list of their accomplishments is truly amazing. An historian colleague who has published extensively on the history of women religious and the U.S. Catholic mission movement remarked that the Holy Family "foundresses were an intrepid lot, as were the Sisters, all the way through their history!" Her comment certainly sums up the story of these remarkable women and their mission in Central America and therefore serves as a fitting conclusion to their story.

Appendix A

Holy Family Sisters Who Have Worked in Belize

Names	Nationality	Period of Service
Sr. Mary Rita Mather	United States	1898–1901; 1911–1914
Sr. Mary Dominica Bee	United States	1898–1901
Sr. Mary Emmanuel Thompson	United States	1898–1901
Sr. Mary Stephen Fortier	United States	1898–1901
Sr. Mary Colombe Cook	United States	1899–1904
Sr. Mary Imelda Green	United States	1899–1904
Sr. Mary Charles Hernández	Cuba	1901–1907
Sr. Mary of the Rosary Landry	United States	1902–1907
Sr. Mary Eusebia Birmingham	Dominica, West Indies	1904–1907
Sr. Mary Gertrude Miller	United States	1905–1908
Sr. Mary Bernadette Elback	United States	1907–1911
Sr. Mary Helena Plaisance	United States	1907–1910
Sr. Mary Bernard Bacon	United States	1907–1908
Sr. Mary Inez Soler	Cuba	1907–1913
Sr. Mary Francis Borgia Hart	Jamaica	1908–1913
Sr. Mary Bernardine Stanford	United States	1909–1910; 1939–1959

Sr. Mary Philip Goodman	United States	1909–1912
Sr. Mary Agnes Frankson	Jamaica	1910
Sr. Mary Edmond Ogaldez	Belize	1911–1912
Sr. Marie Louise Goodman	United States	1912–1936
Sr. Mary Fidelis Osborne	British Guiana	1913–1924
Sr. Mary Joannes Rigaud	United States	1917–1921
Sr. Mary Francis Harrison	United States	?–1927
Sr. Mary Cyrilla Eaglin	United States	1917–1918
Sr. Mary of Lourdes Gray	United States	1927–1935
Sr. Mary Florence Aguet	Belize	1928–1936; 1937–1959
Sr. Miriam of Jesus Chastang	United States	1931–1937
Sr. Mary Cecilia Green	United States	1931–1936; 1937–1959
Sr. Mary Alfrida Barrow	Jamaica	1935–1947
Sr. Mary Stanislaus Sampson	British Guiana	1935–1937
Sr. Mary Damian Llorens	United States	1936–1946
Sr. Mary Gabriella Guidry	United States	1936–1946
Sr. Mary Lydia Lawes	United States	1939–1942
Sr. Mary of the Rosary Heisser	United States	1940–1955
Sr. Mary Joseph Xavier Meikle	Jamaica	1944–1959
Sr. Mary Bertille Hazeur	United States	1946–1956
Sr. Mary Eleanor Gillett	Belize	1947–1965
Sr. Barbara Marie Francis	Belize	1947–1959
Sr. Mary Loyola Mitchell	Belize	1948–1951
Sr. Mary Carolyn Leslie	Belize	1949–1951; 1955–1963
Sr. Rita Marie Ramirez	Belize	1953–1959
Sr. Helen Marie Pradier	United States	1950–1951
Sr. Mary Adrian Johnson	United States	1952–1959
Sr. Mary Elma (David) Olivera	Belize	1955–1963; 1974–1977
Sr. Mary Reparata Toles	United States	1956–1959
Sr. Marie Therese Calvey	United States	1956–1959
Sr. Mary Elaine Vavasseur	United States	1959–1968
Sr. Mary Gloria (Placidus) Lewis	United States	1959–1961; 1962–1963
Sr. Mary Vianney François	United States	1959–1965
Sr. Marie de Montfort Breaux	United States	1959–1966
Sr. Mary Lorene LeBlanc	United States	1959–1964; 1970–1971
Sr. Mary Delphine Townsend	United States	1959–1966
Sr. Mary Henriette Lazare	United States	1960–1968

Sr. Dorothy Marie Stuart	Belize	1962–1967; 1971–1976
Sr. Mary Vincent Ferrer Gill	Belize	1963–1967
Sr. Mary Rita Austin Méndez	Belize	1964–1967; 1971–1976
Sr. Mary Jacinta Blanchard	United States	1965–1968; 1974–1977
Sr. Mary Jude Thadine Gremillion	United States	1965–1969
Sr. Mary Bernice Thornton	United States	1965–1971
Sr. Marie Yvette Ozene	United States	1966–1969; 1971–1974
Sr. Joan Flores	Belize	1966–1971; 1972–1978; 1998–2004
Sr. Mary Bonaventure Jackson	United States	1967–1971
Sr. Mary Cecilia Higinio	Belize	1967–1973
Sr. Mary Joseph Ann Gillett	Belize	1968–1971; 2004–2005
Sr. Mary Joycelyn Francisco	Belize	1968–1971
Sr. Mary Bridget Thompson	Belize	1968–1970
Sr. Donna Marie Tizano	United States	1969–1970; 1972–1973
Sr. Mary Rebecca Carlos Castillo	Belize	1969–1972; 1973–1977; 2001–2008
Sr. Mary Joseph Charles	United States	1969–1972
Sr. Theresa Sue Joseph	United States	1970–1972; 1980–1990; 1998–2001
Sr. Mary Malachy Blair	United States	1970–1972
Sr. Mary Joseph Ellen Cavalier	United States	1971–1974; 1977–1980; 1992–1994
Sr. John Mary Jackson	United States	1971–1974; 1977–1980
Sr. Sheila Marie Williams	United States	1971–1973; 1996–1998
Sr. Jean Martínez	Belize	1971–1973; 1974–1979; 1998–?; 2001–2007
Sr. Evelyn Estrada	Belize	1974–1981
Sr. Mary Leona Bruner	United States	1974–1977
Sr. Mary Avila Thomas	United States	1975–1976; 1977–1983
Sr. Mary Elyswith López	Belize	?–1979
Sr. Mary Joseph Jones	United States	1977–1978
Sr. Sienna Marie Braxton	United States	1978–1981
Sr. Jennie Jones	United States	1978–1981
Sr. Germaine Henry	United States	1978–1981
Sr. Mary Innocente Wiltz	United States	1979–1982
Sr. Ann Michelle Mercier	United States	1981–1986

Sr. Mary Clare of Assisi Pierre	United States	1981–1992
Sr. Hortensia Maria Flowers	Belize	1982–1991; 1995–1998
Sr. Margaret Mary King	United States	1983–1986
Sr. Dorothy Jones	United States	1983–1987
Sr. Mary Judith Therese Barial	United States	1987–2001; 2004–2005
Sr. Mary Lucia Carl	United States	1987–1993
Sr. Barbara Alice Battiste	United States	1990–1994
Sr. Andria Marie Donald	Jamaica	1993–1996
Sr. Lisa Langlois	United States	1994–1995
Sr. Mary Laura Mercier	United States	1995–1996
Sr. Patricia Hardy	United States	2001

Appendix B

Holy Family Sisters from Belize

1. Sr. Mary Aimee de Jesus (Mary Augustine Thompson); from Belize City; entered the congregation in 1894; was never assigned to Belize; left the congregation in 1906
2. Sr. Margaret Mary (Adriana Kuylen); from Dangriga; entered in 1902; was never assigned to Belize; died in 1962
3. Sr. Mary Gerard (Margaret A. Sorel); from Belize City; entered in 1906; was assigned to Dangriga; left the congregation in 1928
4. Sr. Mary Edmund (Guadalupe Ogaldez); from Dangriga; entered in 1908; was assigned to Dangriga where she died in 1912; first Garifuna to enter the congregation
5. Sr. Mary Frederica (Catherine Elizabeth Broaster); from Belize City; entered in 1908; was never assigned to Belize; died in 1912
6. Sr. Mary des Anges (Mary of the Angels) (Mary Agnes Trumbach); from Belize City; entered in 1910; was never assigned to Belize; died in 1958
7. Sr. Mary Agatha (Margaret Edilia Lind); from Belize City; entered in 1910; was never assigned to Belize; died in 1958
8. Sr. Mary Innocente (Feliciana Sebastiana); from Punta Gorda; entered in 1913; was never assigned to Belize; died in 1917
9. Sr. Mary Beatrice (Lucretia Evangelista Flowers); from Dangriga; entered in 1913; was never assigned to Belize; died in 1973
10. Sr. Mary Florence (Iver Florence Aguet); from Belize City; entered in 1914; was assigned to Dangriga; died in 1974
11. Sr. Mary Felix (Rafaela Juana Alamilla); from Corozal City; entered in 1928; was never assigned to Belize; died in 1998

12. Sr. Mary Juanita (Caroline Young); from Belize City; entered in 1929; was never assigned to Belize; died in 1979
13. Sr. Mary Loyola (Iris Veronica Mitchell); from Belize City; entered in 1933; was assigned to Dangriga; died in 1994
14. Sr. Catherine Henrietta, formerly Sr. Effigenia (Catherine Henrietta Ferguson); from Belize City; entered in 1934; was never assigned to Belize
15. Sr. Mary Eleanor (Evelyn Leonora Gillett); from San Ignacio; entered in 1935; was assigned to Dangriga; died in 2007
16. Sr. Mary Martin de Porres (Agnes Lenore Michael); from Belize City; entered in 1935; was never assigned to Belize; died in 2004
17. Sr. Michael Marie (Amalia Aguet); from Belize City; entered in 1936; was never assigned to Belize; died in 1981
18. Sr. Barbara Marie (Elsie Leonora Francis); from Belize City; entered in 1940; assigned to Dangriga; served as first general councilor of the congregation from 1978 to 1986; died in 2008
19. Sr. Esther Marie (Ann Estero); from Dangriga; entered in 1945; was never assigned to Belize
20. Sr. Mary Tekakwitha (Teresita Lilia Vega); from Belize City; entered in 1945; was never assigned to Belize; served as first general councilor from 1974 to 1978; served as superior general from 1978 to 1986
21. Sr. Mary Carolyn (Marie Louise Leslie); from Belize City; entered in 1946; was assigned to Dangriga
22. Sr. Rita Marie (Rosita Maria Ramirez); entered in 1946; was assigned to Dangriga; left the congregation in 1965
23. Sr. Adela Enriquez; entered in 1946; was never assigned to Belize; left the congregation in 1947
24. Sr. Mary Joseph Ann (Simona Rebecca Gillett); from San Ignacio; entered in 1947; was assigned to Dangriga
25. Sr. Elma (formerly Sr. Mary David) (Elma Olivera); from Belize City; entered in 1947; was assigned to Dangriga
26. Sr. Mary Vincent Ferrer (Kathleen Teresa Gill); entered in 1949; was never assigned to Belize; left the congregation in 1970
27. Sr. Sarita (formerly Sr. Joycelin) (Sarita Francisco); entered in 1949; was not assigned to Belize; left the congregation in 1972
28. Sr. Josita Marie (Almira Ogaldez); from Dangriga; entered in 1949; was never assigned to Belize
29. Sr. Maria Goretti (Marcella Elizabeth Menzies); from Belize City; entered in 1949; was never assigned to Belize; left the congregation in 1983
30. Sr. Mary Bridget (Hilda Thompson); entered in 1953; was assigned to Dangriga; left the congregation in 1970
31. Sr. Mary Bernard Therese (Emily Thomas); entered in 1954; was never assigned to Belize; left the congregation in 1964

32. Sr. Dorothy Marie (Daisy Theresa Stuart); from Belize City; entered in 1954; was assigned to Dangriga; died in 2006
33. Sr. Evelyn (formerly Sr. Mary Angela) (Evelyn Estrada); from Dangriga; entered in 1955; was assigned to Dangriga
34. Sr. Mary Virgilius (Laura Dorothy Davis); entered in 1955; was never assigned to Belize; left the congregation in 1956
35. Sr. Mary Rita Austin (Adela Marta Méndez); from Dangriga; entered in 1958; was assigned to Dangriga; left the congregation in 1978
36. Sr. Hortensia Maria (Catherine Flowers); from Belize City; entered in 1959; was assigned to Dangriga
37. Sr. Joan (formerly Sr. Robert Louise) (Joan Flores); from Seine Bight; entered in 1959; was assigned to Dangriga
38. Sr. Veronica Ruth (formerly Sr. Peter Chanel) (Veronica Ruth Lambey); from Seine Bight; entered in 1959; was never assigned to Belize
39. Sr. Mary Rebecca Carlos (Isabella Agatha Castillo); from Dangriga; entered in 1959; was assigned to Dangriga
40. Sr. Mary Anna Augusta (Myrna Rose Joseph); entered in 1960; was never assigned to Belize; left the congregation in 1970
41. Sr. Zoila (formerly Sr. John Patrick) (Zoila Leonor Casanova); entered in 1961; was never assigned to Belize; left the congregation in 1970
42. Sr. Mary Naomi (Matilda Sabal); entered in 1962; was never assigned to Belize; left the congregation in 1965
43. Sr. Cecilia (formerly Sr. Basil) (Cecilia Higinio); entered in 1962; was assigned to Dangriga; left the congregation in 1973
44. Sr. Mary Jeremy (Frances Jean López); entered in 1963; was never assigned to Belize; left the congregation in 1969
45. Sr. Mary Matthias (Margaret Cortona Elizio); entered in 1963; was never assigned to Belize; left the congregation in 1965
46. Sr. Jean (Jean Joseph Martínez); from Seine Bight; entered in 1968; was assigned to Dangriga
47. Sr. Mary Elyswith (Isolene Elyswith López); from Dangriga; entered in 1972; was assigned to Dangriga; left the congregation in 1979
48. Sr. Nirisse Marie (Elizabeth Marie Serano); entered in 1993; was never assigned to Belize but made her postulancy in Dangriga; left the congregation in 1995
49. Sr. Maria Areni (Veronica Areni Castillo); entered in 1993; was never assigned to Belize but made her postulancy in Dangriga; left the congregation in 1995
50. Sr. Alma Marie (Hortensia Maria Fisher); entered in 1994; was never assigned to Belize; left the congregation in 2000

Appendix C

Reflections of Three Lay People Who Were Taught by the Holy Family Sisters in Belize

Sylvia Flores

In October of last year [2008], the Catholic Church of the United States of America honored and celebrated the significant contribution of religious communities who sent out missionaries to minister to the needs of God's people around the world. It is a great privilege for me to reflect on the contribution of one such religious community—the Sisters of the Holy Family of New Orleans, Louisiana. Theirs was a young community, just fifty-seven years since their founding when its very young Superior General, Mother Austin Jones, answered the call of God and the challenge of the then Bishop of Belize, Rev. Salvatore di Pietro, to send a few sisters on a mission to British Honduras (Belize) to assist in the education of the children of Dangriga. The Bishop was experiencing difficulty in finding and sending teachers in Belize City to teach the Garifuna children of Dangriga because the children did not speak English and spoke only the Garifuna language, a language they did not understand. This was during the colonial period, a time when the Garifuna people experienced much discrimination in Belize and so it would not have been surprising that the Bishop found it difficult to find persons who would be willing to teach these children.

Such is the backdrop against which Mother Austin Jones would answer the call to minister to the needs of God's children. Often as I have reflected on the decision of Mother Austin, I ponder anew what thoughts may have crossed her mind as she tried to discern such a call. How welcoming was her spirit in answering this challenge to come to an unknown land, a land she had probably not heard of before? How would the people receive her and her sisters? And how would her own community feel about her decision to send her sisters to this foreign land? Would they be able to cope with the food, the climate, and in those early days when telephone communication was not available and transportation took an entire week from New Orleans, would they be able to cope with these harsh realities? Was there dissent in the community when Mother Austin finalized her decision about bringing the first missionaries to British Honduras? While Mother Austin and her sisters may have pondered all these, nonetheless her response was a signature "YES"; and while she may have responded not only in view of her own vow of obedience to the will of God, the decision also marked her own profound desire to bring that extra measure of love to the least of God's children—the same love that had motivated her foundress, Mother Henriette Delille, to minister to the needs of the black children of New Orleans. It would be this same love that would, for more than one hundred years, seal the commitment of the Sisters of the Holy Family to the children and the people of Belize.

More than one hundred years of continuous service is no easy feat by any stretch of the imagination. What was it that kept the Sisters of the Holy Family coming for so many years? There is an easy answer—LOVE—the greatest lesson ever taught by Christ himself. There is a special love that the people of Belize and particularly of Dangriga have for the Sisters of the Holy Family, evidenced by the many deep relationships that have evolved over time. Those of us who have been privileged to be their students are forever grateful for the quality of education they fostered, but more than this for the love with which they nurtured our spirits and instilled in us the pride that we, too, are God's chosen people.

The Sisters of the Holy Family taught me throughout my primary school years, first at Sacred Heart and then for the last two years at Holy Ghost. Since I lived on the south side of Dangriga, I transferred there when the school was first opened. I graduated from there in 1965. Throughout these years, I was taught by only two lay teachers. All my other teachers were sisters. Sister Marie de Montfort [Breaux], who was my teacher at Sacred Heart School for three consecutive years, remains my favorite teacher. Her child-like confidence and pleasing personality were disarming. It took only a smile from her to have her students forget their mischief. Even today, that smile remains her signature entrance to one's heart.

After I graduated from Holy Ghost Primary School, I attended an Anglican high school because I had won a scholarship there for having gotten the highest test score on the school's entrance exam. I never, however, divorced myself from the sisters during those years. In fact, when I did not have classes on certain days at my school, I would sit in on classes at Austin High School. Along with Sister Marie de Montfort, the sisters who most inspired me were Sister Mary Lorene [LeBlanc] and Sister Dorothy Marie [Stuart], both of whom are now deceased, and Sister Clare of Assisi [Pierre]. I worked with Sister Clare when I was a teacher at Ecumenical High School. I found her to be such an endearing person and one who will commit her time, effort, and resources in making a positive difference in the lives of her students and any young person who comes in contact with her. She is a woman of creative and innovative imagination. Her ideas are always refreshing, but most of all it is her compassionate and nonjudgmental spirit that endear her to so many people and especially those of us in Belize.

Unfortunately, as a result of their diminishing numbers due mainly to ageing and no newer vocations, our sisters are no longer in Belize, but the stark evidence of their love and commitment to our country remains in the continuing presence of Sacred Heart, Holy Angels, and Holy Ghost Primary Schools, and Delille Academy, a four-year secondary institution. And while Austin High School, an institution they founded, merged into what is today referred to as

Ecumenical High School, the thousands of their students who attended and graduated from Austin High School continue to relive the incomparable quality of education fostered by the Sisters of the Holy Family. Many are the teachers who have taught with the sisters—teachers who recognize the able leadership of the sisters in the administration of their institutions. It is well known in Belize that the sisters not only led by example but also fostered the need for necessary teacher training in order to create increasing levels of excellence in the classroom environment.

There is no doubt that there are many students who were taught and fostered by the love of the sisters and have gone on to higher levels of achievement and success in their lives. They humbly acknowledge that were it not for those early and formative years, it would have been perhaps difficult for them to go on and to build on that foundation. In 1998, Belize celebrated the centenary year of the presence and mission of the sisters in Belize. That celebration was, undoubtedly, the biggest celebration ever in our community as we laid out the red carpet to welcome the many sisters who came for the celebration. The presence of many past students and the success of the celebration spoke pointedly to the spirit of a grateful community. It was a moment that rekindled that undying love that had been ignited in 1898. The outpouring of emotions evidenced by the hugs, tears, expressions of gratitude, and unspoken thoughts was a signature moment which convinced the sisters that the seeds of love they had planted had borne fruit in the lives of the "little children." And how poignant are the words of Christ in the sisters' mission that—"unless a grain of wheat dies, it remains only a seed. . . ." The sisters' mission to Belize was in essence a dying to self. They had left their families and friends behind in New Orleans to answer that call even when they did not answer [ask] why. They had risked their own lives traveling in open waters across the Gulf of Mexico and the Caribbean. They knew not what measure of misfortune they would encounter, but they came. But when the "wheat" grew, they were there to reap the harvest of their love.

While we lament the fact that the sisters are no longer in Belize, we are heartened by the presence of the Associates of the Sisters of the Holy Family, an organization of laypersons once taught by the

Sisters, who try to exemplify the charisms of the sisters in our community. This year [2008], the Associates in Belize celebrate ten years since their founding. There are thirty-two Associate members, twenty-three of whom are active members in Dangriga. It is a vibrant group that meets every second Monday of the month. We attend mass and organize activities to meet the spiritual needs of the community. In an effort to mark the ten-year anniversary of our mission in Dangriga, we raised funds to construct a 40-by-52 feet ferro-concrete building and in April 2008 we led the way in inaugurating it. It is called the Henriette Delille Spiritual Life Center, and we hope it will serve as a tribute to the Holy Family Sisters and a symbol of their enduring legacy to our people and community. As Associates, we remain prayerful, hopeful and faithful that our beloved sisters will once again die [unto themselves] to make real another harvest of wheat in Belize.

Sylvia Flores was the first female mayor of Dangriga, serving two consecutive terms from 1988 to 1994. She also was Speaker of the Belize House of Representatives from 1998 to 2001 and President of the Senate from 2001 to 2003. While in the House, she held the positions of Minister of Defense, National Emergency Manager, and Minister of Human Development and Housing. She chaired the Holy Family Sisters' Centennial Celebration in 1998 and raised funds for the Sisters in New Orleans in 2005 after Hurricane Katrina destroyed their motherhouse and most of their schools and other institutions.

Eric López

The Holy Family Sisters were invited from New Orleans to come to British Honduras to teach the Garifuna children of Dangriga. The nuns were assigned to Sacred Heart School, the only Catholic school in Dangriga then. The sisters arrived in 1898 and there were four of them who were to be stationed here. The inhabitants learned to live with the nuns and the sisters learned to live with them even though they did not understand their language. But patience and perseverance were qualities that the sisters had. I know this because I taught with them for many years. They were excellent masters of the classroom. When a child did not attend school, the principal or the classroom teacher would go looking for that child at home or wherever and bring them to school the following day. The parents in those days had great respect for the sisters, so much so that many parents granted parental authority to the sisters. I am certain that many young men would not have become real men had the sisters not taken them into their fold. The sisters were not only disciplinarians but were women who had motherly love. This is why the people of Dangriga had so much reverence for the Sisters of the Holy Family.

The sisters, apart from being in the classrooms, also taught the parts of the mass to the older people and this was in Latin in the early days. They also started prayer groups in the church like the St. Agnes Sodality. This was a group of women who were instructed by the sisters and attended mass every Sunday. The sisters also formed choir groups and taught the members to sing the high masses, as they were called in those days. I can recall when the Bishop would come from Belize City to administer the sacrament of Confirmation to the primary school children. The entire Catholic community would look forward to those days because the celebration of the mass would be so grand. The sisters would decorate the church with the help of the bigger boys they had taught. People would look forward to the singing and there were sisters who had very beautiful voices and could sing on many levels. I recall those masses as very solemn. The people prided themselves in having been taught how to sing so beautifully.

Because there was no teacher training in the early days, the sisters employed their older students as pupil teachers. Under the able leadership of the sisters those pupil teachers sat and passed the colonial exams and were able to teach at higher levels in the classroom. Some of these same pupil teachers became the very best of our education system in Belize and the very same teachers who were employed by the Catholic school management to go and teach the Mayan and Kekchi Indian people in the far rural communities of the Orange Walk, Cayo, and Corozal Districts. The sisters were visionaries and wanted to elevate their students. They felt that some of their students had the potential to do a higher level of service. That is how the idea of Austin High School, a high school for girls, began. Austin High School was named after the superior general of the Sisters of the Holy Family who had brought the first set of missionary sisters to Belize.

When the student numbers began to increase, the sisters opened a school on the south side of Dangriga. Holy Ghost School was opened sometime around 1963 just a short time after Hurricane Hattie, a storm that destroyed Dangriga in 1961. Its first principal was Sr. Lorene Le Blanc under whom I taught for a few years. The sisters were a set of visionary women as we have come to understand so many years later. They had seen where our community would grow and much of this population growth would occur on the south side of Dangriga. Today, as we look back, we can see the student population on the south side still exploding. The government of Belize is now seeing the need to physically expand the school. Holy Ghost School is now about forty-five years [old] and while there are no longer sisters serving many people, even those who are not Catholic can remark that the best days of Holy Ghost School were under the administration of the sisters. For a long time, the best teachers were from Holy Ghost School and the most diligent students were from there also. People like me can only look back on those days as days of academic accomplishments. Perhaps because I am from the south of Dangriga I am somewhat biased.

I want to say something about the sisters' experience back in or around 1946. There was a great fire in Dangriga that destroyed the Sacred Heart School and the Sisters of the Holy Family convent, which were both wooden buildings. This was a fire that totally destroyed much of the assets of the church and those of the sisters. One would think that school would be suspended for many weeks but that was not what happened—not with the sisters. Mr. Henry Bowman, who was the Stann Creek District's wealthiest man and who was also a Catholic, provided one of his huge buildings for the use of the sisters and also for classes for the students. In three days [actually only one day] the students were back to school and the sisters were there once again to provide hope and courage to our community. On account of this fire, the church, together with the sisters, began to make plans for the construction of a new Sacred Heart School and this would be a concrete building. So began "Cordi Jesu," the new concrete school building. While I cannot say if the sisters had any funds associated with the new building, I dare say that they helped to organize the students' brigade to carry sand from the beaches for the construction of the school building. Men in the parish also assisted in the construction of the building.

The sisters, as I have said earlier, had organized the St. Agnes Sodality, a young women's group within the church. From this group would come many young women who would join the sisters as nuns. There were more than a dozen young women who joined the order, many of whom came back to assist in the education of our people. While there have been no new vocations for many years from Dangriga, we can proudly say that part of the fruits of the sisters' love for our community came in the form of the young women who had chosen to become nuns. I am certain that there are still a few of these sisters in the order. I want to say that if there were ever the opportunity for the sisters to open a university in Belize, they would probably have done so. But in those early days, a high school education was like a university education for us. It was the highest one could go to, and Austin High School, the first high school for girls, founded by the sisters, became our local "university."

Our community of Dangriga owe an enormous debt of gratitude to God and to the Sisters of the Holy Family, and to the sisters I say, God bless your community for many more years.

Eric López is a retired teacher who was taught by the Holy Family Sisters and later taught with them at Holy Ghost School.

EUGENE HERNÁNDEZ

The Sisters of the Holy Family along with the Jesuits of the Missouri Province laid the foundation for Catholic education in Dangriga and influenced the religio-cultural formation of Garinagu [plural form of Garifuna] in the town and villages of the Stann Creek District.

My first association was with the Sisters at age five, in what was referred to as the "Primer" (grade two). Grade one was called ABC. It is hard to remember what Sr. Cecilia [Green] taught but you can't forget the songs and religious hymns, the catechism and her insistence on keeping our slates clean. One of the most impressionable memories is that she was "my" teacher rather than "our" teacher. Probably it was the weight of the slates since she had to deal with the individual child for the basics of arithmetic, writing, and drawing. I don't remember how she taught reading since we shared the Primer reading book. But somehow, we learned to read.

We left Sr. Cecilia in what is now the Infant Division and moved on to the Middle Division where the boys were separated from the girls and where the nuns taught mainly girls. Sister Cecilia's Holy Family influence did not surface again until she became the principal at Faber House following the fire, which leveled the convent and Sacred Heart Church and the first two classes. Standards Four and Five of the upper division were transferred to Downtown Dangriga. She had not lost her gentleness and "every child a sacred trust" attitude.

In Standard Six, boys and girls were again combined and we boys were brought under the heavy discipline of Sr. Joseph Xavier [Meikle]. Here, it was obvious that the nuns were determined that "every child was not only a sacred trust" but he was to be brought up "by hand," and the old adages of "spare the rod and spoil the child" and "education makes a bloody entrance" were well applied. In my case it seemed that it was a mold into which I had unfortunately been poured. I was under the ever-watchful eye of Sr. Joe. She single-handedly took charge of what I became. Early in my entrance into Standard Six, Sr. Joe took me under her wings. She insisted that I take the "First Teachers' Exam" along with the older students. I passed and credit Sr. Joe for setting me on my career track as a teacher. My mother used to say that Sr. Joe saw in me what nobody else saw and that she followed up by pushing me to succeed. Even after passing the "Second Teachers' Certificate Exam," when I tried to slip from beneath "the hand" she found a way to bring me back.

What do I tell my children and my grandchildren about the Christian foundation that girths my being? It was the productive love and inspiration of the Sisters of the Holy Family embedded in the unselfish guidance and dedication that were woven into the fabric of the mission of the sisters.

Eugene Hernández, who was taught by the Sisters of the Holy Family at Sacred Heart School, is a retired teacher.

NOTES

Introduction

1. Gerald Costello, *Mission to Latin America: The Successes and Failures of a Twentieth-Century Crusade* (Maryknoll, NY: Orbis Books, 1979).

2. See for instance John Tracy Ellis, *American Catholicism* (Chicago: University of Chicago Press, 1956); Thomas McAvoy, *A History of the Catholic Church in the United States* (Notre Dame, IN: University of Notre Dame Press, 1969); James Hennesey, *American Catholics: A History of the Roman Catholic Community in the United States* (Oxford: Oxford University Press, 1981); Jay P. Dolan, *The American Catholic Experience: A History from Colonial Times to the Present* (New York: Doubleday, 1985); Philip Gleason, *Keeping the Faith: American Catholicism Past and Present* (Notre Dame, IN: University of Notre Dame Press, 1987). Paul Kollman noticed this gap in Catholic history when he wrote: "Standard histories of U.S. Catholicism have not made missionary activity by U.S. Catholics beyond their borders a central feature of their narratives." Paul Kollman, C.S.C., "The Promise of Mission History for U.S. Catholic History," *U.S. Catholic Historian* 24, no. 3 (Summer 2006): 2.

3. This was especially true of small congregations involved in missionary work. The archives of the Maryknolls and the Jesuits are examples of those that are well organized.

4. Donna Whitson Brett and Edward T. Brett, *Murdered in Central America: The Stories of Eleven U.S. Missionaries* (Maryknoll, NY: Orbis Books, 1988).

5. See Edward T. Brett, *The U.S. Catholic Press on Central America: From Cold War Anticommunism to Social Justice* (Notre Dame, IN: University of Notre Dame Press, 2003), which attempts, among other things, to show how U.S. Catholic missionaries in Central America played a large role in changing American Catholic perceptions of U.S. policy in the isthmus.

6. Committee on the Church in Latin America, National Conference of Catholic Bishops, *Sharing Faith across the Hemisphere* (Washington, DC: United States Catholic Conference, 1997).

7. Dana L. Robert, *American Women in Mission: A Social History of Their Thought and Practice* (Macon, GA: Mercer University Press, 1997). For more recent contributions on female missionaries and their unique role, see Dana L. Robert, ed., *Gender Bearers, Gender Barriers: Missionary Women in the Twentieth Century* (Maryknoll, NY: Orbis Books, 2002); Susan Fitzpatrick Behrens, "From Symbols of the Sacred to Symbols of Subversion to Simply Obscure: Maryknoll Women Religious in Guatemala, 1953–1967," *The Americas* 51, no. 2 (October 2004): 189–216; and Susan Fitzpatrick Behrens, "Maryknoll Sisters, Faith, Healing, and the Maya Construction of Catholic Communities in Guatemala," *Latin American Research Review* 44, no. 3 (2009): 27–49.

8. Angelyn Dries, O.S.F., *The Missionary Movement in American Catholic History* (Maryknoll, NY: Orbis Books, 1998).

9. Ibid., 1.

10. Ibid., 56–57.

11. John Thomas Gillard, S.S.J., *The Catholic Church and the American Negro* (Baltimore: St. Joseph's Society Press, 1929); and Gillard, *Colored Catholics in the United States* (Baltimore: Josephite Press, 1941).

12. Albert S. Foley, *God's Men of Color: The Colored Catholic Priests of the United States, 1854–1954* (New York: Farrar Straus, 1955).

13. Albert S. Foley, "Adventures in Black Catholic History: Research and Writing," *U.S. Catholic Historian* 5, no. 1 (1986): 103–18.

14. Marilyn Wenzke Nickels, *Black Catholic Protest and the Federated Colored Catholics, 1917–1933: Three Perspectives on Racial Justice* (New York: Garland, 1988).

15. Stephen J. Ochs, *Desegregating the Altar: The Josephites and the Struggle for Black Priests, 1871–1960* (Baton Rouge: Louisiana State University Press, 1990).

16. For an example of how deep-seated Catholic racism was in mid-nineteenth-century southern Louisiana and how extreme its effects could be, see Stephen J. Ochs, *A Black Patriot and a White Priest: André Cailloux and Claude Paschal Maistre in Civil War New Orleans* (Baton Rouge: Louisiana State University Press, 2000).

17. Cyprian Davis, *The History of Black Catholics in the United States* (New York: Crossroad, 1990).

18. See Michael J. McNally, "A Minority of a Minority: The Witness of Black Women Religious in the Antebellum South," *Review for Religious* 40 (March 1981): 260–69; Sister M. Reginald Gerdes, O.S.P., "To Educate and Evangelize: Black Catholic Schools of the Oblate Sisters of Providence (1828–1880)," *U.S. Catholic Historian* 7, nos. 2 and 3 (Spring 1988; Summer 1988): 183–99.

19. Diane Batts Morrow, *Persons of Color and Religious at the Same Time: The Oblate Sisters of Providence, 1828–1860* (Chapel Hill: University of North Carolina Press, 2002).

20. Carol K. Coburn, "An Overview of the Historiography of Women Religious: A Twenty-Five-Year Retrospective," *U.S. Catholic Historian* 22, no. 1 (Winter 2004): 2.

21. Evangeline Thomas, *Women Religious History Sources: A Guide to Repositories in the United States* (New York: R. R. Bowker, 1983); Elizabeth Kolmer, *Religious Women in the United States: A Survey of the Influential Literature from 1950 to 1983* (Wilmington, DE: Michael Glazier, 1984).

22. For more on this topic see Coburn, "An Overview of the Historiography of Women Religious," from which the above information comes.

23. Some of the most notable works to appear since the Conference on the History of Women Religious began are: Jo Ann Kay McNamara, *Sisters in Arms: Catholic Nuns through Two Millennia* (Cambridge, MA: Harvard University Press, 1996); Carol K. Coburn and Martha Smith, *Spirited Lives: How Nuns Shaped Catholic Culture and American Life, 1836–1920* (Chapel Hill: University of North Carolina Press, 1999); Marjorie Noterman Beane, *From Framework to Freedom: A History of the Sister Formation Conference* (Lanham, MD: University Press of America, 1993); Lora Ann Quiñonez and Mary Daniel Turner, *The Transformation of American Catholic Sisters* (Philadelphia: Temple University Press, 1992); Amy L. Koehlinger, *The New Nuns: Racial Justice and Religious Reform in the 1960s* (Cambridge, MA: Harvard University Press, 2007).

24. Two notable exceptions are Behrens, "From Symbols of the Sacred," 189–216; and Behrens, "Maryknoll Sisters," 27–49.

25. While the ground floor of the New Orleans Holy Family Motherhouse was flooded in Hurricane Katrina in 2005, destroying virtually everything located there, the congregational archives were fortunately stored on the second floor and therefore survived.

26. Since the Jesuits were in charge of Sacred Heart Parish in Stann Creek (Dangriga), where the Holy Family Sisters taught, the author corresponded with David Miros, the archivist for the Midwest Province Archives in St. Louis, where the Jesuit Belize materials are kept. There was very little in these archives, however, on the Holy Family Sisters, and what was there was of no value for this study.

Chapter 1. Foundation and Growth in New Orleans

1. Some of the information in Part I was earlier published in a greatly abbreviated form in Edward T. Brett, "African American Missionaries in

Central America: The Sisters of the Holy Family in Belize," *U.S. Catholic Historian* 24, no. 3 (Summer 2006): 75–94; and also in Edward T. Brett, "Race Issues and Conflict in Nineteenth- and Early Twentieth-Century Religious Life: The New Orleans Sisters of the Holy Family," *U.S. Catholic Historian* 29, no. 1 (Winter 2011): 113–27.

2. A letter from Fr. Matharus Antillach to Sister Austin Jones, May 17, 1899, found in the Belize Collection of the Archives of the Sisters of the Holy Family, New Orleans, Louisiana (hereafter cited as Belize Collection), shows conclusively that Addie Saffold worked in the "Infant School" until May 1899, when she returned to New Orleans for her year of novitiate.

3. Until the last three or four decades, "Carib" was used by non-natives to identify this indigenous people. More recently, however, "Garifuna" has replaced "Carib."

4. O. Nigel Bolland writes that by 1802, about 150 Garifuna had settled in the Stann Creek area. See O. Nigel Bolland, *Belize: A New Nation in Central America* (Boulder and London: Westview Press, 1986), 25. William David Setzekorn states that the black Caribs have been in southern Belize since 1797. See William David Setzekorn, *Formerly British Honduras: A Profile of the New Nation of Belize* (Athens: Ohio University Press, 1981), 62.

5. Richard Buhler, *A History of the Catholic Church in Belize* (Belize: BISRA (Belize Institute for Social Research and Action), Occasional Publications No. 4, 1976), 35.

6. Ibid., 12.

7. Setzekorn, *Formerly British Honduras*, 42; Buhler, *History of the Catholic Church in Belize*, 34; Dries, *Missionary Movement*, 289 note 29. For the Mercy Sisters' early work in British Honduras see Mary Hermenia Muldrey, R.S.M., *Abounding in Mercy: Mother Austin Carroll* (New Orleans: Habersham, 1988), 207–10, 218, 224, 226, 231–32, 238–39, 247, 266, 271, 323–24. Muldrey shows how the Mercy Sisters' mission in British Honduras became a pawn in a game between German American and Irish American church leaders. This further illustrates how prelates often attempted to control sisters working in their diocese and how the sisters tried to cope with such tactics. In 1914 the Mercy Sisters in British Honduras severed their affiliation with the Mercy Sisters of New Orleans and became an independent community. In 1931, however, they joined the Providence, Rhode Island, regional community of Mercy Sisters and have remained affiliated with them ever since. See Sister Yvonne Hunter, R.S.M., *The Sisters of Mercy in Belize, 1883–1983* (Cumberland, RI: Sisters of Mercy, Province of Providence Communications, 1984), for more information on the Sisters of Mercy in Belize. This work is valuable to the researcher in that it contains many verbatim entries from the sisters' archival records at St. Catherine's Convent in Belize City.

8. *Notations from the St. Catherine Convent Annals (Belize)*, a photocopy of the handwritten original, in Belize Collection.

9. Sister Mary Francis Borgia Hart, S.S.F., "Violets in the King's Garden: A History of the Sisters of the Holy Family of New Orleans" (New Orleans: Unpublished typed manuscript, 1931), 462. Hereafter cited as "Violets."

10. Ibid., 462; Sister Mary of the Rosary [Heisser], "Builders of Belize (2) Holy Family Sisters," *National Studies: A Journal of Social Research and Thought*, (November 1973): 15. Letter from Salvatore Di Prieto, S.J., to "Your Grace" [the archbishop of New Orleans], April 13, 1898, in Belize Collection.

11. Sister Mary Francis Borgia Hart, S.S.F., *Violets in the King's Garden: A History of the Sisters of the Holy Family of New Orleans* (New Orleans: Privately printed, 1976), revised and abbreviated edition, 50. Hart is not a professional historian and both the long and abbreviated versions of her work are not completely trustworthy. Most of her facts are based on documents found in the Belize Collection in the New Orleans Archives, but a substantial number come from interviews with her fellow sisters or from their recollections and cannot always be substantiated. At times she makes hagiographical-like statements that idealize her subjects and that in a few rare instances are definitely untrue. Nevertheless, her *Violets in the King's Garden* is a valuable source for historians if used with caution and common sense. I cite both this 1976 book and the original 1931 typescript, "Violets" (note 9 above).

12. There had been some earlier Protestant African American missionary efforts in Liberia and other parts of Africa as well as in Haiti. See Sandy D. Martin, *Black Baptists and African Missions: The Origin of a Movement, 1880–1915* (Macon, GA: Mercer University Press, 1989); John Saillant, "Missions in Liberia and Race Relations in the United States," in *The Foreign Missionary Enterprise at Home: Explorations in North American Cultural History*, ed. Daniel H. Bays and Grant Wacker (Tuscaloosa: University of Alabama Press, 2003), 13–28; and Laurie F. Maffey-Kipp, "The Serpentine Trail: Haitian Missions and the Construction of African-American Religious Identity," in Bays and Wacker, *Foreign Missionary Enterprise at Home*, 29–43. Only a few U.S. Catholic missionary endeavors had occurred prior to that of the Holy Family Sisters. New York Franciscans became the first U.S. female religious to become involved in foreign missionary work when they sent sisters to teach in Jamaica in 1879. In the 1880s, Sisters of Charity began teaching missions in Jamaica and the Bahamas, while Mercy Sisters opened schools in Jamaica and British Honduras. These three congregations seem to be the first U.S. female communities to undertake the education of black children overseas, and the Sisters of the Holy Family appear to be the fourth to do so. See Dries, *Missionary Movement*, 43–57. The Oblate Sisters of Providence, the first community of African American sisters, founded in 1829, opened a

school in Cuba for Afro-Cubans in 1900. Shortly thereafter they would send missionaries to Colombia and Costa Rica. Theirs was the second Catholic African American missionary enterprise in history. For more on their mission work, see William M. Montgomery, "The Oblate Sisters of Providence: The Origins of Their Mission to Latin America," *U.S. Catholic Historian* 24, no. 2 (Spring 2006): 41–55; and William M. Montgomery, "Mission to Cuba and Costa Rica: The Oblate Sisters of Providence in Latin America, 1900–1970" (Ph.D. dissertation, The Catholic University of America, Washington, DC, 1997).

    13. For the genealogy of Henriette Delille see Cyprian Davis, O.S.B., *Henriette Delille: Servant of Slaves, Witness to the Poor* (New Orleans: Archives of the Archdiocese of New Orleans, 2004), 2–16, 98–99.

    14. Herbert Asbury, *The French Quarter: An Informal History of the New Orleans Underworld* (Atlanta: Mockingbird Books, 1976), 97.

    15. Virginia Meacham Gould and Charles E. Nolan, *Henriette Delille: "Servant of Slaves"* (New Orleans: Sisters of the Holy Family, 1999), 4. Gould and Nolan are professional historians with doctoral degrees in history. Their twenty-two-page *Henriette Delille: "Servant of Slaves"* is based on archival sources from a variety of religious congregations, male and female, in Louisiana, Maryland, Missouri, Massachusetts, Illinois, and Kentucky as well as from archival sources in France. (A list of their archival sources is found on page 22 of their pamphlet.) Thus, in the current writer's opinion, it is the best source for the life of Delille prior to the publication of Cyprian Davis's *Henriette Delille*. Unfortunately, however, Gould and Nolan did not footnote their materials, thereby making it difficult to track down exact archival sources.

    16. Asbury, *The French Quarter*, 96–101.

    17. Gould and Nolan, *Henriette Delille*, 2; Davis, *Henriette Delille*, 13. Hart writes that Henriette's parents' "faith and love of God took deep root in her own young heart," thereby insinuating that her father played an important role in her life. But this is merely wishful thinking on Hart's part. There is absolutely no evidence to support Hart's contention.

    18. Joseph H. Fichter, "The White Church and the Black Sisters," *U.S. Catholic Historian* 12, no. 1 (Winter 1994): 37; Onita Estes-Hicks, "Henriette Delille: Free Woman of Color, Candidate for Roman Catholic Sainthood, Early Womanist," in *Perspectives on Womanist Theology*, ed. Jacquelyn Grant, Black Church Scholars Series, vol. 7 (Atlanta, GA: ITC Press, 1995), 44; Sister Audrey Marie Detiege, *Henriette Delille, Free Woman of Color: Foundress of the Sisters of the Holy Family* (New Orleans: Sisters of the Holy Family, 1976), 17–19. Prior to her death in 1989, Detiege spent nearly two decades gathering information for a proposed biography of Delille that was never completed. In 1976, however, she published a fifty-one-page pamphlet

summarizing her findings. Unfortunately the pamphlet does not contain footnotes and therefore it is sometimes difficult to trace her sources. Nevertheless, Detiege's work is valuable and sophisticated in its quality. It should be noted that documents have recently been found that indicate that, while a teenager in the early 1820s, Delille may have given birth to one or two boys, each named Henry Bocno, both of whom died at an early age. As journalist Carol Glatz states, "One death record from the St. Louis Cathedral sacramental register listed Henry Bocno as the son of Henriette Delille. Other records that were found gave conflicting information, such as one record referring to Henry as the son of 'Marie.' Another record named the mother as 'Henriette Sarpy.'" Charles Nolan notes, however, that the sacramental register may have been in error. Delille could have taken in an abandoned child, and the priest who recorded the boy's death in the register may have mistaken her for the birth mother. See Carol Glatz, "Mother Henriette Delille Declared Venerable," *Clarion Herald* (April 3, 2010), 1 and 6.

19. Detiege, *Henriette Delille*, 18–25; Davis, *Henriette Delille*, 22–26, 30. Davis points out that there is no written evidence from that period of Henriette's life to confirm that Delille and Gaudin were students at Fontière's school. Sister Mary Bernard Deggs, however, who in her younger years would have had contact with some of the pioneer Holy Family Sisters, wrote in the 1890s that Gaudin had attended the school. Sister Mary Bernard Deggs, *No Cross, No Crown: Black Nuns in Nineteenth-Century New Orleans*, ed. Virginia Meacham Gould and Charles E. Nolan (Bloomington: Indiana University Press, 2002), 10. Davis further notes that Fontière's school was the only one in New Orleans at the time open to free women of color; and since both Delille and Gaudin had some formal education, they almost certainly must have been students there. Davis, *Henriette Delille*, 30. Jesuit sociologist Joseph Fichter claims that in 1830, when Henriette was eighteen, her siblings registered as white in the U.S. Census, but she did not. He interprets this omission to mean that she refused to pass for white, preferring to identify with her African American heritage. See Joseph H. Fichter, "A Saintly Person of Color," *America* (February 29, 1992): 157. Fichter does not cite a source for his claim, and the author could find no verification of it in the 1830 census. Thus, it seems that Fichter's claim is incorrect.

20. The "Rules and Regulations for the Congregation of the Sisters of the Presentation of the Blessed Virgin Mary" is in the middle of a notebook located in the Holy Family Archives in New Orleans. For more on this document see Davis, *Henriette Delille*, 36–38.

21. Gould and Nolan, *Henriette Delille*, 11–13. In the 1730s and 1740s the Ursuline Sisters in New Orleans created the Children of Mary, a confraternity of laywomen who catechized and sponsored slaves for baptism. Free women of color were involved in the confraternity from the beginning and as

time went on became its driving force. Delille's great-grandmother, grandmother, and mother took part in this ministry and passed it on to Henriette. Thus, when Father Rousselon formed Delille, Gaudin, and Charles into a quasi-formal religious community, the archbishop saw this as an extension of the traditional lay-confraternity movement. The three Afro-Creole women, however, envisioned it as much more—an important step toward the fulfillment of their dream to eventually become a traditional, vowed religious congregation. For an excellent treatment of the Children of Mary lay-confraternity movement and its eventual evolution into a religious congregation, see Emily Clark and Virginia Meacham Gould, "The Feminine Face of Afro-Catholicism in New Orleans, 1727–1852," *William and Mary Quarterly*, 59, no. 2 (April 2002): 409–48. See also Virginia Meacham Gould, "Henriette Delille, Free Women of Color, and Catholicism in Antebellum New Orleans, 1727–1852," in *Beyond Bondage: Free Women of Color in the Americas*, ed. David Barry Gaspar and Darlene Clark Hine (Urbana and Chicago: University of Illinois Press, 2004), 271–85.

22. Davis, *Henriette Delille*, 53.

23. Hart, *Violets*, 10; Deggs, *No Cross*, 10; Detiege, *Henriette Delille*, 41–43. Detiege points out that there is no official written record of their novitiate with the Religious of the Sacred Heart. Evidence comes from the recollections of Mother Juliette Gaudin and an autograph book given to Henriette by the Sacred Heart Sisters and signed by some of their members. Fichter speculates that they made their novitiate under the "episcopally approved subterfuge" that they had been taken on by the Religious of the Sacred Heart as housekeepers or maids. This theory is supported by the statement of the historian Roger Baudier, who writes that Holy Family Sisters had served in a domestic capacity for the Religious of the Sacred Heart. Gould and Nolan add that St. Michael's was an ideal place to send them since it was secluded from New Orleans and no one would therefore have known them. See Fichter, "White Church and Black Sisters," 42; Roger Baudier, *The Catholic Church in Louisiana* (New Orleans: Hyatt, 1939), 198; and Virginia Meacham Gould and Charles E. Nolan, "Researchers Explore Delille's Formation in Convent, LA," *Servant of the Poor: Newsletter of Friends of Henriette Delille* (Summer 2004): 1, 5. Also see Davis, *Henriette Delille*, 62–63 and 70 note 19.

24. Davis, *Henriette Delille*, 63. Hart and Detiege claim, but without any documentation, that they took vows on October 15, 1852. See Hart, *Violets*, 10; and Detiege, *Henriette Delille*, 43.

25. Davis, *Henriette Delille*, 59, 63.

26. Tracy Fessenden, "The Sisters of the Holy Family and the Veil of Race," *Religion and American Culture: A Journal of Interpretation* 10, no. 2 (2000): 197.

27. Davis, *History of Black Catholics*, 107. Between 1830 and 1862 the Louisiana state government and that of the city of New Orleans passed a series of laws that severely restricted the rights and activities of *gens de couleur libre*. In such a hostile environment it is understandable that Archbishop Blanc might have decided that it was best that the transition of the Holy Family women from a pious association to a vowed religious community be kept from the public. See Gould and Nolan in Deggs, *No Cross*, 4.

28. See comments of Gould and Nolan in Deggs, *No Cross*, 215 note 59.
29. Deggs, *No Cross*, 89.
30. Hart, *Violets*, 1.
31. Ibid., 14; Baudier, *Catholic Church in Louisiana*, 377.
32. Translated from the French and quoted in [Sisters of the Holy Family] *The Greatest Gift of All: A Pictorial Biography of Mother Henriette Delille* (New Orleans: Heritage of America Foundation Press, 1992), 38.
33. Detiege, *Henriette Delille*, 42. They were listed this way also in British Honduras by Bishop Frederick Hopkins: "In 1898, the Sisters of the Holy Family (colored) came to the Mission." Frederick C. Hopkins, "The Catholic Church in British Honduras (1851–1918)," *Catholic Historical Review* 4, no. 3 (October 1918): 311. The Oblate Sisters of Providence were also omitted from the list of female religious congregations in the Baltimore Archdiocesan Catholic Directories and listed instead under charitable associations. Morrow, *Persons of Color*, 115–41.
34. White congregations working with African Americans also seem to have taken this low-keyed approach. Historian Suellen Hoy writes of the Sisters of the Blessed Sacrament: "They also shunned publicity and avoided politics, especially in black neighborhoods. From unpleasant experiences they had learned that their efforts were less likely to provoke hostile or violent reactions if they eluded public notice." Suellen Hoy, "Lives on the Color Line: Catholic Sisters and African Americans in Chicago, 1890s–1960s," *U.S. Catholic Historian* 22, no. 1 (Winter 2004): 74.
35. Deggs, *No Cross*, 24–25. Sister Borgia Hart adds more details on this point: "[P]rotests against the Habit were registered by another Congregation who thought the bonnet resembled too closely that of their lay Sisters, and that the collar or guimpe could easily be mistaken for theirs. Very slight changes with the addition of the Cord of St. Joseph in white wool satisfied the malcontents." Hart, *Violets*, 20.
36. Hart, *Violets*, 20. It was not unusual for white congregations of sisters to also supplement their income by taking in sewing.
37. Ibid., 19.
38. Ibid.
39. Deggs, *No Cross*, 28–29. "[D]ark as the head of a jet pine" could be a misreading of Deggs's handwriting. Jet pin—referring to the small black

spheres capping straight pins at the time—seems to fit the context better. The author thanks one of the anonymous readers of this manuscript for pointing this out.

40. Deggs writes: "The differences between Sisters Juliette Gaudin and Josephine Charles were so striking that it caused the establishment of a new house or rather split house." Deggs, *No Cross*, 14.

41. Mary Francis Borgia Hart, "A History of the Congregation of the Sisters of the Holy Family of New Orleans" (Master's thesis, Xavier College, 1939), 23.

42. See comments of Gould and Nolan in Deggs, *No Cross*, 6–7. Diane Batts Morrow takes issue with Gould and Nolan's interpretation. She argues that "the Holy Family Sisters themselves imposed color, class, and caste restrictions on their membership" and that Gould and Nolan are unconvincing when they claim that "from their inception the sisters identified racially with the black slave and free people they evangelized." Correspondence from Diane Batts Morrow to the author, August 14, 2004; and Diane Batts Morrow, review of Deggs, *No Cross, No Crown*, in *Catholic Historical Review* 89, no. 1 (January 2003): 122. Cyprian Davis and Joseph Fichter agree with Morrow. See Davis, *History of Black Catholics*, 108; and Fichter, "White Church and Black Sisters," 36. Sister Sylvia Thibodeaux, superior general of the Holy Family Congregation from 1998 to 2006, claims that from the congregation's founding until the present many of the light-skinned, Franco–African American sisters have either consciously or unconsciously had a sense of superiority and entitlement resulting from the cultural mores of New Orleans society. She thinks that this attitude has had harmful effects on the community throughout its history and that the sisters must face up to it in order to eradicate it. Interview with Sister Sylvia Thibodeaux, May 12, 2008.

43. Hart, *Violets*, 71–72.

44. Deggs, *No Cross*, 9–10.

Chapter 2. Mother Austin Jones and the Early Mission

1. Deggs, *No Cross*, 187.

2. Gould and Nolan in Deggs, *No Cross*, xiii, 181.

3. John Hope Franklin and Alfred A. Moss, Jr., *From Slavery to Freedom: A History of African Americans* (New York: McGraw-Hill, 1994), 260–62; Gould and Nolan in Deggs, *No Cross*, 182–83; John B. Alberts, "Black Catholic Schools: The Josephite Parishes of New Orleans during the Jim Crow Era," *U.S. Catholic Historian* 12, no. 1 (Winter 1994): 82.

4. In his otherwise superb study, *A Class of Their Own: Black Teachers in the Segregated South* (Cambridge and London: Belknap Press of Harvard

University Press, 2007), Adam Fairclough makes no mention of the Sisters of the Holy Family or their contributions to the education of African Americans in the South. He is likewise silent on the Oblates of Providence. Although his book concentrates primarily on public schools, he takes care to mention the important contributions of Baptists to "dozens of elementary and secondary [African American] schools in Louisiana, Virginia, and other states" (11). Thus, it seems puzzling that he would ignore the important educational work of black Catholic sisters.

5. In the Garifuna language, "Garinagu" is the plural of "Garifuna." However, in this study the author will use Garifuna for singular and plural in order to avoid confusion.

6. Francis B. Arana, Sr., *The Garifuna Teachers: Their Contribution to Education in Belize* (Belize: No publisher listed, 2002), 4–5; "Lengthy Account of the Mission," *Woodstock Letters* 23 (1910), 345, quoted in Dries, *Missionary Movement*, 56.

7. *Response to God's Love: Commemorative Yearbook* (Belize: Privately printed, 1998), 27; *"We Celebrate Our Catholic Heritage,"* Three-page typed paper dated February 23, 1996, Belize Collection. Interviews with Sisters Boniface Adams, Barbara Marie Francis, and Eleanor Gillett, S.S.F., July 2003. Dries, *Missionary Movement*, 54; Muldrey, *Abounding in Mercy*.

8. Two-page typed paper in celebration of the 75th anniversary of the Sisters in Belize (1973), Belize Collection.

9. Hart, *Violets*, 23.

10. Sister Mary of the Rosary, "Builders of Belize (2)," 15–18.

11. Letter from the Sisters of the Holy Family to the Rt. Rev. S. Di Pietro, S.J., Vicar Apostolic of British Honduras, undated, Belize Collection.

12. Contract between the Right Rev. Salvatore Di Pietro, S.J., Vicar Apostolic of British Honduras, and Rev. Mother Austin of "the Holy Family" in New Orleans, Belize Collection. In a handwritten letter to Mother Austin from Father Frederick Hopkins, dated December 24, 1898, we learn that the British Honduran government, due to diminished revenues, had reduced grant-in-aid to schools by 20 percent, thereby cutting aid to Catholic schools by about $1,000 per annum. Thus, we know that in 1898 government support to Sacred Heart School did exist, but we do not know to what extent. From a handwritten note on the back of a March 22, 1904, copy of the original contract between Mother Austin and Bishop Di Pietro, we also know that Bishop Frederick Hopkins, Di Pietro's successor, at some unspecified time raised the sisters' salary from $60 to $80 and that new provisions by the British Honduran government gave the sisters about $140 in additional revenue. This note is dated December 1924 and signed by Bishop J. A. Murphy, S.J., who was the third vicar apostolic of Belize. The note does not state when the

additional revenue was instituted or whether the $140 was a monthly stipend or an annual sum. Both documents are in the Belize Collection.

13. Historians Carol Coburn and Martha Smith note that in the nineteenth and early twentieth centuries, "American sisters received salaries from parish schools that rarely met their basic living expenses." They add that it was common to underpay and devalue the work of sister-teachers and that at times they received no salaries at all. Likewise, pastors or bishops often promised adequate living accommodations that did not always materialize. It was not uncommon for some pastors to actually ask nuns to pay for their own housing. Indeed, after accepting an assignment in 1885 to teach at St. Augustine's School in Mother Austin's hometown of Donaldsonville, the Sisters of the Holy Family were obliged to live in a barn owned by the Sisters of Charity. The building was partitioned in half, with the sisters living on one side and the farm animals on the other. See Coburn and Smith, *Spirited Lives*, 144–45; Hart, *Violets*, 30.

14. The term "nun" canonically refers only to religious women who live a contemplative or cloistered life behind closed doors. Those who are involved in a more activist apostolate are limited to the title "sister" or "mother." To avoid redundancy of terms, however, the author will on rare occasion resort to the colloquial "nun" to refer to the Holy Family Sisters.

15. Letter from Salvatore Di Pietro, S.J., to "Your Grace," April, 13, 1898, Belize Collection.

16. Ibid.

17. "Nassau Papers," *The Children of Providence* (1921–1922), 7, quoted in Dries, *Missionary Movements*, 47.

18. Hart, "Violets," 463.

19. This was also true for the New Orleans–based Mercy Sisters. The Jesuits in British Honduras were also frequently forced to leave the country due to illness. See Hunter, *Sisters of Mercy in Belize;* and Buhler, *History of the Catholic Church in Belize.*

20. Hart, "Violets," 464–65; *The (Belize) Clarion* (February 16, 1935); and "Sisters who are Buried in Stann Creek Cemetery," one typed page taken from Stann Creek church records. Both are located in the Belize Collection. A letter from M. Antillach, S.J., to Mother Austin Jones, May 17, 1899, Belize Collection, notes that Sr. Emmanuel Thompson had returned to New Orleans slightly more than a year after her arrival in Stann Creek. Although the letter does not give the reason for her return, it may have been for health reasons.

21. When the Mercy Sisters first heard the "Carib" (Garifuna) language upon their arrival in Belize City in 1883, they recorded their impressions in their Annals: "Carib, a dialect which seemed to our ears a sort of cross

between Chinese and Hottentot." Annals of St. Catherine's Convent, Belize City, quoted in Hunter, *Sisters of Mercy*, 11.

22. Hart, "Violets," 463. In the nineteenth and early twentieth centuries, African American Protestant missionaries working in Africa "were not as ethnocentric as white missionaries, but they did condemn indigenous African cultures as inferior." See Walter L. Williams, "The Missionary: Introduction," in *Black Americans and the Missionary Movement in Africa*, ed. Sylvia M. Jacobs (Westport, CT: Greenwood Press, 1982), 132. The decision of the Holy Family missionary sisters in British Honduras to teach in English and limit their pupils' use of their native tongue to outside the classroom may be an indication of a similar attitude. It must be said, however, that nowhere in the archives of the Holy Family Sisters in British Honduras does one find any document in which a sister refers to the Garifuna people or their culture as inferior. Bishop Di Pietro does so, however, noting that the sisters should be able to "civilize not only the children but the adults" (see note 16 above), but there is no indication from archival material that the sisters held a similar attitude.

23. The Belize Collection contains Sister Mary Dominica's "1st Class Provisional Certificate" dated May 3, 1898, and her "Honorary Teacher's Certificate, First Class" dated February 11, 1899. A letter from Father Frederick Hopkins to Mother Austin, December 24, 1898, Belize Collection, notes that Sister Rita Mather as well as Sister Dominica had received first-class teacher's certificates.

24. "Prospectus: Convent of Our Lady of Mercy, Belize City," cited in Hunter, *Sisters of Mercy*, 15.

25. Sylvia M. Jacobs, "The Historical Role of Afro-Americans in American Missionary Efforts in Africa," in *Black Americans and the Missionary Movement in Africa*, ed. Jacobs, 25.

26. *Golden Rays through Clouded Years, 1898–1948* (Belize: The Commercial Press, 1948).

27. This comes from the handwritten recollections of an elderly Dangriga woman who had been a student of the sisters when they first came to Sacred Heart. The two-page document is dated May 10, 1989, Belize Collection. The woman's name is unclear but appears to be L. Califis or Califo.

28. Mary of the Rosary Heisser, "Builders of Belize," 17.

29. Ibid. "Report on the Stann Creek Mission" (1948), 5, Belize Collection; "Response to God's Love," 5; photocopied page 8 from "Call to Serve," Belize Collection. "Call to Serve" is a Belize church publication with information on all Catholic religious congregations working in Belize.

30. Letter from M. Antillach, S.J., to Mother Austin Jones, May 17, 1899, Belize Collection.

31. Ibid.

32. Ibid.

33. Letter to the author from Sister M. Carolyn Leslie, S.S.F., archivist, Sisters of the Holy Family, New Orleans, April 26, 2004.

34. Typed notes from a 1989 taped interview of the recollections of Leopoldina Arana (at the time 86 years old), Victoria Sorenzo (83 years old), Amelia Cayetana Ramos (84 years old), Clothilda Servio (95 years old), Belize Collection. From these notes it is evident that Sister Emmanuel returned to Stann Creek.

35. Hart, "Violets," 463.

Chapter 3. Trouble with the Bishop

1. Arana, *Garifuna Teachers*, 5; Hunter, *Sisters of Mercy in Belize*, 73–74.

2. Handwritten letter from Bishop Frederick C. Hopkins to Mother Elizabeth [Bowie], July 4, 1910, Belize Collection.

3. Ibid.

4. Ibid.

5. Handwritten letter from Sister Bernadette to Archbishop Blenk, July 4, 1916, Belize Collection.

6. Handwritten letter from Bishop Hopkins to Mother Elizabeth, January 25, 1917, Belize Collection.

7. Handwritten letter from Bishop Hopkins to "Very Rev. and dear Father" [Jules B. Jeanmard], October 4, 1917, Belize Collection.

8. Ibid.

9. Ibid.

10. Ibid.

11. Typed copy of original letter from "Your Lordship's humble servant in Christ [Jules B. Jeanmard]" to Right Reverend Frederick C. Hopkins, S.J., October 20, 1917, Belize Collection. Jeanmard was soon named the first bishop of the new Diocese of Lafayette, Louisiana. This diocese by 1928 contained about 25 percent of all black U.S. Catholics, making it the nation's diocese with the largest number of Catholic African Americans. Although Jeanmard held some of the stereotypical racist views of white Southerners, he nevertheless seems to have had some sympathy, albeit paternalistic, for black Catholics. As a result of pressure from Cardinal Amleto Cicognani, the apostolic delegate to the United States, he reluctantly agreed in 1934 to accept four African American priests into his diocese to work at all-black parishes, but under the direct supervision of a white priest in a nearby parish. This white priest soon had to be replaced due to his racial biases and belligerent behavior. The four black priests, members of the Divine Word Missionary Society and

the first graduates of this congregation's new seminary for African Americans at Bay St. Louis, Mississippi, eventually gained the respect of Jeanmard, who wrote glowing reports on their ministry to Cicognani. The Lafayette Diocese was the first in the South to accept black priests and remained the only one to do so until the 1940s. In 1941 there were nine black Divine Word priests working in the Lafayette Diocese. In 1947, Jeanmard again broke new ground when he accepted the diocese's first African American candidate for the priesthood. Although the young man left the seminary after one year, a second candidate, Louis Le Doux, was ordained in 1952, thus making Jeanmard the first bishop in the Deep South to ordain a black man for the diocesan clergy. It seems that Jeanmard's benign paternalism toward blacks over time evolved into respect and admiration at least for black priests. See Ochs, *Desegregating the Altar*, 261–62, 331–59, 404–5.

12. "Your Lordship's humble servant in Christ" [Jeanmard] to Hopkins, October 20, 1917. The Holy Family Sisters were not alone in occasionally allowing their missionaries in British Honduras to return home for a short visit. Sister Yvonne Hunter reports: "It was the policy of the Reverend Mother [of the Sisters of Mercy] to bring the Sisters periodically to the Motherhouse in New Orleans for a change of climate." Hunter, *Sisters of Mercy*, 27.

13. The health problems that plagued the Holy Family Sisters also plagued the other missionary orders and congregations working in British Honduras, and Bishop Hopkins was well aware of this. Several Jesuits and Sisters of Mercy died from tropical sicknesses while serving in British Honduras; and countless others, including Bishop Di Pietro, were forced to leave the colony for extended periods because they had contracted yellow fever, malaria, or numerous other diseases. Indeed, as Bishop Hopkins himself reports, all three Mount Carmel Sisters who came to the colony in 1899 to staff a school in Orange Walk had to close their mission and return to New Orleans after only two years due to constant sickness. See Hopkins, "The Catholic Church in British Honduras," 311.

14. "Your Lordship's humble servant in Christ" [Jeanmard] to Hopkins, October 20, 1917.

15. Ibid.
16. Ibid.
17. Ibid.
18. Ibid.
19. Ibid.

20. Much later, in the late 1970s and again in the 1990s, attempts would be made by the Holy Family Sisters to create an indigenous community of sisters in Belize. These attempts, which are discussed in chapter 8, failed.

21. Hart, "Violets," 465.

22. In 1931, Sister Mary of Lourdes Gray was the first to take her final vows in Stann Creek; in 1935, Sister Mary Cecilia Green did likewise. Both were U.S.-born sisters assigned to British Honduras. Hart, "Violets," 465.

23. Handwritten letter from Bishop Hopkins to Mother Elizabeth, November 23, 1917, Belize Collection.

24. Ibid.

25. The Sisters of the Holy Family, because of their extensive teaching commitments, would only have been able to take college classes during the summer months. But, due to the school segregation laws of Louisiana, there was no institution of higher learning open to them in New Orleans when Hopkins was writing his letters (1910–1917). Xavier University, the only black Catholic university in the United States, opened its doors in 1916 but was not certified to grant college credits for prospective teachers until years later. Since nuns were not permitted to attend secular colleges and universities, most congregations sent their sisters during the summer months to Catholic University in Washington, DC, but Catholic University, like virtually all Catholic institutions of higher learning at this time, refused to accept blacks. (Catholic University only lifted its ban on African American students in 1931.) It seemed that the Holy Family Sisters' problem was finally solved beginning in June 1921, when, at the request of Monsignor John E. Burke, director of the Board for Mission Work among the Colored, six Sisters of Charity of Seton Hill College in Greensburg, Pennsylvania, volunteered to come to New Orleans each summer to conduct specially arranged, six-week-long college semesters for Holy Family nuns at the latter's motherhouse. Loyola University of New Orleans agreed to grant credit for the courses and the Board of Missions paid the fees. As a result of this program, some Holy Family Sisters assigned to British Honduras were undoubtedly better educated than their predecessors. Unfortunately, however, in 1938, when Loyola University was attempting to obtain certification from the Southern Association of Colleges, its president, Father Harold Gaudin, S.J., fearing protests about granting credits to blacks, terminated the program. He also removed all transcript records for black sisters who had matriculated there. As a result, those women who had taken courses but had not yet earned their bachelor degrees lost all the credits they had earned and had to retake their coursework at Xavier. See Hart, *Violets*, 78; Davis, *History of Black Catholics*, 215–18; and Joseph H. Fichter, "First Black Students at Loyola University: A Strategy to Obtain Teacher Certification," *Journal of Negro Education* 56 (Fall 1987): 535–49. The author thanks Sister Patricia Byrne, C.S.J., for making him aware of Fichter's article.

26. Dries, *Missionary Movement*, 47.

27. In their publications on the Catholic Church in Belize, Jesuit writers say very little about the four congregations of religious women who worked

there in collaboration with the Society of Jesus. Bishop Hopkins, in his eleven-page "Catholic Church in British Honduras," devotes only twenty-six lines to the Sisters of Mercy, four to the Mount Carmel Sisters, who came to British Honduras in 1899 but left after only two years in the colony, ten to the Congregation of Pious Missions (Pallottine Sisters), and six to the Holy Family Sisters, whom he lists with "(colored)" after their introduction. Gilbert Garragahn, S.J., in his three-volume *The Jesuits of the Middle United States* (www.Jesuitarchives.org), has one chapter on Jesuit home and foreign missions. Although he discusses in detail the work of the Jesuits in British Honduras, he makes no mention whatsoever of any of the congregations of sisters who staffed the schools of the Jesuit parishes there. Buhler, whose 96-page *History of the Catholic Church in Belize* ends in the year 1950, mentions the Mercy Sisters on sixty-five lines, the Pallottines on ninety-one, the Mount Carmel nuns on seventeen, and the Holy Family Sisters on nineteen. His neglect of the Holy Family Congregation is amazing, considering that by 1950 they had served in British Honduras for fifty-two years. The white Mount Carmel Sisters, who receive only two lines fewer than the Holy Family, had spent only two years there.

28. Hopkins, "The Catholic Church in British Honduras," 310–11.
29. Buhler, *History of the Catholic Church in Belize,* 70.
30. Muldrey, *Abounding in Mercy,* 312.
31. Hunter, *Sisters of Mercy,* 26.
32. The Propagation of the Faith is the Vatican institution in charge of foreign missions.
33. Hunter, *Sisters of Mercy,* 28.
34. Muldrey, *Abounding in Mercy,* 323–24.
35. Hunter, *Sisters of Mercy,* 35–48.
36. St. Catherine Convent Archives, quoted in ibid., 48.
37. In the period from 1914 to 1931, Bishop Hopkins and his episcopal successors recruited the vast majority of postulants for the British Honduras foundation from Ireland. See Hunter, *Sisters of Mercy,* 61. In 1931, on orders from the Vatican, the Mercy Sisters in British Honduras affiliated with the Mercy Sisters of Providence, Rhode Island.

Chapter 4. The 1920s to the Second Vatican Council

1. Hart, *Violets,* 81.
2. Ibid.
3. Records: Sacred Heart School, Stann Creek, Belize Collection. The records begin in 1936 and end in 1948.

4. Typed letter from Bishop Joseph A. Murphy, S.J., to Mother Elizabeth, October 16, 1936, Belize Collection.

5. "Report on the Stann Creek Mission" (no date but from the 1940s), eight typed pages, Belize Collection; Sister Mary of the Rosary, "Builders of Belize," 17.

6. Sacred Heart School: Records, Belize Collection.

7. As Angelyn Dries points out, "[S]tandard mission theory identified women missionaries as 'auxiliary' to the task of mission. Women sometimes used the term themselves, but little evidence is found that they estimated themselves or what they did as less important than the clergy. Over the decades, women's attention to the health, education, and spiritual needs of people built up the social service and educational institutions wherever they served." Angelyn Dries, "U.S. Catholic Women and Mission: Integral or Auxiliary?" *Missiology: An International Review* 33, no. 3 (July 2005): 301.

8. Karen M. Kennelly, C.S.J., "Foreign Missions and the Renewal Movement," *Review for Religious* 49 (May–June 1990): 451–59.

9. "Report on the Stann Creek Mission" (1948), 6; Sacred Heart School: Records.

10. Sister Mary of the Rosary, "Builders of Belize," 17; *Response to God's Love*, 5.

11. Kennelly, "Foreign Missions," 455.

12. "Religious Vocations to Sisters of the Holy Family, 1894–2001," Belize Collection.

13. Interview with Sister Barbara Marie Francis, July 2003.

14. Ibid.

15. Ibid. Undated correspondence from Sister Barbara Marie Francis to the author, received in September 2004; *Response to God's Love*, 76. Sister Barbara Marie died on February 12, 2008.

16. Interview with Sister Eleanor Gillett, July 2003.

17. Ibid.

18. Undated correspondence from Sister Rebecca Carlos Castillo to the author, received in September 2004.

19. Ibid.

20. Undated correspondence from Sister Esther Marie Estero to the author, received in September 2004.

21. Undated correspondence from Sister Veronica Ruth Lambey to the author, received in September 2004.

22. Undated correspondence from Sister Joan Flores to the author, received in September 2004.

23. *Response to God's Love*, 4, 49–58.

24. Ibid. "With the appointment of Father Marin as pastor [of Sacred Heart] in January 1948, Stann Creek became a Diocesan parish, instead of a

Jesuit mission as before. It is the only place in the colony so classed." From "Report on the Stann Creek Mission" (1948), 6, Belize Collection. Later, Jesuits would again serve at Sacred Heart.

25. *Response to God's Love*, 4, 53–58.

26. Interview with Sister Mary Bertille Hazeur, July 2003.

27. Ibid.

28. Interview with Sister Mary Adrian Johnson, July 2003.

29. Ibid.

30. Until the early 1980s and in some cases even later, it was common for female religious communities to be charged with this work. As one nun told the current writer, "it exhausted the sisters."

31. Interview with Sister Carolyn Leslie, July 2003.

32. For the hurricane see reports in the *New Orleans Times-Picayune*, November 3, 1961; and "Hurricane Hattie—A Harrowing Ten Days," *Jesuit Bulletin* [St. Louis] (February 1962): 12.

33. Typed notation entitled "Newspaper accounts of Hurricane 'Hattie' in Belize and Stann Creek, British Honduras, Central America," Belize Collection.

Chapter 5.   Changes in the 1950s through the Early 1970s

1. See McNamara, *Sisters in Arms*, 613–14.

2. Koehlinger, *New Nuns*, 6.

3. Ibid., 6.

4. Ibid., 6–7.

5. Patricia Byrne, "In the Parish but Not of It: Sisters," in *Transforming Parish Ministry: The Changing Roles of Catholic Clergy, Laity, and Women Religious*, ed. Jay P. Dolan, R. Scott Appleby, Patricia Byrne, and Debra Campbell (New York: Crossroad, 1990), 109–200.

6. Quiñonez and Turner, *Transformation*, 67.

7. Byrne, "In the Parish," 140–41; Quiñonez and Turner, *Transformation*, 67; Sally Witt, C.S.J., *Sisters of the North Country: The History of the Sisters of Saint Joseph of the Diocese of Ogdensburg, Watertown, New York* (Watertown, NY: Sisters of St. Joseph, 2005), 129.

8. Koehlinger, *New Nuns*, 24–27.

9. Ibid., 27.

10. Byrne, "In the Parish," 154.

11. Cardinal Leon Joseph Suenens, *The Nun in the World: New Dimensions of the Modern Apostolate* (Westminster, MD: Newman Press, 1963), as cited by Byrne, "In the Parish," 157.

12. Mary Schneider, *The Transformation of American Women Religious: The Sister Formation Conference as Catalyst for Change (1954–1964)* (South Bend, IN: Charles and Margaret Hall Cushwa Center for the Study of American Catholicism, University of Notre Dame, 1986). See also Beane, *From Framework to Freedom*.

13. Angelyn Dries, "Living in Ambiguity: A Paradigm Shift Experienced by the Sister Formation Movement," *Catholic Historical Review* 79, no. 3 (July 1993): 486–87.

14. Quiñonez and Turner, *Transformation*, 11–15, 20–22; Witt, *Sisters of the North Country*, 199 and 203.

15. From the LCWR's mission statement. See http://www.lcwr.org

16. Mary Ewens, O.P., "Women in the Convent," in *American Catholic Women: A Historical Explanation*, ed. Karen Kennelly, C.S.J. (New York: Macmillan, 1989), 41.

17. "Decree on the Appropriate Renewal of Religious Life," in *The Documents of Vatican II*, ed. Walter M. Abbot, S.J. (New York: Guild Press, 1966), 469.

18. Later, in 1979 at the Third Latin American Bishops' Conference at Puebla, Mexico, the bishops expanded on what they had proclaimed at Medellín, Colombia, calling on the church to make "a preferential option for the poor." For more on these conferences see Edward L. Cleary, *Crisis and Change: The Church in Latin America Today* (Maryknoll, NY: Orbis Books, 1985); Enrique Dussel, *De Medellín a Puebla: Una década de sangre y esperanza* (Mexico City: Centro de Estudios Ecuménicos, 1979); and John Eagleson and Philip Scharper, eds., *Pueblo and Beyond* (Maryknoll, NY: Orbis Books, 1979).

19. Byrne, "In the Parish," 164.

20. Ibid., 166.

21. Quiñonez and Turner, *Transformation*, 74.

22. The Superior General's 1958–1964 Report to the Holy Family Congregation, Archives of the Holy Family Sisters, New Orleans.

23. The juniorate program refers to the formation of sisters who have completed their novitiate and taken temporary vows. In other words, they were not yet fully professed.

24. The Superior General's 1958–1964 Report.

25. As a result of the influence of the SFC and LCWR, between 1959 and the early 1970s many female religious congregations throughout the United States established junior colleges for the training of their young sisters. Thus, the Holy Family Sisters were following a familiar pattern and were not unique.

26. The Superior General's 1958–1964 Report.

27. Theresa A. Rector, "Black Nuns as Educators," *Journal of Negro Education* 51, no. 3 (1982): 249.

28. The Superior General's 1964–1970 Report to the Holy Family Congregation, Archives of the Holy Family Sisters, New Orleans.

29. During the 1970s, at least four Holy Family Sisters who would later be assigned to Belize studied at the College of St. Teresa in Winona. Correspondence from Sister Joan Flores to the current author, August 2010.

30. The Superior General's 1958–1964 Report.

31. Correspondence from Sister Joan Flores to the author, August 2010. Several professed sisters joined those in the formation program in these classes at Notre Dame Seminary.

32. Program information found in the Archives of the Holy Family Sisters, New Orleans.

33. Correspondence from Sister Carolyn Leslie to the author, August 2010.

34. Ibid.

35. Correspondence from Sister Joan Flores and Sister Carolyn Leslie to the author, August 2010.

36. Correspondence from Sister Coletta Dunn, O.S.F., to the author, August 11, 2010.

37. Correspondence from Sister Marie Colette Roy, O.S.F., to the author, August 12, 2010. He thanks Sisters Angelyn Dries, O.S.F., and Justine Peter, O.S.F., for putting him in touch with Sisters Coletta and Colette.

38. Correspondence from Sisters Carolyn Leslie and Joan Flores to the author, August 2010. The Liturgy of the Hours is the Divine Office, communal prayers taken from the Roman breviary, which were prayed daily by the sisters.

39. Correspondence from Sister Joan Flores to the author, August 2010.

40. Ibid.

41. Correspondence from Sister Carolyn Leslie to the author, August 2010.

42. Correspondence from Sister Joan Flores to the author, August 2010.

43. Correspondence from Sister Carolyn Leslie to the author, August 2010.

44. Ibid.

45. Louise Marie Bryan, "History of the National Black Sisters' Conference," in *Celibate Black Commitment: Report of the Third Annual National Black Sisters' Conference* [August 9–15, 1970, University of Notre Dame] (Pittsburgh: NBSC, 1971), 2–9. Bryan gives August 1968 as the founding date for the Conference, but Cyprian Davis and Jamie Phelps list August 1969. See *The Survival of Soul: National Black Sisters' Conference Position Paper, 1969*, in *"Stamped With the Image of God": African Americans as God's Image in*

Black, ed. Cyprian Davis and Jamie Phelps (Maryknoll, NY: Orbis Books, 2003), 114–16.

46. M. Shawn Copeland, "A Cadre of Women Religious Committed to Black Liberation: The National Black Sisters' Conference," *U.S. Catholic Historian* 14, no. 1 (Winter 1996): 123. Copeland, who played an important role in the early years of the Conference and was one of its leading officers, was at the time a Dominican nun. She has since left the convent and is today a professor of theology at Boston College.

47. Ibid., 123–24.

48. Correspondence from Sister Sylvia Thibodeaux to the author, August 2010.

49. Copeland, "A Cadre of Women Religious," 130 note 23.

50. Ibid., 135.

51. Ibid., 138.

52. Ibid., 137 note 35.

53. Ibid., 139. Interview with M. Shawn Copeland, June 24, 2010.

54. Correspondence from Sister Jean Flores to the author, August 2010.

55. Copeland, "A Cadre of Women Religious," 142–43. Interview with Copeland, June 24, 2010; interview with Sister Sylvia Thibodeaux, August 31, 2010.

56. In her June 24, 2010, interview with the author, M. Shawn Copeland, a longtime leader in the NBSC, remarked that over the years she has come to believe that these sisters had a valid point.

57. Correspondence from Sister Sylvia Thibodeaux to the author, August 2010.

58. Interview with Sister Sylvia Thibodeaux, August 31, 2010.

59. According to Holy Family oral tradition, when Mother Josephine Charles sent a novice wearing the new religious habit of the congregation to Archbishop Perché of New Orleans, he angrily demanded that the novice remove the clothing because she was of African descent and therefore had no right to dress as a sister. See Davis, *History of Black Catholics*, 107–8; Hart, *Violets*, 20–21; and Brett, "Race Issues and Conflict," 121–22.

60. As with most other female religious congregations, Sister Borgia Hart notes that religious vocations to the Holy Family Congregation were increasing in the late 1950s and early 1960s. See Hart, *Violets*, 116.

61. For this expansion, see Hart, *Violets*, 101–19.

62. For instance, after the Sisters of Charity of Nazareth came to Dangriga in the mid-1970s to do mission work, two Garifuna women, Sisters Barbara Flores and Rose Johnson, joined their congregation. Had admission into that community been closed to black women, there is certainly a good possibility that they would have chosen to enter the Holy Family Congregation.

The author thanks Sister Mary Ellen Doyle for her correspondence, dated July 24, 2007, informing him of the Garifuna sisters in her community.

63. Letter from Rev. Wm. P. Thro, S.J., to Mother Anselm, March 11, 1968, Belize Collection.

64. Ibid.

65. Ibid.

66. Ibid.

67. Ibid.

68. Letter from Sister Cecilia Higinio to the Honourable George Price, Premier, September 29, 1971, Belize Collection.

69. Letter from Rev. Howard C. Oliver, S.J., to the Honourable George Price, Premier, September 28, 1971, Belize Collection.

70. Letter from Rev. Howard C. Oliver, S.J., Chairman [of the committee for the Stann Creek Ecumenical High School] to Mr. E. P. York, Minister of Education, October 8, 1971, Belize Collection.

71. *Response to God's Love,* 5. A one-page, untitled document on the history and status of Ecumenical High School, dated May 17, 1990, Belize Collection, makes it clear that the school was "the amalgamation of three christian [sic] schools." Yet the author could find no mention of the name of the Methodist school.

72. Letter from Bishop R. L. Hodapp, S.J., to Mother Rose of Lima Hazeur, S.S.F., May 9, 1974, Belize Collection.

73. Letter from Father Howard C. Oliver, S.J., to Mother Rose of Lima Hazeur, S.S.F., April 25, 1974.

74. Ibid.

75. [Ecumenical High School] Staff List, 1978–1979, Belize Collection. Sister Joseph Ellen Cavalier, who served as the last principal of Austin High School in 1974, taught at Ecumenical from 1977 to 1980 and again from 1992 through 1994. She had later returned to Dangriga for two summers where she worked with Sister Judith Therese Barial in her Christian Youth Enrichment program, emphasizing the need for Belizean young people to retain their traditional culture. (Interview with Sister Joseph Ellen Cavalier, May 8, 2008.) Sister Jennie Jones taught at Ecumenical from 1977 to 1980. Since then she has taught at Holy Family schools in the United States.

76. Untitled one-page document on the history and status of Ecumenical High School, May 17, 1990, Belize Collection.

77. Ibid.

78. Ibid.

79. The Christian Youth Enrichment program and its eventual transformation into Delille Academy is discussed in chapter 7.

80. Letter from Sister Hortensia Maria Flowers to Sister Carolyn Leslie, February 1995, Belize Collection.

81. *News from Holy Family Convent–Dangriga*. One-page, single-spaced document, Belize Collection. Although undated, internal contents make it clear that it is from 1995.

82. Letter from Sister Hortensia Maria Flowers to Sister Carolyn Leslie, February 1995, Belize Collection. Sisters who were over fifty-five could apply to the Ministry of Education for an exemption from mandatory retirement. This was a time-consuming process, however, and there was no guarantee that a sister's request would be granted.

83. Interviews with Sisters Clare of Assisi Pierre and Carolyn Leslie, May 8, 2008, and with Sister Sylvia Thibodeaux, May 12, 2008.

84. When the author could find no example of the existence of a Catholic-Protestant ecumenical high school prior to 1974, he sent a query to the Yale-Edinburgh University Missions List, a global record of scholars who specialize in Catholic or Protestant missionary history. Although he received several replies, no one knew of the existence of a joint Catholic-Protestant high school that predated that of Ecumenical High in Dangriga. Professor Elizabeth Koepping of the Divinity School of the University of Edinburgh knew of several such schools in the United Kingdom, but none predated 1975. She referred the current author to the forty-four-page online *Joint Protestant-Roman Catholic Schools, Colleges and Universities, International Directory, 2007* (www.nicie.org/archive/internationaldirectory04.pdf). There, nineteen ecumenical high schools, colleges, and universities are listed in the United Kingdom, one in the United States, and one in Australia. The oldest is St. Aidan's Church of England High School–St. John Fisher Catholic High School. Although these two schools began to integrate their resources and faculty in 1973, they remained separate schools with separate names and identities. St. Cuthbert is cited as the "first Joint Catholic and Church of England Comprehensive school in Britain." St. Cuthbert's was originally a Catholic high school in Devon, which needed to increase its enrollment in order to become financially secure. The Anglicans of the area had long sought an Anglican secondary school but did not anticipate having enough students to justify the construction of a new facility. Consequently, after several months of negotiations, the Catholic Diocese of Plymouth and the Anglican Diocese of Exeter reached an agreement in 1975 to transform St. Cuthbert into the United Kingdom's first joint Catholic-Protestant high school. See *Joint Protestant-Roman Catholic Schools, Colleges and Universities, International Directory, 2007*, especially 10–11. The author thanks Professor Koepping for bringing this directory to his attention. It is interesting to note that the *Directory* does not list the establishment of Ecumenical High School of Dangriga in 1974. This is an oversight that needs to be corrected.

85. Interview with Sister Joseph Ellen Cavalier, the last principal of Austin High School, May 8, 2008.

Chapter 6.   Problems over Language and Inculturation

1. "Inculturation" is a term used in Roman Catholic missiology and defined by Aylward Shorter as "the creative and dynamic relationship between the Christian message and a culture or cultures." See Aylward Shorter, *Towards a Theology of Inculturation* (Maryknoll, NY: Orbis Books, 1988), 11. Proponents of this form of evangelization claim that it can be traced back as far as Saint Paul, as well as to Saint Patrick in Ireland in the fifth century, to Saints Cyril and Methodius in Eastern Europe in the ninth century, and to the Jesuits Matteo Ricci and Adam Schall von Bell in China in the seventeenth century. By the end of the seventeenth century, however, the papacy began to favor a more Eurocentric approach to Christian evangelization in an attempt to foster Roman Catholic uniformity. Inculturation was revived by the Second Vatican Council, especially in its document, *Gaudium et Spes*, which noted that Christianity should be taught in a way that is familiar to the people being evangelized, so that they do not view the faith as foreign to their way of life and therefore as irrelevant. For more on this topic see Shorter, *Towards a Theology of Inculturation*; and Peter Schineller, *A Handbook on Inculturation* (New York: Paulist Press, 1990).

2. For the movement for independence see Bolland, *Belize*; Assad Shoman, *Party Politics in Belize, 1950–1986* (Benque Viejo del Carmen, Belize: Cobula Productions, 1987); J. Fernández, *Belize: Case Study for Democracy in Central America* (Brookfield, VT: Gower, 1989); and Setzekorn, *Belize*, 215–35. The discussion of the struggle for independence in this study, however, is taken from Edward T. Brett, "Belize, national independence movement," in *International Encyclopedia of Revolution and Protest*, ed. Immanuel Ness (London and New York: Blackwell, 2009), 1:365–66.

3. Although the name of the city of Stann Creek now officially became Dangriga, the name of the district remained Stann Creek. The author wishes to thank Ms. Sylvia Flores, former mayor of Dangriga, for providing him with the official date of the city's name change.

4. Letter from R. L. Hodapp, S.J., D.D., Bishop of Belize, to Sister Rose of Lima Hazeur, S.S.F., March 30, 1974, Belize Collection.

5. Ibid.

6. Ibid.

7. Ibid.

8. The eight were Sisters Esther Marie Estero, who entered the congregation in 1945; Josita Marie Ogaldez, who entered in 1949; Evelyn Estrada, who entered in 1955; Veronica Ruth Lambey, Rebecca Carlos Castillo, and Joan Flores, all of whom entered in 1959; Jean Martínez, who entered in 1968; and Elyswith López, who entered in 1972.

9. Letter from Sister Sienna Marie Braxton to Mother Tekakwitha Vega, undated but from sometime in the summer of 1978, Belize Collection.

10. Letter from Mother M. Tekakwitha Vega to Sister Sienna Braxton, September 6, 1978, Belize Collection.

11. Letter from Sister Sienna Braxton to Mother Tekakwitha Vega, September 12, 1978, Belize Collection.

12. Letter from Sister Germaine Henry to Mother Tekakwitha Vega, undated but from September 1978, Belize Collection.

13. Letter from Sister Jennie Jones to Mother Tekakwitha Vega, undated but from September 1978, Belize Collection.

14. Letter from Sister John Mary Jackson to Mother Tekakwitha Vega, undated but from September 1978, Belize Collection.

15. Author's telephone interview with Sister John Mary Jackson, October 5, 2004.

16. Letter from Sister Joseph Ellen Cavalier to Mother Tekakwitha Vega, September 23, 1978, Belize Collection. In a more recent letter to the author, Sister Joseph Ellen notes: "My feelings today are exactly the same. I felt then, as I do now, that our praying in Garifuna was one way of our being more closely united with our Garifuna sisters." Letter from Sister Joseph Ellen Cavalier to the author, October 20, 2004.

17. Letter from Sister Jean Martínez to Mother Tekakwitha Vega, September 30, 1978, Belize Collection.

18. Ibid. In 1974, two Sisters of Charity of Nazareth, Sister Mary Lynn Fields and Sister Susan Gatz, spent the summer in Dangriga with the Garifuna people. The president of the Kentucky-based congregation, Sister Barbara Thomas, had sent them at the request of the Jesuits to look into possible mission work there. In 1975 the Sisters of Charity began assisting the Jesuit pastor of Sacred Heart Parish, and soon four members of the congregation were working full-time in Belize. Their primary apostolate was to develop lay leadership, and consequently they set up a lay ministry program in Dangriga. Soon the sisters expanded this program to the Cayo and San Antonio Districts. Eventually the congregation extended their apostolate to include education and health care. By the end of the twentieth century there were six Sisters of Charity of Nazareth assigned to mission work in Belize. Unlike the Sisters of the Holy Family, the Charity Congregation had previous missionary experience in India and elsewhere before beginning their labors in Belize. See Sister Mary Ransom Burke, S.C.N., *We Drank the Water: Nazareth in Belize* (Louisville, KY: Harmony House, 2003).

19. Letter from Sister Jean Martínez to Mother Tekakwitha Vega, September 30, 1978, Belize Collection.

20. Ibid.

21. Letter from Sister Stephen [Franco] to all priests and religious men and women of Belize, September 17, 1978, Belize Collection.
22. Ibid.
23. Letter from Sister Evelyn Estrada to Mother Tekakwitha Vega, September 28, 1978, Belize Collection.
24. Ibid.
25. Ibid.
26. Ibid.
27. Ibid.
28. This decree of the general council was transcribed and sent to the author by Sister Carolyn Leslie, archivist of the Holy Family Sisters. The original can be found in the Holy Family Archives in New Orleans.
29. Letter from Mother Tekakwitha Vega to the Sisters of Dangriga, October 24, 1978, Belize Collection.
30. Ibid.
31. Belizean Creoles are English-speaking people of mixed African and European ancestry. They are descendants of British woodcutters and their African slaves and comprise about half of the population of modern-day Belize. Most live in Belize City. According to William David Setzekorn, "the urban Creole still hesitates to accept this strange Negro [the Garifuna] who speaks an Indian language-form and retains Indian cultural traits." He adds that the Garifuna likewise holds "a certain amount of hostility toward the Creole," although in the latter decades of the twentieth century this mutual dislike for each other had begun to gradually break down. See Setzekorn, *Formerly British Honduras*, 18–23.
32. The council members in 1978 were North American Sisters Mary de Chantal St. Julien, Jean Carter, Maria Petra Simms, and M. Boniface Adams. The Belizeans were Sister Barbara Marie Francis, who served in Dangriga from 1947 to 1959, and Sister Carolyn Leslie, who served there from 1949 to 1951 and from 1955 to 1963. This information was sent to the author by Sister Carolyn Leslie in answer to his query, in a letter dated July 21, 2007. Lists of council members can be found in the Holy Family Archives in New Orleans.
33. Letter from Sister Sienna Marie Braxton to Mother Tekakwitha Vega, December 23, 1978, Belize Collection.
34. Letter from Sister Sienna Marie Braxton to Mother Tekakwitha Vega, February 18, 1979, Belize Collection.
35. Letter from Sister Jennie Jones to Mother Tekakwitha Vega, March 25, 1979, Belize Collection.
36. Interview with Sister Sylvia Thibodeaux, May 12, 2008.
37. Reservations were also established for the Maya.
38. Bollard, *Belize*, 26.
39. Setzekorn, *Formerly British Honduras*, 22.

40. Letter from Sister Carolyn Leslie to the author, September 23, 2004.
41. Letter from Sister Joseph Ellen Cavalier to the author, October 20, 2004; telephone call from Sister John Mary Jackson to the author, October 5, 2004. Although she did not respond to my inquiry in 2004, later in July 2010, after reading this chapter, Sister Jean Martínez in a telephone conversation with the author stated that she "agreed with every word of chapter 6."
42. Letter from Sister Sienna Marie Braxton to the author, October 9, 2004. Sister Sienna died at the motherhouse in New Orleans on April 13, 2007.
43. "Religious Vocations to Sisters of the Holy Family, 1894–2001," Belize Collection; 2007 letter from Sister Carolyn Leslie to the author.
44. In 1972 there were 117,103 sisters in Latin America. The number increased to 128,875 by 2001 and grew to 138,123 by 2004. See *Statistical Yearbook of the Church, 2003;* and *Catholic Almanac, 2006.* These statistics can also be found on the "Religion in Latin America" website of the University of Texas at Austin.
45. *Catholic Almanac, 2006.* Growth rates in all five Central American countries were less dramatic from 2001 to 2004.
46. *Catholic Almanac, 2006.* The *Statistical Yearbook of the Church, 2003* puts the 2001 number of sisters in Belize much lower at only 63. If this is correct, it would mean a 36 percent reduction.
47. As will be shown later, there are other reasons that must be taken into consideration when attempting to determine why an indigenous community did not succeed.
48. Sister Barbara Flores, responses to questions from the author, February 7, 2008.
49. Ibid.
50. Ibid.

Chapter 7.   Mission Experiences of Three Holy Family Sisters

1. Letter from Mother M. Tekakwitha Vega, S.S.F., to Sisters of the Holy Family, Dangriga, Belize, March 6, 1980, Belize Collection.
2. Ibid.
3. See Byrne, "In the Parish."
4. Interview with Sister Clare of Assisi Pierre, July 2003.
5. Ibid.
6. Ibid.
7. Ibid.
8. Ibid.

9. See letter from Mother Rose de Lima Hazeur, S.S.F., to Rev. James Short, S.J., March 13, 1987, and letter from Mother Rose de Lima Hazeur, S.S.F., to Sister Clare of Assisi [Pierre], May 22, 1987, both in Belize Collection.

10. Letter from Mother Rose de Lima Hazeur, S.S.F., to Rev. James Short, S.J., September 11, 1987, Belize Collection.

11. Ibid.

12. Ibid.

13. Sister Lucia Carl, "My Perspective as an American on Belize and Belizean Life," three-paged, undated, typed document, Belize Collection.

14. Ibid.

15. Interview with Sister Clare of Assisi Pierre, July 2003.

16. Interview with Sister Clare of Assisi Pierre, May 8, 2008.

17. Ibid.

18. Interview with Sister Clare of Assisi Pierre, July 2003.

19. Ibid.

20. Letter from Father Frank Schmidt to Sister Clare of Assisi Pierre, February 29, 1992, Belize Collection.

21. Letter from Father Schmidt to Sister Clare of Assisi Pierre, June 3, 1992, Belize Collection.

22. In the twentieth century, several Jamaican women joined the Holy Family Congregation. Five of these have served in Belize. For the list of sisters who have worked in Belize since 1898, see Appendix A.

23. Sister Hortensia Maria Flowers, "House Report, Dangriga Town, Belize, Central America, 1994–1995," 2–3; *News from Holy Family Convent–Dangriga*, 1995, Belize Collection.

24. Interview with Sister Judith Barial, July 2003.

25. Ibid.

26. Ibid.; "Holy Family Sister Initiates CYE Program," one-page document dated September 25, 1989, Belize Collection.

27. "Holy Family Sisters helps [sic] young people of Dangriga through C.Y.E.," one-page, undated article (probably written in 1995), Belize Collection.

28. Ibid.

29. Interview with Sister Judith Barial, July 2003.

30. During the formative years from 1989 to 1991, the CYE received financial aid and support from the Blanch Walsh Charity Trust ($2,500 for operating costs) and the Little Way Association of England ($1,600 for the purchase of sewing machines). Mission clubs from St. Mary's Academy of New Orleans and Regina Caeli High School of Compton, California, also provided funds, as did family and friends of the sisters in the United States.

See "Delille's History," in *Horizon*, the Delille Academy Yearbook, 2001, 2; and "Holy Family Sisters helps [sic] young people of Dangriga through C.Y.E."

31. Interview with Sister Judith Barial, July 2003; "Holy Family Sister Initiates CYE Program"; *Response to God's Love*, 81.

32. "Holy Family Sister Initiates CYE Program."

33. Letter from Mother M. Rose de Lima Hazeur, S.S.F., to Mr. Austin Flores, Principal of Ecumenical High School, February 17, 1990, Belize Collection. Due to lack of available personnel, the Holy Family Sisters were unable to replace Sister Judith at Ecumenical High.

34. E-mail from Sister Clare of Assisi Pierre to the author, August 10, 2009.

35. "Grant Application, Hackett Foundation, for Christian Youth Enrichment Program," 1990, Belize Collection.

36. Ibid.

37. Ibid.

38. Ibid.

39. "Holy Family Sisters helps [sic] young people of Dangriga through C.Y.E."

40. Letter from Sister Clare of Assisi Pierre to "Dear Sir/Madam," June 10, 1991, Belize Collection.

41. Ibid.

42. Letter from Sister Clare of Assisi Pierre and Sister Judith Therese Barial to the Most Rev. O. P. Martin, D.D., June 10, 1991, Belize Collection.

43. *Response to God's Love*, 81; "Delille's History," *Horizon*, 2.

44. "Holy Family Sisters helps [sic] young people of Dangriga through C.Y.E."

45. "Delille's History," *Horizon*, 2.

46. "Holy Family Sisters helps [sic] young people of Dangriga through C.Y.E."

47. Interview with Sister Judith Barial, July 2003.

48. Ibid.

49. *Response to God's Love*, 81.

50. Ibid. Letter from Mother M. de Chantal St. Julien to Sister M. Judith Therese Barial and Staff, June 18, 1996, Belize Collection. In this letter Mother de Chantal congratulates Sister Judith and her staff on government approval for the CYE and Delille Junior Academy.

51. Letter from Sister Theresa Sue Joseph to Sister Sylvia Thibodeaux, September 28, 1998, Belize Collection.

52. Ibid.

53. Ibid.

54. Letter from Sister Judith Barial to Mother Mary de Chantal [St. Julien], March 30, 1997, Belize Collection.
55. Ibid.
56. "Delille's History," *Horizon*, 2.
57. Ibid.
58. Letter from Sister Judith Barial to Sister Tekakwitha Vega and Sister Carolyn Leslie, September 19, 1999, Belize Collection.
59. Interview with Sister Judith Barial, July 2003.
60. "Delille's History," *Horizon*, 2.
61. Interview with Sister Judith Barial, July 2003.
62. Ibid.
63. Interview with Sister Clare of Assisi Pierre, July 2003.

Chapter 8. Withdrawal from Belize

1. "Future Ministry of the Sisters of the Holy Family in Belize: A Questionnaire," November 10, 1991, Belize Collection.
2. Sixth standard is the equivalent of the eighth grade in the United States.
3. Ten-page document sent by the four sisters at Dangriga to the sisters at the motherhouse in New Orleans, November 10, 1991, 10, Belize Collection.
4. Ibid., 1.
5. Ibid.
6. Ibid. Acculturation refers to the intercultural borrowing between diverse peoples that results in new, blended patterns.
7. Ibid. The four sisters were Clare of Assisi Pierre, Judith Barial, Lucia Carl, and Barbara Alice Battiste.
8. Interview with Sister Clare of Assisi Pierre, May 8, 2008.
9. Ibid.
10. The proceedings of this General Chapter are mentioned in an undated document, "Challenge for the Future," Belize Collection, which was sent sometime in 1998 by Bishop Martin to the Holy Family Sisters.
11. See chapter 3.
12. Letter from Mother M. de Chantal St. Julien to Most Rev. Osmond Martin, December 15, 1994, Belize Collection.
13. Ibid.
14. Ibid.
15. Arthur Jones, "Holy Family Mission: Local Schools, Africa and Belize (Sister Sylvia Thibodeaux named head of Holy Family)," *National Catholic Reporter* (March 5, 1999).

16. Sister Sylvia Thibodeaux, "To Encourage Bishop Martin" (a summary of his meeting with Archbishop Ekpu), September 26, 1995, Belize Collection.

17. Ibid.

18. Ibid.

19. Minutes from the Sisters of the Holy Family Meeting of Sisters from Belize, September 28, 1995, Belize Collection.

20. See chapter 6.

21. Ibid.

22. Bishop Osmond Martin, "Challenge for the Future," Belize Collection.

23. Ibid.

24. Correspondence from Sister Jean Martínez to the author, August 24, 2010. Interview with Sister Clare of Assisi Pierre, May 8, 2008.

25. His remarks at a meeting with Sister Sylvia Thibodeaux make this clear. See Sister Clare of Assisi Pierre to Bishop Osmond P. Martin regarding the ministry of Sister Jean Martínez in Belize, February 17, 2004, Belize Collection. The meeting took place on February 11, but Sister Clare's report is dated February 17, evidently the day she drew it up.

26. Letter from Sister Jean Martínez to Prime Minister Said Musa, May 13, 2003, Belize Collection. Correspondence from Sister Jean Martínez to the author clarifying some points in her letter, August 24, 2010.

27. Letter from Sister Jean Martínez to Prime Minister Said Musa, May 13, 2003, Belize Collection.

28. Sister Jean Martínez, "Report on Meeting with Most Rev. Bishop O. P. Martin, D.D., Bishop of Belize City and Belmopan," September 2, 2003, Belize Collection.

29. Ibid.

30. Correspondence from Sister Jean Martínez to the author clarifying some points in her letter, August 24, 2010.

31. Sister Jean Martínez, "Towards the Foundation of an Indigenous Community of Sisters for Belize: Familiarization Phase, Journal of Visits to Schools, October 2003–January 2004," Belize Collection.

32. Correspondence from Sister Jean Martínez to the author, August 24, 2010.

33. Sister Jean Martínez, "Towards the Foundation of an Indigenous Community."

34. Ibid.

35. Sr. Clare of Assisi Pierre to Bishop Osmond P. Martin regarding the ministry of Sr. Jean Martínez in Belize, February 17, 2004, Belize Collection.

36. Ibid.

37. Presumably this means that the Holy Family Congregation will assume responsibility for any financial transactions conducted by Sister Jean concerning the purchase or rental of land for the indigenous foundation. It seems, however, that no land had been leased or bought, so this became a moot point.

38. Sister Clare to Bishop Martin regarding the ministry of Sister Jean, February 17, 2004.

39. Letter from Sister Sylvia Thibodeaux to Most Rev. Osmond Martin, February 27, 2004, Belize Collection.

40. Correspondence from Sister Carolyn Leslie to the author, October 29, 2008.

41. Virtually every Holy Family Sister whom the author has interviewed since 2003 has made this assertion.

42. Interview with Sister Clare of Assisi Pierre, May 8, 2008.

43. Letter from Sister Sylvia Thibodeaux to Peter Castillo, Principal of Delille Academy (cc: Most Rev. Osmond Martin), August 3, 2004, Belize Collection.

44. Letter from Most Rev. Osmond P. Martin to Sister Sylvia Thibodeaux, November 22, 2004, Belize Collection.

45. Press release, Press Release Archives, Government of Belize, March 13, 2003, April 24, 2003; *Army Reserve Magazine* (Spring 2003).

46. Interview with Sister Judith Barial, July 2003.

47. Letter from Sister Judith Barial to Rev. Paysee of the Mission Cooperative Plan, Archdiocese of New Orleans, October 13, 2004; Address (speaker's name not listed) given on the dedication of the Sister Judith Barial Library at Delille Academy, November 25, 2003. Both documents found in Belize Collection.

48. Address given on the dedication of the Sister Judith Barial Library.

49. Letter from Sister Judith Barial to Rev. Paysee of the Mission Cooperative Plan, October 13, 2004.

50. Ibid.

51. Dawn Gibeau, "Lay Associates Flock to Religious Orders," *National Catholic Reporter* (February 16, 1996).

52. Interview with Sister Sylvia Thibodeaux, May 12, 2008.

53. Testimony of Sylvia Flores, composed at the request of the author and sent to him in January 2009.

54. Ogaldez is a Belizean Garifuna, Flowers is from Belize but is not a Garifuna, Donald is a Jamaican, and Joseph is from the United States.

55. Sister Josita Marie Ogaldez, "Catechesis in Independence and Red Bank Villages, Stann Creek District, Belize," July 7–21, 2008.

56. Ibid.

57. Ibid.

58. Ibid.

Conclusion

1. Correspondence from Sister Carolyn Leslie to the author, August 2010.
2. "Since 1883 only thirty-one Belizean women joined the Sisters of Mercy. The last sister joined in 1964, a whole generation ago." Channel 5 (Belize) newscast, September 29, 1999, www.channel5belize.com.
3. Interview with Sister Eleanor Gillett, July 2003.
4. Sylvia Flores, "Foreword" to "Response to God's Love," 2.
5. Letter from Sister Tekakwitha Vega to the Sisters of the Holy Family, Dangriga, Belize, March 6, 1980, Belize Collection.
6. By the 1980s the Holy Family Sisters in Belize were becoming more involved in working with other female congregations. In 1980, Pallottine Sister Stephen Franco was hired to teach at Delille Academy, where she lived in community with the Holy Family Sisters. After serving as principal of Delille Academy, Sister Jean Martínez taught at Muffles College in Orange Walk. The sisters were also frequently involved in conferences and workshops with other congregations where such topics as inculturation and social justice were discussed and studied.
7. Interview with Sister Clare of Assisi Pierre, July 2003.
8. Telephone interview with Sister Jean Martínez, July 14, 2010.
9. Jean Martínez, "Arise! Adelante! Go Forth! Garifuna Healing Rites: An Instrument for Evangelization at Sacred Heart Church in Dangriga, Belize," Master's thesis, Institute for Black Catholic Studies, Xavier University of Louisiana, 2005.
10. Jean Martínez, *"Furendei Wama; Afarenha Wama, Lun Wareidagu! Let Us Learn; Let Us Share; Let Us Heal!* A Practicum for Healing," Sacred Heart Parish, Dangriga.
11. See Hunter, *Sisters of Mercy in Belize*, 170–71.

BIBLIOGRAPHY

Archives

Sisters of the Holy Family, New Orleans, LA, Belize Collection

Interviews

Adams, Sister Boniface, July 2003
Barial, Sister Judith Therese, S.S.F., July 2003
Cavalier, Sister Joseph Ellen, S.S.F., May 8, 2008
Copeland, M. Shawn, June 24, 2010
Francis, Sister Barbara Marie, S.S.F., July 2003
Gillett, Sister Eleanor, S.S.F., July 2003
Hazeur, Sister Mary Bertille, S.S.F., July 2003
Jackson, Sister John Mary, S.S.F., October 5, 2004
Johnson, Sister Mary Adrian, S.S.F., July 2003
Leslie, Sister Carolyn, S.S.F., July 2003, May 8, 2008
Martínez, Sister Jean, S.S.F., July 14, 2010
Pierre, Sister Clare of Assisi, S.S.F., July 2003, May 8, 2008
Thibodeaux, Sister Sylvia, S.S.F., May 12, 2008, August 31, 2010

Correspondence with Author

Braxton, Sister Sienna Marie, S.S.F., October 9, 2004
Byrne, Sister Patricia, C.S.J., August 2004
Castillo, Sister Rebecca Carlos, S.S.F., September 2, 2004
Cavalier, Sister Joseph Ellen, S.S.F., October 20, 2004
Doyle, Sister Mary Ellen, S.C.N., July 24, 2007
Dries, Sister Angelyn, O.S.F., April 2006, May 2010, December 2010
Dunn, Sister Coletta, O.S.F., August 11, 2010
Estero, Sister Esther Marie, S.S.F., September 2004
Flores, Sister Barbara, S.S.F., February 7, 2008

Flores, Sister Joan, S.C.N., September 2004, August 2010
Flores, Sylvia, October 2008, September 2009, December 2009, May 2010, June 2010
Francis, Sister Barbara Marie, S.S.F., September 2004
Koepping, Elizabeth, June 12, 2008
Lambey, Sister Veronica Ruth, S.S.F., September 2004
Leslie, Sister Mary Carolyn, S.S.F., April 26, 2004, September 23, 2004, July 21, 2007, October 29, 2008, August 2010
Martínez, Sister Jean, S.S.F., August 24, 2010
Miros, David, June 2010, July 2010
Morrow, Diane Batts, August 14, 2004
Nolan, Charles, June 2005
Pierre, Sister Clare of Assisi, S.S.F., August 10, 2009
Roy, Sister Marie Colette, O.S.F., August 12, 2010
Thibodeaux, Sister Sylvia, S.S.F., August 2010
Witt, Sister Sally, C.S.J., May 2010

Reflections

The three written reflections of Appendix C, by Sylvia Flores, Eugene Hernández, and Eric López, were provided by Sylvia Flores.

Books, Articles, and Other Sources

Abbot, Walter M., ed. *The Documents of Vatican II*. New York: Guild Press, 1966.
Alberts, John B. "Black Catholic Schools: The Josephite Parishes of New Orleans during the Jim Crow Era." *U.S. Catholic Historian* 12, no. 1 (Winter 1994): 77–98.
Arana, Francis B., Sr. *The Garifuna Teachers: Their Contribution to Education in Belize*. Belize: No publisher listed, 2002.
Asbury, Herbert. *The French Quarter: An Informal History of the New Orleans Underworld*. Atlanta: Mockingbird Books, 1976.
Baudier, Roger. *The Catholic Church in Louisiana*. New Orleans: Hyatt, 1939.
Bays, Daniel H., and Grant Wacker, eds. *The Foreign Missionary Enterprise at Home: Explorations in North American Cultural History*. Tuscaloosa: University of Alabama Press, 2003.
Beane, Marjorie Noterman. *From Framework to Freedom: A History of the Sister Formation Conference*. Lanham, MD: University Press of America, 1993.

Behrens, Susan Fitzpatrick. "From Symbols of the Sacred to Symbols of Subversion to Simply Obscure: Maryknoll Women Religious in Guatemala, 1953–1967." *The Americas* 51, no. 2 (October 2004): 189–216.

———. "Maryknoll Sisters, Faith, Healing, and the Maya Construction of Catholic Communities in Guatemala." *Latin American Research Review* 44, no. 3 (2009): 27–49.

Bolland, O. Niger. *Belize: A New Nation in Central America.* Boulder and London: Westview Press, 1986.

Brett, Donna Whitson, and Edward T. Brett. *Murdered in Central America: The Stories of Eleven U.S. Missionaries.* Maryknoll, NY: Orbis Books, 1988.

Brett, Edward T. "African-American Missionaries in Central America: The Sisters of the Holy Family in Belize." *U.S. Catholic Historian* 24, no. 3 (Summer 2006): 75–94.

———. "Belize, national independence movement." In *International Encyclopedia of Revolution and Protest,* edited by Immanuel Ness, 1:365–66. London and New York: Blackwell, 2009.

———. "Race Issues and Conflict in Nineteenth- and Early Twentieth-Century Religious Life: The New Orleans Sisters of the Holy Family." *U.S. Catholic Historian* 29, no. 1 (Winter 2011): 113–27.

———. *The U.S. Catholic Press on Central America: From Cold War Anticommunism to Social Justice.* Notre Dame, IN: University of Notre Dame Press, 2003.

Bryan, Louise Marie. "History of the National Black Sisters' Conference." In *Celibate Black Commitment: Report of the Third Annual National Black Sisters' Conference* [August 9–15, 1970, University of Notre Dame], 2–9. Pittsburgh: NBSC, 1971.

Buhler, Richard. *A History of the Catholic Church in Belize.* Belize: BISRA (Belize Institute for Social Research and Action), Occasional Publications No. 4, 1976.

Burke, Sister Mary Ransom. *We Drank the Water: Nazareth in Belize.* Louisville, KY: Harmony House, 2003.

Byrne, Patricia. "In the Parish but Not of It: Sisters." In *Transforming Parish Ministry: The Changing Roles of Catholic Clergy, Laity, and Women Religious,* edited by Jay P. Dolan, R. Scott Appleby, Patricia Byrne, and Debra Campbell, 109–200. New York: Crossroad, 1990.

Catholic Almanac, 2006. Huntington, IN: Our Sunday Visitor, 2000.

Channel 5 (Belize) Newscast (September 29, 1999). www.channel5belize.com.

Clark, Emily, and Virginia Meacham Gould. "The Feminine Face of Afro-Catholicism in New Orleans, 1727–1852." *William and Mary Quarterly* 59, no. 2 (April 2002): 409–48.

Cleary, Edward L. *Crisis and Change: The Church in Latin America Today*. Maryknoll, NY: Orbis Books, 1985.
Coburn, Carol K. "An Overview of the Historiography of Women Religious: A Twenty-Five-Year Retrospective." *U.S. Catholic Historian* 22, no. 1 (Winter 2004): 1–26.
Coburn, Carol K., and Martha Smith. *Spirited Lives: How Nuns Shaped Catholic Culture and American Life, 1836–1920*. Chapel Hill: University of North Carolina Press, 1999.
Committee on the Church in Latin America, National Conference of Catholic Bishops. *Sharing Faith across the Hemisphere*. Washington, DC: United States Catholic Conference, 1997.
Copeland, M. Shawn. "A Cadre of Women Religious Committed to Black Liberation: The National Black Sisters' Conference." *U.S. Catholic Historian* 14, no. 1 (Winter 1996): 123–44.
Costello, Gerald. *Mission to Latin America: The Successes and Failures of a Twentieth-Century Crusade*. Maryknoll, NY: Orbis Books, 1979.
Davis, Cyprian. *Henriette Delille: Servant of Slaves, Witness to the Poor*. New Orleans: Archives of the Archdiocese of New Orleans, 2004.
———. *The History of Black Catholics in the United States*. New York: Crossroad, 1990.
Davis, Cyprian, and Jamie Phelps. *"Stamped with the Image of God": African Americans as God's Image in Black*. Maryknoll, NY: Orbis Books, 2003.
Detiege, Sister Audrey Marie. *Henriette Delille, Free Woman of Color: Foundress of the Sisters of the Holy Family*. New Orleans: Sisters of the Holy Family, 1976.
Deggs, Sister Mary Bernard. *No Cross, No Crown: Black Nuns in Nineteenth-Century New Orleans*. Edited by Virginia Meacham Gould and Charles E. Nolan. Bloomington: Indiana University Press, 2002.
Dolan, Jay P. *The American Catholic Experience: A History from Colonial Times to the Present*. New York: Doubleday, 1985.
Dolan, Jay P., R. Scott Appleby, Patricia Byrne, and Debra Campbell, eds. *Transforming Parish Ministry: The Changing Roles of Catholic Clergy, Laity, and Women Religious*. New York: Crossroad, 1990.
Dries, Angelyn. "Living in Ambiguity: A Paradigm Shift Experienced by the Sister Formation Movement." *Catholic Historical Review* 79, no. 3 (July 1993): 478–87.
———. *The Missionary Movement in American Catholic History*. Maryknoll, NY: Orbis Books, 1998.
———. "U.S. Catholic Women and Mission: Integral or Auxiliary?" *Missiology: An International Review* 33, no. 3 (July 2005): 301–11.
Drusine, Helen. "The Garifuna." *American Legacy* (Fall 2008): 15–19.

Dussel, Enrique. *De Medellín a Puebla: Una década de sangre y esperanza.* Mexico City: Centro de Estudios Ecuménicos, 1979.

Eagleson, John, and Philip Scharper, eds. *Pueblo and Beyond.* Maryknoll, NY: Orbis Books, 1979.

Ellis, John Tracy. *American Catholicism.* Chicago: University of Chicago Press, 1956.

Estes-Hicks, Onita. "Henriette Delille: Free Woman of Color, Candidate for Roman Catholic Sainthood, Early Womanist." In *Perspectives on Womanist Theology,* edited by Jacquelyn Grant, 41–54. Black Church Scholars Series 7. Atlanta, GA: ITC Press, 1995.

Ewens, Mary. "Women in the Convent." In *American Catholic Women: A Historical Explanation,* edited by Karen Kennelly, 17–47. New York: Macmillan, 1989.

Fairclough, Adam. *A Class of Their Own: Black Teachers in the Segregated South.* Cambridge and London: Belknap Press of Harvard University Press, 2007.

Fernández, J. *Belize: Case Study for Democracy in Central America.* Brookfield, VT: Gower, 1989.

Fessenden, Tracy. "The Sisters of the Holy Family and the Veil of Race." *Religion and American Culture: A Journal of Interpretation* 10, no. 2 (2000): 187–224.

Fichter, Joseph H. "First Black Students at Loyola University: A Strategy to Obtain Teacher Certification." *Journal of Negro Education* 56 (Fall 1987): 535–49.

———. "A Saintly Person of Color." *America* (February 29, 1992): 156–57.

———. "The White Church and the Black Sisters." *U.S. Catholic Historian* 12, no. 1 (Winter 1994): 31–48.

Foley, Albert S. "Adventures in Black Catholic History: Research and Writing." *U.S. Catholic Historian* 5, no. 1 (Winter 1986): 103–18.

———. *God's Men of Color: The Colored Catholic Priests of the United States, 1854–1954.* New York: Farrar Straus, 1955.

Franklin, John Hope, and Alfred A. Moss, Jr. *From Slavery to Freedom: A History of African Americans.* New York: McGraw-Hill, 1994.

Garragahn, Gilbert. *The Jesuits of the Middle United States.* Vol. 3. www.Jesuitarchives.org.

Gaspar, David Barry, and Darlene Clark Hine, eds. *Beyond Bondage: Free Women of Color in the Americas.* Urbana and Chicago: University of Illinois Press, 2004.

Gerdes, Sister M. Reginald. "To Educate and Evangelize: Black Catholic Schools of the Oblate Sisters of Providence (1828–1880)." *U.S. Catholic Historian* 7, nos. 2 and 3 (Spring 1988; Summer 1988): 183–99.

Gibeau, Dawn. "Lay Associates Flock to Religious Orders." *National Catholic Reporter* (February 16, 1996).
Gillard, John Thomas. *Colored Catholics in the United States*. Baltimore: Josephite Press, 1941.
———. *The Catholic Church and the American Negro*. Baltimore: St. Joseph's Society Press, 1929.
Glatz, Carol. "Mother Henriette Delille Declared Venerable." *Clarion Herald* (April 3, 2010), 1, 6.
Gleason, Philip. *Keeping the Faith: American Catholicism Past and Present*. Notre Dame, IN: University of Notre Dame Press, 1987.
Golden Rays through Clouded Years, 1898–1948. Belize: The Commercial Press, 1948.
Gould, Virginia Meacham. "Henriette Delille, Free Women of Color, and Catholicism in Antebellum New Orleans, 1727–1852." In *Beyond Bondage: Free Women of Color in the Americas*, edited by David Barry Gaspar and Darlene Clark Hine, 271–85. Urbana and Chicago: University of Illinois Press, 2004.
Gould, Virginia Meacham, and Charles E. Nolan. *Henriette Delille: "Servant of Slaves."* New Orleans: Sisters of the Holy Family, 1999.
———. "Researchers Explore Delille's Formation in Convent, LA." *Servant of the Poor: Newsletter of Friends of Henriette Delille* (Summer 2004).
Grant, Jacquelyn, ed. *Perspectives on Womanist Theology*. Atlanta, GA: ITC Press, 1995.
Hart, Sister Mary Francis Borgia. "A History of the Congregation of the Sisters of the Holy Family of New Orleans." Master's thesis, Xavier College, 1939.
———. "Violets in the King's Garden: A History of the Sisters of the Holy Family of New Orleans." Unpublished typed manuscript, 1931.
———. *Violets in the King's Garden: A History of the Sisters of the Holy Family of New Orleans*. New Orleans: Privately printed, 1976.
[Heisser], Sister Mary of the Rosary. "Builders of Belize (2) Holy Family Sisters." *National Studies: A Journal of Social Research and Thought* 15 (November 1973).
Hennesey, James. *American Catholics: A History of the Roman Catholic Community in the United States*. Oxford: Oxford University Press, 1981.
Hopkins, Frederick C. "The Catholic Church in British Honduras (1851–1918)." *Catholic Historical Review* 4, no. 3 (October 1918): 304–14.
Hoy, Suellen. "Lives on the Color Line: Catholic Sisters and African Americans in Chicago, 1890s–1960s." *U.S. Catholic Historian* 22, no. 1 (Winter 2004): 67–92.

Hunter, Sister Yvonne. *The Sisters of Mercy in Belize, 1883–1983.* Cumberland, RI: Sisters of Mercy, Province of Providence Communications, 1984.

Jacobs, Sylvia M., ed. *Black Americans and the Missionary Movement in Africa.* Westport, CT: Greenwood Press, 1982.

———. "The Historical Role of Afro-Americans in American Missionary Efforts in Africa." In *Black Americans and the Missionary Movement in Africa,* edited by Sylvia M. Jacobs, 5–30. Westport, CT: Greenwood Press, 1982.

Joint Protestant-Roman Catholic Schools, Colleges and Universities, International Directory, 2007. www.nicie.org/archive/internationaldirectory04.pdf.

Jones, Arthur. "Holy Family Mission: Local Schools, Africa and Belize." *National Catholic Reporter* (March 5, 1999).

Kennelly, Karen M., ed. *American Catholic Women: A Historical Explanation.* New York: Macmillan, 1966.

———. "Foreign Missions and the Renewal Movement." *Review for Religious* 49 (May–June 1990): 445–63.

Koehlinger, Amy L. *The New Nuns: Racial Justice and Religious Reform in the 1960s.* Cambridge, MA: Harvard University Press, 2007.

Kollman, Paul. "The Promise of Mission History for U.S. Catholic History." *U.S. Catholic Historian* 24, no. 3 (Summer 2006): 1–18.

Kolmer, Elizabeth. *Religious Women in the United States: A Survey of the Influential Literature from 1950 to 1983.* Wilmington, DE: Michael Glazier, 1984.

Maffey-Kipp, Laurie. "The Serpentine Trail: Haitian Missions and the Construction of African-American Religious Identity." In *The Foreign Missionary Enterprise at Home: Explorations in North American Cultural History,* edited by Daniel H. Bays and Grant Wacker, 29–43. Tuscaloosa: University of Alabama Press, 2003.

Martin, Sandy D. *Black Baptists and African Missions: The Origin of a Movement, 1880–1915.* Macon, GA: Mercer University Press, 1989.

Martínez, Jean. "Arise! Adelante! Go Forth! Garifuna Healing Rites: An Instrument for Evangelization at Sacred Heart Church in Dangriga, Belize." Master's thesis, Xavier University of Louisiana, 2005.

McAvoy, Thomas. *A History of the Catholic Church in the United States.* Notre Dame, IN: University of Notre Dame Press, 1969.

McNally, Michael J. "A Minority of a Minority: The Witness of Black Women Religious in the Antebellum South." *Review for Religious* 40 (March 1981): 260–69.

McNamara, Jo Ann Kay. *Sisters in Arms: Catholic Nuns through Two Millennia.* Cambridge, MA: Harvard University Press, 1996.

Montgomery, William M. "Mission to Cuba and Costa Rica: The Oblate Sisters of Providence in Latin America, 1900–1970." Ph.D. dissertation, The Catholic University of America, Washington, DC, 1997.

———. "The Oblate Sisters of Providence: The Origins of Their Mission to Latin America." *U.S. Catholic Historian* 24, no. 2 (Spring 2006): 41–55.

Morrow, Diane Batts. *Persons of Color and Religious at the Same Time: The Oblate Sisters of Providence, 1828–1860.* Chapel Hill: University of North Carolina Press, 2002.

———. Review of Sister Mary Bernard Deggs, *No Cross, No Crown: Black Nuns in Nineteenth-Century New Orleans,* edited by Virginia Meacham Gould and Charles E. Nolan. *Catholic Historical Review* 89, no. 1 (January 2003): 121–23.

Muldrey, Mary Hermenia. *Abounding in Mercy: Mother Austin Carroll.* New Orleans: Habersham, 1988.

National Black Sisters' Conference. *Celibate Black Commitment: Report of the Third Annual National Black Sisters' Conference* [August 9–15, 1970, University of Notre Dame]. Pittsburgh: NBSC, 1971.

Nickels, Marilyn Wenzke. *Black Catholic Protest and the Federated Colored Catholics, 1917–1933: Three Perspectives on Racial Justice.* New York: Garland, 1988.

Ochs, Stephen J. *A Black Patriot and a White Priest: André Cailloux and Claude Paschal Maistre in Civil War New Orleans.* Baton Rouge: Louisiana State University Press, 2000.

———. *Desegregating the Altar: The Josephites and the Struggle for Black Priests, 1871–1960.* Baton Rouge: Louisiana State University Press, 1990.

Quiñonez, Lora Ann, and Mary Daniel Turner. *The Transformation of American Catholic Sisters.* Philadelphia: Temple University Press, 1992.

Rector, Theresa A. "Black Nuns as Educators." *Journal of Negro Education* 51, no. 3 (1982): 238–53.

Response to God's Love: Commemorative Yearbook. Belize: Privately printed, 1998.

Robert, Dana L. *American Women in Mission: A Social History of Their Thought and Practice.* Macon, GA: Mercer University Press, 1977.

———, ed. *Gender Bearers, Gender Barriers: Missionary Women in the Twentieth Century.* Maryknoll, NY: Orbis Books, 2002.

Saillant, John. "Missions in Liberia and Race Relations in the United States." In *The Foreign Missionary Enterprise at Home: Explorations in North American Cultural History,* edited by Daniel H. Bays and Grant Wacker, 13–28. Tuscaloosa: University of Alabama Press, 2003.

Schineller, Peter. *A Handbook on Inculturation.* New York: Paulist Press, 1990.

Schneider, Mary. *The Transformation of American Women Religious: The Sister Formation Conference as Catalyst for Change (1954–1964)*. South Bend, IN: Charles and Margaret Hall Cushwa Center for the Study of American Catholicism, University of Notre Dame, 1986.

Setzekorn, William David. *Formerly British Honduras: A Profile of the New Nation of Belize*. Athens: Ohio University Press, 1981.

Shoman, Assad. *Party Politics in Belize, 1950–1986*. Benque Viejo del Carmen, Belize: Cobula Productions, 1987.

Shorter, Aylward. *Towards a Theology of Inculturation*. Maryknoll, NY: Orbis Books, 1988.

[Sisters of the Holy Family]. *The Greatest Gift of All: A Pictorial Biography of Mother Henriette Delille*. New Orleans: Heritage of America Foundation Press, 1992.

Statistical Yearbook of the Church, 2003. Vatican City: Libreria Editrice Vaticana, 2003.

Thomas, Evangeline. *Women Religious History Sources: A Guide to Repositories in the United States*. New York: R. R. Bowker, 1983.

Williams, Walter L. "The Missionary: Introduction." In *Black Americans and the Missionary Movement in Africa*, edited by Sylvia M. Jacobs, 131–34. Westport, CT: Greenwood Press, 1982.

Witt, Sally. *Sisters of the North Country: The History of the Sisters of Saint Joseph of the Diocese of Ogdensburg, Watertown, New York*. Watertown, NY: Sisters of St. Joseph, 2005.

INDEX

Adams, M. Boniface, Sr., 198n.32
aggiornamento, 58, 60, 78, 80, 84
Aguet, M. Florence, Sr., 55
Aliquot, Marie Jeanne, 17–18, 22
Alpaugh, Marie Magdalene, Sr., 22
Anglicans, 54, 148, 165
    and creation of Ecumenical High School, 80–84, 195n.84
Antillach, Matharus, Fr., 15, 183n.20
    letter concerning Addie Saffold, 37–38, 183n.20
Apostolic Letter to the Religious of Latin America, 126
Arana, Leopoldina, 185n.34
Archdiocese of New Orleans. *See* New Orleans, Archdiocese of
Asbury, Herbert, 16
Augustine, Lazarus, Fr., 134–35
Austin High School, 53, 56–57, 60, 146, 165–66, 168, 170, 194n.75
    in reflections, 165–70
    transition to Ecumenical High School, 79–82

"baby school," 37–38, 53, 175n.2
Baker, M. Bernard, Sr., 33
Barial, M. Judith Therese, Sr., 108, 201n.50, 202n.7
    and CYE, 83, 116–20, 194n.75
    and Delille Academy, 122–23, 132, 137–39, 148
    and Delille Junior Academy, 119–21
    and Ecumenical High School, 114–16, 151, 201n.33
    inculturation, 123–24, 149, 152
    and NBSC, 76
    self-transformation of, 123–24
Bartholomew, Mother Mary, 73
Battiste, Barbara Alice, Sr., 202n.7
BEC (Belize Estate and Produce Company), 85–86
Bee, M. Dominica, Sr., 13, 38, 184n.23
Belize
    climate, 32, 43–44, 78, 164
    Constitution, 87
    Department of Education, 35–36
    educational system of, 35–36, 119, 139–40, 171, 202n.2
    history of, 34–35, 59, 61, 85–88, 198n.31
    hurricanes, 61, 86
    independence movement, 9, 59, 85–88, 127, 196n.2
    poverty in, 114, 117–18, 134, 136, 141–42, 145, 150–51. *See also* Dangriga (Stann Creek), poverty in
    tropical disease in, 32–33, 52, 186n.13
Belizean Conscientization Committee, 94
Belize City, 198n.31
    Hurricane Hattie, 61
    Mercy Sisters arrive in 1883, 14–15, 144–45, 175n.7
    political and labor strife in, 86–88
    See also Creoles, in Belize
Belize Estate and Produce Company (BEC). *See* BEC (Belize Estate and Produce Company)

Belmopan, 58, 133–34, 154
Black Catholic Clergy Caucus. *See* National Black Catholic Clergy Caucus
Blanc, Archbishop Antoine, 18–19, 180n.27
Blenk, Archbishop James H.
  episcopal authority and Holy Family Sisters, 41–43
  and Sisters of Mercy, 49–50
Board for Mission Work among the Colored, 187n.25
Bocno, Henry, 177n.18
Bolland, O. Nigel, 175n.4
Bonille, Cecile, 17
Bowie, Mother M. Elizabeth, 51–52
  conflict with Bishop Hopkins, 40–47
Bowman, Henry, 169
Bowman, William, 52
Braxton, Sienna Marie, Sr.
  and controversy over communal prayer, 90–91, 95–99, 103, 149
  death of, 199n.42
Breaux, Marie de Montfort, Sr., 77, 165
British Honduras. *See* Belize
Buhler, Richard, Fr., 48, 187n.27
Burke, Monsignor John E., 187n.25
Byrne, Patricia, Sr., 66, 70, 187n.25

Cardinal Stritch College, 72–74
Carib(s). *See* Garifuna
Carib Settlement Day, 88
Carl, M. Lucia, Sr., 124, 149–50, 202n.7
  delay in salary compensation of, 113–14
  inculturation, 108
  at Lafon Nursing Home, 111
  work with elderly, 111–13
Carlos Castillo, Rebecca, Sr. *See* Castillo, Rebecca Carlos, Sr.

Carlow University. *See* Mount Mercy College
Carroll, Mother Austin, 28–29, 48–49
Carter, Jean, Sr., 198n.32
Castillo, Rebecca Carlos, Sr., 56, 74, 139, 154, 196n.8
Catholic University, 72–73, 187n.25
Cavalier, Joseph Ellen, Sr.
  and controversy over communal prayer, 93, 98, 197n.16
  and cultural sensitivity, 93
  and Ecumenical High School, 83, 194n.75
Cayetano, Fabian, 121
Cayo District, 154, 168, 197n.18
Charles, Mother Josephine, 18, 181n.40
  and Chloe Preval controversy, 22–23, 178n.21
  conflict with Archbishop Perché over religious habit, 193n.59
Children of Mary, 178n.21
Christian Youth Enrichment (CYE). *See* CYE (Christian Youth Enrichment)
Cicognani, Cardinal Amleto, 185n.11
Civil Rights Act of 1875, 27
CMSW (Conference of Major Superiors of Women), 68, 73, 75. *See also* LCWR (Leadership Conference of Women Religious)
Coburn, Carol, 6, 183n.13
Code of Canon Law, 65
College of Mount St. Joseph, 72
College of St. Teresa, 72, 192n.29
Conditae a Christo, 65
Conference of Major Superiors of Women (CMSW). *See* CMSW (Conference of Major Superiors of Women)

Conference on the History of
  Women Religious, 6–7, 174n.23
Congregation of Pious Missions. *See*
  Pallottine Sisters (Congregation
  of Pious Missions)
Congregation of the Sisters of the
  Presentation of the Blessed
  Virgin Mary, 18, 178n.20
conscientization, 95
Constitution on the Sacred Liturgy,
  95
Copeland, M. Shawn
  and NBSC, 76, 193n.46, 193n.56
Corozal, 49, 154, 168
Costello, Gerald, 1
Creoles
  in Belize, 8, 39–40, 87, 98, 102,
    129, 147, 198n.31
  in New Orleans, 16, 22, 26, 101–2,
    179n.21
CYE (Christian Youth Enrichment),
  83, 113, 117, 123, 125, 194n.75
  concept and origin of, 116
  curriculum, 116
  finances of, 120–21, 200n.30
  growth, 118–19

Dangriga (Stann Creek)
  Bishop Di Pietro requests teachers
    for, 28–29
  creation of Ecumenical High
    School in, 79–84
  evolution of technical training in,
    114–24, 137–40
  Garifuna migration to, 34–35
  Holy Family Sisters' arrival in, 13,
    15
  Holy Family Sisters assigned to,
    53–54, 156–59
  Holy Family Sisters consent to
    teach in, 28–32
  Holy Family Sisters' early years
    in, 33, 38–47

Holy Family Sisters withdraw
    from, 129–37
  and Hurricane Hattie, 61
  ministry to elderly in, 111–14
  Mother Mary of the Sacred
    Heart's visit to, 51
  name change to Dangriga, 88
  opening of Austin High School in,
    53
  poverty in, 41, 43, 47, 60, 108, 112,
    116–18, 128, 144, 150–52
  union activities in, 86–87
  See also Austin High School;
    CYE; Delille Academy;
    Ecumenical High School;
    Garifuna, culture of; Jesuits;
    Sacred Heart Parish; Sacred
    Heart School; Sisters of Charity
    of Nazareth; Sisters of the Holy
    Family
Daughters of Charity, 55
Davis, Cyprian, Fr., 5, 19, 177n.15,
  178n.19, 181n.42, 192n.45
Debreuil, Cecile, 16
Deggs, M. Bernard, Sr.
  on attendance of Congregation's
    founders at Sister Marthe
    Fontière's school, 178n.19
  comments on Mother Austin
    Jones, 26
  on discrimination against Holy
    Family Sisters, 22
  on establishment of Chartres
    Street convent, 22–23
  on personalities of Srs. Juliette
    Gaudin and Josephine Charles,
    181n.40
  on poverty of Congregation in
    early years, 24–25
Delille, Jean-Baptiste, 17
Delille, Mother Henriette, 127, 140,
  148, 151, 164, 177n.18, 178n.19,
  178n.21

Delille, Mother Henriette, (*cont.*)
  ancestry and birth, 16–17
  and Congregation of the Sisters of the Presentation of the Blessed Virgin Mary, 18
  foundress and first mother superior of Holy Family Sisters, 17–21
  and Marie Jeanne Aliquot, 17–18, 22
  novitiate with Religious of the Sacred Heart, 19, 179n.23
  obituary, 20–21
  and Sr. Marthe Fontière, 17
  and Society of the Holy Family, 18
Delille Academy, 84, 165, 205n.6
  becomes four-year high school, 122
  controversy over its philosophy, 132, 135, 137
  curriculum, 119
  development of technical training programs, 114–24, 137–40
  as innovation in Belizean education system, 139–40, 148
  and Sr. Judith Barial, 122–23, 138–39
  and Sr. Rebecca Carlos Castillo, 56
Delille Junior Academy, 119–22, 201n.50
DeLisle Junior College, 72
Detiege, Audrey Marie, Sr., 21, 177n.18, 179n.23, 179n.24
Dias, Marie Josephe, 16
Di Pietro, Bishop Salvatore, 25, 33, 40, 143, 163, 184n.22
  contract with Mother Austin Jones, 28–31, 44–47, 50, 144–45, 182n.12
  health problems of, 186n.13
  Jesuit Superior General for British Honduras, 28
  named vicar apostolic of Belize, 28
  and Sisters of Mercy, 48–50, 144–45
Divine Word Missionary Society, 185n.11
Dominican Sisters, 73
Donald, Andria Marie, Sr., 84, 114, 141, 204n.54
Doyle, Mary Ellen, Sr., 193n.62
Drexel, Mother Katherine, 41
Dries, Angelyn, Sr., 3, 5, 32, 68, 189n.7
Dubay, Thomas, Fr., 73
Duffel, Mother Marie Anselm, 72, 75, 80
Dunn, Coletta, Sr., 73

Ecclesiae Sanctae, 69
Ecumenical High School, 126, 165–66, 194n.75, 201n.33
  conception and origin of, 80–83, 194n.71
  first ecumenical high school to be established, 195n.84
  and Sr. Clare of Assisi Pierre, 109–10, 150
  and Sr. Judith Barial, 114–16, 125, 151
  sisters' withdrawal from faculty of, 84, 113, 120, 125, 201n.33
ecumenism, 70, 84, 148
Ekpu, Bishop Patrick, 130–31, 137
Elback, M. Bernadette, Sr., 41–43, 45
Estero, Esther Marie, Sr., 56–57, 196n.8
Estrada, Evelyn, Sr., 95–96, 103, 196n.8
Eucharistic Dominicans, 73
Ewens, Mary, 68

Fairclough, Adam, 181n.4
Fazende, Mary Ann, Sr., 13
femme(s) de couleur libre, 16–18, 178n.19, 178n.21. See also *gens de couleur libre*
Fessenden, Tracy, 19
Fichter, Joseph, Fr., 178n.19, 179n.23, 181n.42
Fields, Mary Lynn, Sr., 197n.18
Fifteenth Amendment, 27
Flores, Barbara, Sr., 105, 107, 109, 193n.62
Flores, Joan, Sr., 56–57, 74, 196n.8
Flores, Sylvia, 116, 122, 140, 149
  on name change of Stann Creek to Dangriga, 196n.3
  reflection on Holy Family Sisters, 163–67
Flowers, Hortensia Maria, Sr., 83–84, 116, 125, 141, 204n.54
Foley, Albert S., Fr., 4–5
Fontière, Marthe, Sr., 17
Fortier, M. Stephen, Sr., 13, 38
Francis, Barbara Marie, Sr., 54–56, 60, 189n.15, 198n.32
Francis, Richard, Fr., 58
Franciscan Handmaidens of the Most Pure Heart of Mary, 56
Franciscan Sisters, 73–74
Franco, Stephen, Sr., 94, 205n.6
free person(s) of color. See *femme(s) de couleur libre*; *gens de couleur libre*

García, Russell, 116
Garifuna
  culture of, 34–35, 98, 102, 105–7, 109–10, 112, 123, 126, 131, 145, 152–53, 184n.22, 205n.9
  ethnic stratification of, 102–3
  history of, 13, 34–35, 175n.4, 198n.31
  Holy Family Sisters' proposal for indigenous religious community, 40, 43–45, 99–100, 129–37
  language of, 34, 88–106, 124, 129–30, 145, 149, 175n.3, 182n.5, 183n.21, 197n.16. *See also* Sisters of the Holy Family, controversy over communal prayer
  priests, 58, 147
  sisters, 33, 56–57, 88–107, 123, 139, 149, 152, 193n.62, 197n.16, 204n.54
  Settlement Day, 88
  teachers, 59
  See also Dangriga (Stann Creek); Sisters of the Holy Family
Garifuna Settlement Day, 88
Garragahn, Gilbert, Fr., 187n.27
Gatz, Susan, Sr., 197n.18
Gaudin, Harold, Fr., 187n.25
Gaudin, Mother Juliette, 178n.21, 179n.23, 181n.40
  and Chloe Preval controversy, 22–23
  as member of original community, 18, 179n.23
  and Propagation of the Faith, 29
  as student at Fontière school, 17, 178n.19
Gaudium et Spes, 69, 196n.1
General Chapter, Ninth, 129, 202n.10
General Workers Union (GWU). *See* GWU (General Workers Union)
gens de couleur libre, 18, 22–23, 26, 101, 180n.27. See also *femme(s) de couleur libre*
Gillard, John, Fr., 4
Gillett, M. Eleanor, Sr., 55–57, 147
Goodman, Marie Louise, Sr., 56

Gordon, Reuben, 121
Gould, Virginia Meacham, 23, 177n.15, 179n.23, 181n.42
Gray, Mary of Lourdes, Sr., 33, 187n.22
Green, M. Cecilia, Sr., 170–71
Grey, Martin de Porres, Sr. (Patricia), 75
GROWTH (program), 117
GWU (General Workers Union), 86–87

Hart, M. Francis Borgia, Sr.
  on absence of segregation in Sacred Heart School, 39
  on Chloe Preval controversy, 23
  on Holy Family Sisters soliciting alms, 24
  on Mother Austin Jones's concern for Stann Creek mission, 15
  opposition of Bishop Hopkins to her transfer from mission, 42–43
  on opposition of Sisters of St. Joseph to Holy Family Sisters' religious habit, 180n.35
  on religious vocations to Holy Family Sisters, 193n.60
  on ridicule of Holy Family Sisters, 19–20
  trustworthiness as historian, 176n.11, 177n.17, 179n.24
Hazeur, M. Bertille, Sr., 59–60
Hazeur, Mother Rose de Lima, 111, 113, 150
Heisser, Mary of the Rosary, Sr., 36
Henriette Delille Spiritual Life Center, 140, 167
Henry, Germaine, Sr.
  and controversy over communal prayer, 90–92, 99, 103
Hernández, Eugene, 170–71
Higinio, Mary Cecilia, Sr., 82

Hodapp, Bishop Robert, 81, 83, 88–89, 99, 134
Holy Angels School, 53, 57, 59, 165
Holy Family Associates, 140, 154, 166–67
Holy Family Sisters. *See* Sisters of the Holy Family
Holy Ghost School, 54, 57, 165, 169–70
Holy Redeemer School, 15, 35, 48, 55, 147
Hopkins, Bishop Frederick C., 184n.23, 187n.25, 188n.37
  increase of Holy Family Sisters' salary, 182n.12
  listing Holy Family Sisters as "colored," 180n.33
  power struggle with Holy Family Sisters, 40–50, 78, 145, 186n.13
  power struggle with Mercy Sisters, 47–50, 145
  and proposal for indigenous religious community, 40, 43–45, 47, 129
House of the Holy Family, 20–21
Hoy, Suellen, 180n.34
Hunter, Yvonne, Sr., 48, 175n.7, 186n.12
Hurricane Hattie, 61, 169
Hurricane Katrina, 139, 167, 174n.25

Independence (village of), 141
independence movement in Belize, 9, 59, 85–88, 127, 196n.2. *See also* Belize, history of
infant school. *See* "baby school"
Institute for Black Catholic Studies, 153

Jackson, John Mary, Sr., 93
Jacobs, Sylvia, 35
Jeanmard, Jules B., Fr., 41–45, 47
  as bishop, 185n.11

Jesuits, 4, 15, 38, 40, 46, 52, 74, 87, 151
  absence of information on female religious congregations in writings, 187n.27
  delinquent payment of Sr. Lucia Carl's salary, 113–14
  and Ecumenical High School, 79–84, 148
  education of elite, 28
  illness in British Honduras, 183n.19, 186n.13
  inculturation, 106, 196n.1
  influence on Garifuna religio-cultural formation, 170
  and Pupil-Teacher Training Center, 36, 146–47
  and religious vocation of Sr. Eleanor Gillett, 55–56
  in Sacred Heart Parish, 42, 58, 75, 189n.24
  and Sacred Heart School, 13
  and Sisters of Charity of Nazareth, 197n.18
  transfer of British Honduras from English to Missouri Jesuit Province, 28
Jim Crow laws, 27, 47, 144
John Paul II, Pope, 126
Johnson, M. Adrian, Sr., 59–60, 77
Johnson, Rose, Sr., 193n.62
John XXIII, Pope, 58, 66, 69
Jones, Jennie, Sr., 83, 90, 92, 99, 103, 194n.75
Jones, Mother M. Austin, 8, 40, 102, 175n.2, 183n.13
  accompanying first missionary sisters to Stann Creek, 13–16
  called most capable and successful Holy Family mother superior, 26
  contract with Bishop Di Pietro, 29–31, 41, 44–45, 47, 144, 163
  election as mother superior, 25–27
  first mother superior to speak English as native language, 26
  and Stann Creek mission, 13–16, 28–32, 37–38, 42, 144, 163–64
  years prior to election as mother superior, 26
Joseph, Theresa Sue, Sr., 115, 120, 141
Josephites, 4–5
Jourdan, Mother Mary of Sacred Heart, 51

Kekchi Indians. *See* Q'eqchi Indians
King, Martin Luther, Jr., 75
Knopp, John, Fr., 36
Koehlinger, Amy, 65–67
Koepping, Elizabeth, 195n.84
Kollman, Paul, Fr., 172n.2
Kolmer, Elizabeth, Sr., 6
Ku Klux Klan, 27

Labor and Unemployed Association (LUA). *See* LUA (Labor and Unemployed Association)
Lafon Nursing Home, 111
Lambey, Veronica Ruth, Sr., 56–57, 60, 196n.8
Langlois, Lisa, Sr., 114
Lazare, M. Henriette, Sr., 81
LCWR (Leadership Conference of Women Religious), 75, 191n.25
  and higher education, 72–73, 191n.25
  origin of, 68
  and SFC, 68, 71–75, 191n.25
  See also CMSW (Conference of Major Superiors of Women)
Leadership Conference of Women Religious (LCWR). *See* LCWR (Leadership Conference of Women Religious)
LeBlanc, M. Lorene, Sr., 165, 169

Le Doux, Louis, 185n.11
Leibe, C. J., Fr., 15
Leo XIII, Pope, 65
Le Propagateur, 20
Leslie, M. Carolyn, Sr., 60, 103, 146, 198n.32
Leveau, Henriette, 16
Little Office of the Blessed Virgin Mary, 74
Liturgy of the Hours, 74, 140, 192n.38
López, Eric, 167–170
López, M. Elyswith, Sr., 91, 97–100, 103, 196n.8
Loyola University of New Orleans, 72–73, 111, 187n.25
LUA (Labor and Unemployed Association), 86

Malcolm X, 75
Marin, Philip, Fr., 58, 189n.24
Marist Fathers, 73
Martin, Bishop Osmond P.
  aid for CYE program, 119
  meeting with Bishop Ekpu of Nigeria, 130–31
  and proposal for indigenous religious community, 129–37
  request for missionary sister to work with elderly, 111, 150
  and Sr. Judith Barial, 132, 137–38
  as student at Sacred Heart School, 58, 147
Martin, Eva Regina, Sr., 77, 102
Martínez, Jean, Sr., 74, 196n.8
  and controversy over communal prayer, 93–95, 98–100, 103–4, 152, 199n.41
  and Garifuna culture, 94–95, 104, 152–53
  principal of Delille Academy, 122
  and proposal for indigenous religious community, 100, 131–37, 204n.37
  teacher at Muffles College, 205n.6
Marymount College, 72
Mater et Magistra, 69
Mather, M. Rita, Sr., 13, 38, 42, 184n.23
Maya Mopan, 133
Maya(n), 102, 106, 114, 151, 154, 198n.37
McGlone, Mary, Sr., 2
Medellín Conference, 69–70, 191n.18
Meikle, Joseph Xavier, Sr., 171
Mercy Sisters. *See* Sisters of Mercy
Methodist missionaries, 28
Methodists, 80–83, 148, 194n.71
Miros, David, 174n.26
Morrow, Diane Batts, 6–7, 181n.42
Mount Carmel Sisters, 73, 186n.13, 187n.27
Mount Mercy College, 75
Muffles College, 136, 205n.6
Muldrey, M. Hermenia, Sr., 175n.7
Murphy, Bishop Joseph, 51, 182n.12
Musa, Said, 132–33

Nanette, 16
National Black Catholic Clergy Caucus, 75, 78
National Black Lay Catholic Caucus, 78
National Black Sisters' Conference (NBSC). *See* NBSC (National Black Sisters' Conference)
National Conference of Catholic Bishops, 2
National Office for Black Catholics, 78
National Sisters Committee (NSC). *See* NSC (National Sisters Committee)

NBSC (National Black Sisters' Conference), 75–78, 193n.56. See also *Practicability Study*
New Orleans
- Archdiocese of, 3–4, 18–19, 21, 42, 138
- early history of, 7, 17, 20, 22, 27
- education of children in, 16–17, 27, 35, 46, 55, 178n.19
- expense of sisters' travel to and from, 40–43, 45–46, 164
- Hurricane Katrina, 139, 167, 174n.25
- race issues in, 16, 21, 23, 27, 47, 55, 71, 101–3, 143, 164, 181n.42, 193n.59
- and Sisters of Mercy, 9, 15, 28–29, 46, 48–50, 145, 175n.7
- *See also* Blanc, Archbishop Antoine; Blenk, Archbishop James H.; Creoles, in New Orleans; Delille, Mother Henriette; *femme(s) de couleur libre*; *gens de couleur libre*; Sisters of the Holy Family

Nickels, Marilyn W., 5
Ninth General Chapter. *See* General Chapter, Ninth
Nolan, Charles, 3–4
- on baptismal records of "Henry Bocno," 177n.18
- on color and class within Holy Family community, 181n.42
- expertise on Henriette Delille, 177n.15
- on Henriette Delille's year with Religious of the Sacred Heart, 179n.23
- views on Chloe Preval, 23

Notre Dame Seminary of New Orleans, 73, 192n.31

NSC (National Sisters Committee), 68

Oblate Sisters of Providence, 6, 56, 71, 176n.12, 180n.33, 181n.4
Ochs, Stephen J., 5, 173n.16
Odin, Archbishop Jean-Marie, 22
O'Donovan, M. Stanislaus, Sr., 50
Ogaldez, Josita Marie, Sr., 141, 196n.8, 204n.54
Ogaldez, M. Edmond, Sr., 33
Oliver, Howard, Fr., 82–83
Orange Walk, 136, 154, 168, 186n.13, 205n.6

Pacem in Terris, 69
Pallottine Sisters (Congregation of Pious Missions), 55, 94
- contact with Holy Family Sisters, 146, 205n.6
- drowning of two sisters and Bishop Hopkins, 40
- mentioned in Jesuit publications, 187n.27
- ministry in Belize, 154–55

Paul VI, Pope, 67, 69
Penet, M. Emil, Sr., 67
People's United Party (PUP). *See* PUP (People's United Party)
Perché, Archbishop Napoléon, 193n.59
Pierre, M. Clare of Assisi, Sr., 74
- and CYE program, 119
- as faculty member at Ecumenical High School, 83–84, 109–10, 125, 149–50
- and Garifuna culture, 109–10, 124, 150, 152
- as local superior in Dangriga, 123
- pastoral ministry of, 109–11, 150
- and proposal for indigenous religious community, 135–36

Pierre, M. Clare of Assisi, Sr., (cont.)
  questionnaire, 126–29
  on Sr. Lucia Carl's work with elderly, 113
  starts charismatic prayer group, 115
  work with Sylvia Flores, 165
Pius XII, Pope, 66–67, 72, 78
plaçage, 16–17
Plaisance, M. Helena, Sr., 40–41
Plessy v. Ferguson, 27
Pomona, 53, 59
Poor Clares, 73
Populorum Progressio, 69
Practicability Study, 76–77
preferential option for the poor, 70, 191n.18
Preval, Chloe, 22–23, 101
Price, George, 61, 82, 86–87
Project DESIGN (Development of Educational Services in the Growing Nation), 77
Propagation of the Faith (Propaganda Fide), 29, 48–49, 188n.32
Protestants, 43, 54, 71, 80–83, 148, 165, 181n.4, 195n.84
  African American Protestant missionaries, 35, 176n.12, 184n.22
  See also Anglicans; Methodists
Punta Gorda, 34, 40, 129
PUP (People's United Party), 86–88
pupil teacher(s), 30, 36–37, 53, 147, 168
Pupil-Teacher Training Center, 36, 126–27, 147
pupil-teacher training program, 30, 36–37, 53–54, 126–27, 145–47, 168

Q'eqchi Indians, 141–42, 168
quadroon balls, 17
Quiñonez, Lora Ann, 66, 70

Ramos, Amelia Cayetana, 185n.34
Raymond, Gilbert, Fr., 22–23
Reconstruction, 27
Red Bank, 114, 141–42
Religious of the Sacred Heart, 19, 179n.23
Reyes, Oscar, 121
Reynolds, Daniel, Br., 13, 28
Robert, Dana, 2
Rousselon, Etienne, Fr., 18–19, 22, 178n.21

Sacred Heart Church, 45, 52–53, 56, 58, 61, 84, 169, 171
Sacred Heart Convent, 31, 52–53, 169, 171
Sacred Heart Parish
  economic problems of, 120–21
  faith healing rituals at, 153
  fire, 52–53, 169, 171
  ministry to elderly, 111–14, 150
  pastoral team of, 105–6, 109–10
Sacred Heart School
  "baby school," 37–38
  bishop and priests who graduated from, 58
  curriculum of, 35, 38, 145
  expansion of physical plant, 51–53
  as government school, 35, 182n.12
  Holy Family Sisters begin teaching, 13, 15
  Holy Family Sisters decide to teach in English, 33–34
  last Holy Family sister to serve, 125
  pupil teacher(s), 30, 36–37, 53, 147, 168
  Pupil-Teacher Training Center, 36, 126–27, 147
  pupil-teacher training program, 30, 36–37, 53–54, 126–27, 145–47, 168
  racially integrated, 38–39

and select school(s), 15, 30–31, 35–36
and student success, 53
Saffold, Addie, 13, 37–38, 175n.2
Salvapan, 133
San Antonio District, 197n.18
Schmidt, Frank, Fr., 113
Schneider, Mary, 67
Second Vatican Council. *See* Vatican II
Seine Bight, 34
select school(s), 15, 30–31, 35–36
Servio, Clothilda, 185n.34
Seton Hill College, 72, 187n.25
Setzekorn, William, 102, 175n.4, 198n.31
SFC (Sister Formation Conference), 67–68, 71–75
Short, James, Fr., 111, 113
Shorter, Aylward, 196n.1
Simms, Maria Petra, Sr., 198n.32
Sister Formation Bulletin, 67
Sister Formation Conference (SFC). *See* SFC (Sister Formation Conference)
Sisters of the Blessed Sacrament, 41, 180n.34
Sisters of Charity, 32, 46, 176n.12, 183n.13
Sisters of Charity of Nazareth
  collaboration with Holy Family Sisters, 109
  comments on Holy Family Sisters, 8, 105–7
  Garifuna women in congregation, 105–7, 193n.62
  liturgy in Garifuna language, 94, 96, 106–7
  origins in Dangriga, 197n.18
Sisters of Charity of Seton Hill College, 72, 187n.25
Sisters of the Holy Family
  arrival in Belize, 8–10, 13–16
  and Austin High School, 53, 146, 165–66, 168, 170
  charism of, 8–9, 38, 56, 60, 71, 74, 108, 111, 140, 148–52, 154
  Chloe Preval controversy, 22–23
  conflict with Archbishop Perché over religious habit, 193n.59
  conflict with Bishop Hopkins, 40–47, 50
  contract with Bishop Di Pietro, 29–31, 41, 45–47, 144, 163
  controversy over communal prayer, 88–105, 129
  decision to accept mission in Dangriga, 28–31
  and Delille Academy, 118–23, 132, 137, 139–40, 148
  early congregational history, 8–10, 16–25
  and Ecumenical High School, 80–84, 113–14, 120, 125, 165–70, 194n.71, 195n.84
  education of sisters, 46, 72–74, 111, 153, 187n.25, 192n.31
  expansion of Holy Family schools, 27, 53–54, 79–80, 138
  financial concerns of, 18, 20–25, 30–31, 41–42, 52, 70, 113–14, 116–17, 120–24, 139, 143, 148, 151, 155, 182n.12, 183n.13
  fire of 1942, 52–53, 169, 171
  as first black Catholic missionaries, 32, 35
  founding of Congregation, 16–19
  health problems in Belize, 32–33, 41, 43–45, 78, 139, 183n.20
  and Hurricane Hattie, 61
  and Hurricane Katrina, 139, 167, 174n.25
  implementation of Vatican II decrees, 70–71
  and inculturation, 88, 114–15, 123–24, 149, 152–53

Sisters of the Holy Family (*cont.*)
  and LCWR and SFC, 72–75
  modification of religious habit, 78–79
  under Mother Austin Jones's leadership, 25–32
  and Mother Henriette Delille, 17–21
  and NBSC, 75–78
  novitiate and formation of, 19, 33, 37–38, 43–45, 51, 72–73, 191n.23, 192n.31
  obituary of Henriette Delille, 20–21
  origin of author's research on, 4, 7–8
  proposal for indigenous religious community, 129–37, 204n.37
  pupil-teacher training, 30, 36–37, 53–54, 126–27, 145–47, 168
  religious vocations to, 54–57, 104–7, 114, 125
  summer work in Belize, 141–42
  See also Austin High School; "baby school"; pupil teacher(s); Sacred Heart Convent; Sacred Heart School; select school(s)
Sisters of Mercy
  affiliation with Rhode Island Province, 188n.37
  Belizean religious vocations to, 205n.2
  comments on Garifuna language, 175n.7, 183n.21
  deaths from tropical sickness, 186n.13
  educational prowess, 46
  health problems in Belize, 183n.19, 186n.12
  hosts of first Holy Family Sisters in British Honduras, 13, 15
  mentioned in Jesuit publications, 187n.27
  and Muffles College, 136
  nineteenth-century missions, 176n.12
  power struggle with Belizean bishops, 9, 47–50, 144–45, 175n.7
  and Sr. Eleanor Gillett, 55, 147
  unwilling to expand to Stann Creek, 28–29
  use of American-based curriculum in Belizean schools, 35
Sisters of the Sacred Heart of Jesus, 105, 130
Sisters of St. Joseph, 22, 73
Smith, Martha, 183n.13
Soberanis Gómez, Antonio, 86
Society of the Holy Family, 18
Sodality of Our Lady, 57, 168, 170
Sorel, M. Gerard, Sr., 29
Sorenzo, Victoria, 185n.34
St. Catherine's Academy, 15, 28, 48
St. Catherine's Convent, 15, 175n.7
St. Catherine's School, 15, 29
St. Hildy's College, 54
St. John's College, 87
St. Joseph High School, 55
St. Julien, Mother Mary de Chantal, 121, 129–31, 198n.32, 201n.50
St. Louis University, 72
St. Mary's Academy, 26, 121, 124, 200n.30
St. Michael's Convent, 19
St. Vincent de Paul Society, 113, 150
Stanford, Bernardine, Sr., 52
Stann Creek. *See* Dangriga (Stann Creek)
Stann Creek College, 80, 82–83
Stuart, Dorothy Marie, Sr., 165
Suenens, Cardinal Leon Joseph, 67

Thibodeaux, Sylvia, Sr.
  and Delille Junior Academy, 120
  establishment of indigenous community in Nigeria, 105, 130
  and NBSC, 76–78
  proposal for indigenous religious community in Belize, 129–32, 135–36, 203n.25
  and Sr. Judith Barial's return to Delille Academy, 137–38
  on social stratification within Holy Family Congregation, 101–2, 181n.42
Thomas, Barbara, Sr., 197n.18
Thomas, Evangeline, Sr., 6
Thompson, Aimee de Jesus, Sr., 29
Thompson, M. Emmanuel, Sr., 13, 38, 183n.20
Thro, William P., Fr., 80–82, 84
Toledo District, 40, 154
Turner, Mary Daniel, 66, 70
Turner, Thomas, 5

Unemployed Brigade, 86
University of Dayton, 76
University of Notre Dame, 76
Ursuline Sisters, 7, 178n.21

Vatican II
  and changes in mission philosophy, 8, 53, 154
  and Delille Academy, 139
  effects on Holy Family Sisters, 9, 58, 70–75, 78–81, 84, 103, 109, 142, 148
  effects on women religious, 9, 60–61, 65–70, 79–80, 103, 107, 148
  and inculturation, 85, 90–103, 106–14, 124, 146, 149–51, 196n.1
  and lay associates, 140
Vavasseur, M. Elaine, Sr., 81
Vega, Mother Tekakwitha
  and controversy over communal prayer, 90–100, 103–4, 149
  evaluation of Holy Family community in Dangriga, 108, 149

Wales, Elizabeth, Sr., 22
Williams, Walter L., 184n.22

Xavier University of New Orleans, 72–73, 153, 187n.25

York, E. P., 83

EDWARD T. BRETT
is professor of history at La Roche College.
He is the author or co-author of a number of books,
including *The U.S. Catholic Press on Central America:
From Cold War Anticommunism to Social Justice*
(University of Notre Dame Press, 2003).

www.ingramcontent.com/pod-product-compliance
Lightning Source LLC
Chambersburg PA
CBHW050441240426
43661CB00055B/2463